Social Movements and Transformation

Series Editor
Berch Berberoglu
Sociology
University of Nevada
Reno, NV, USA

This series tackles one of the central issues of our time: the rise of large-scale social movements and the transformation of society over the last thirty years. As global capitalism continues to affect broader segments of the world's population workers, peasants, the self-employed, the unemployed, the poor, indigenous peoples, women, and minority ethnic groups there is a growing mass movement by the affected populations to address the inequities engendered by the globalization process. These popular mass movements across the globe (such as labor, civil rights, women's, environmental, indigenous, and anti-corporate globalization movements) have come to form a viable and decisive force to address the consequences of the operations of the transnational corporations and the global capitalist system. The study of these social movements their nature, social base, ideology, and strategy and tactics of mass struggle is of paramount importance if we are to understand the nature of the forces that are struggling to bring about change in the global economy, polity, and social structure. This series aims to explore emerging movements and develop viable explanations for the kind of social transformations that are yet to come.

Adam Barrington

The U.S. Labor Movement in the 20th and Early 21st Century

A Critical Analysis

palgrave
macmillan

Adam Barrington
Labor activist and community organizer
Cleveland, OH, USA

Social Movements and Transformation
ISBN 978-3-031-30076-9 ISBN 978-3-031-30077-6 (eBook)
https://doi.org/10.1007/978-3-031-30077-6

This Palgrave Macmillan imprint is published by the registered company Springer Nature Switzerland AG.
The registered company address is: Gewerbestrasse 11, 6330 Cham, Switzerland

Preface and Acknowledgments

My introduction to the labor movement happened, if I had to guess, during the protests leading up to the 2011 Ohio Issue 2 vote. By that time, however, I already knew about unions—my maternal grandfather was a United Auto Workers (UAW) member, and my paternal grandmother spoke glowingly of her union from time to time. My mother worked as an attorney for UAW, and my father, though never having the opportunity to join a union himself, always referred (and refers) to himself as working class. Growing up in a family built by workers, and second and third generation immigrant workers at that, has a way of instilling a sense of class consciousness even when there is no casual talk of radical politics at the dinner table. I wasn't a 'red diaper baby', but with a family like mine, I didn't need to be. Thinking particularly of my father, I'm reminded of the famous quote by William "Big Bill" Haywood: "I've never read Marx's *Capital*, but I've got the marks of capital all over my body."

So, when Issue 2 came around, and the right of collective bargaining in Ohio was placed in serious jeopardy, I was paying close attention. At the time, I was working as a delivery driver at a Chinese restaurant. Though I was not personally involved in a union or labor activism, I knew enough about unions to understand why they are important for working people. Thus, I found myself attending rallies in opposition to Senate Bill 5 (the referendum which would have made Ohio a 'right-to-work' state). The demonstrations against SB5 were electric—workers from both the public and private sectors expressed their shared disgust, anger, and contempt for a bill obviously meant to assault their livelihoods and collective power.

More than disgust, anger, and contempt, though, the demonstrations expressed something greater: solidarity.

If my upbringing gave me a familiarity with unions and working-class identity, the protests against Senate Bill 5 showed me what it meant to put such concepts into action. When SB5 failed, it was a tremendous victory for Ohio workers, and I was among those celebrating the loudest. In 2015, I joined the Cleveland chapter of the Industrial Workers of the World. From that point on, I have been more or less consistently involved in the labor movement in some form or other. In 2017, I moved to Reno, Nevada, after accepting an organizer job with the American Federation of State, County, and Municipal Employees (AFSCME) Local 4041. It was during my two-year stint with Local 4041 that my idealist perspective regarding the labor movement took a turn.

To be fair, AFSCME Local 4041 accomplished the monumental goal of getting the right of collective bargaining signed into law for Nevada state workers in 2019, and this achievement is certainly admirable. However, during my time working as a paid organizer, the contradictions plaguing the labor movement became quite clear. First, the fact that much of the organizing was done by paid staff and not by rank-and-file workers troubled me. The AFSCME international union sent in a troop of organizers, representatives, political consultants, and the like, and these characters made the calls for which workplaces deserved focus, what worker outreach should look like, what would be demanded from the state government, and so on. Second, there was the fact that the responsibility of the paid organizer was to encourage rank-and-file participation without actually nurturing rank-and-file participation. If the rank-and-file workers showed up for a protest outside the governor's mansion, great; if the rank-and-file challenged the predetermined campaign program, not so great.

The international staff functioned like gatekeepers to the levers of power, or at least that is how it seemed to me. The international organizers supervised the local organizers, and thus my work as a local organizer was directed by international staff who were flown into Nevada from around the country. I was sent to various worksites and it was my job to talk to workers and convince them to sign union cards. Even with my idealistic perspective and the sense that I was meaningfully participating in the labor movement, there was something about the job that made me feel more like an insurance salesman than an organizer.

This is not to say that the whole experience was negative, or that my time as a professional organizer was not educational. However, after gathering over a hundred signed union cards from Nevada state workers in Reno and Carson City, I could not help but begin to ask myself whether my work was actually building worker power. Out of all of the workers I signed up, only a handful ever came to a meeting or participated in union activities after signing their cards. Then, those workers who did participate were essentially put under the same kind of supervision by the international staff as the local organizers.

The whole process appeared full of contradictions. Union staff were instructed to say '*our* union' rather than '*the* union' when speaking with members and potential members in order to combat attempts by the employer to 'third party' the union. Fair enough—but how else are workers supposed to perceive an organization that claims to represent them but is effectively controlled by bureaucrats who don't even live in the same state as the membership? Workers who were interested enough to run for representative positions or participate in demonstrations or canvassing events were never given the chance to make meaningful decisions regarding the direction of the organizing campaign. Of course, workers who are new to union activities need assistance and guidance, but it seemed to me that rather than empowering the workers with the skills and knowledge necessary for legitimate rank-and-file organization and mobilization, the AFSCME international was more interested in controlling the membership and ensuring the workers did not get enough of a voice to disrupt the calculated legislative campaign underway in Nevada.

Perhaps this sounds harsh. It is not my goal to paint AFSCME or its paid staff as villains or cold bureaucrats. In fact, many of the international organizers with whom I became acquainted had sympathetic views on radical politics, and a few even belonged to Democratic Socialists of America (DSA). However, whatever their political leanings, when it came to union operations, they followed orders from above the same way I did. In any case, a significant number of dues-paying Local 4041 members expressed frustration with the international staff, who they felt were outsiders flown in to tell the rank and file how to handle their business. Many of the rank-and-file workers I befriended and worked alongside eventually gave up participating in union activities, and some even dropped their membership altogether.

I entered the labor movement as a paid organizer under the assumption that every union wants to build worker power and rank-and-file participation. After two years working in a statewide campaign, I can say with some certainty that this is not the case. Local 4041 is not alone in its shortcomings. Labor has been trapped by its history of class collaborationism and dependency on support from the political mainstream, and the consequence is that unions predominantly function like professional mediators in the workplace and campaign organizations for politicians. It became clear during my time as a professional organizer that if unions want to remain relevant, they have to change how they function and rediscover their revolutionary purpose.

My time with Local 4041 ended on less than amicable terms, but by then I had grown disillusioned with the campaign anyhow. I was fortunate enough to get a state job after being unemployed for a year, and shortly thereafter, I was elected president of the Washoe chapter of Local 4041. My tenure as president would be rather short-lived. I was told on several occasions by AFSCME international organizers stationed in Nevada that the executive board viewed me as an enemy, and so before the year 2020 came to a close, I was replaced by a candidate friendlier to the international union and Local 4041 executive board. I harbor no hard feelings—but the ordeal did seem to validate my suspicion regarding the roles of bureaucrats and paid staff in union operations.

Prior to moving to Nevada, I had already read works by Staughton Lynd and other labor activists who examined the problems in the movement and described a different kind of unionism that would put workers in control and preserve militancy and radicalism. Whether it is labeled democratic unionism, rank-and-file unionism, or solidarity unionism, I figured such a concept could only exist if something was really rotten in labor's mainstream—otherwise, there would be little reason to explore alternatives. Working as a paid organizer for a mainstream union, AFSCME, gave me insight into the bureaucracy and class collaborationism which long ago became dominant features of the labor movement.

I also got to see firsthand AFSCME's longstanding and deep connection to the Democratic Party. I took the job and moved out west in 2017, and 2018 was an election year for Nevada. In April 2018, I attended the American Federation of Labor and Congress of Industrial Organizations' (AFL-CIO) Committee on Political Education (COPE) conference at the Circus Circus Casino in Reno. The event was largely an opportunity for local labor leaders and union staff to rub elbows with candidates whose names would appear on the ballot in November. I remember clearly when I met Steve Sisolak, the gubernatorial candidate who would go on to become the governor of Nevada. One of his staff eagerly asked a few of us if we had any questions for Steve, and I asked him whether he would get rid of 'right-to-work' after getting elected. Sisolak's response was "Well, I think that would certainly even the playing field."

While Nevada is still a 'right-to-work' state, Sisolak did sign state worker collective bargaining into law, for which he deserves some credit. The honeymoon between Sisolak and Local 4041 would be short-lived, however. In 2020, AFSCME filed a lawsuit against the governor for violating the newly signed collective bargaining law when he tried to introduce pay cuts and furloughs without negotiating with the union. I participated in several demonstrations outside the governor's mansion during this time. State workers felt rightfully betrayed—they had after all, knocked doors, phone-banked, and some even signed up with AFSCME's political action fund to give a portion of their dues to, among other projects, Sisolak's gubernatorial campaign.

That Sisolak would campaign as labor's candidate only to turn on workers after getting into office was not surprising. It goes without saying that politicians say one thing and do another. For labor, this phenomenon of political dishonesty is more of a structural guarantee than an unfortunate anomaly. Despite the tremendous financial support and other forms of campaign assistance (canvassing, etc.) it provides candidates, there is no indication that the labor movement holds any kind of meaningful influence in the political arena.

With these experiences in mind, I had determined that, when the time came to write my master's thesis (I was able to attend classes at University of Nevada, Reno, through a benefit from the state which paid a significant amount of my tuition), I would figure out how the labor movement came to be the institutionalized, defanged creature that it is today. It seemed to me that co-optation served as the best explanation for labor's transition from a radical and militant social force to a moderate institution within the power structure. Initially, I wanted to make such a connection using other social movements as examples in addition to the labor movement. I read up on professional activists like DeRay McKesson, the state's absorption of the community mediation movement, and the phenomenon of 'slacktivism'. I also read (and reread) a heavy amount of labor literature hoping to gain a better idea of when the turn took place in the movement.

It might be rather obvious from some of the language contained in this book that its most significant influences come from the Marxist tradition. The writings of not only Marx and Engels but also Gramsci, Lenin, and Althusser offered more than all the bourgeois or non-Marxist sources did in my hunt for theoretical support. This remained the case throughout the process of turning my thesis into a book, though there is less explicit discussion of Marxist theory here than in my thesis.

The major difference between this book and my thesis is the overall conclusion. I found that, in examining labor history and more deeply applying Marxist theory than merely discussing it, I could no longer suggest that co-optation is solely responsible for the current state of the labor movement. It is true that elements of co-optation—particularly institutionalization and professionalization—played a significant role in undermining labor's radicalism and militancy. However, the unfortunate fact remains that labor has, since its early days, carried the germ of conservatism, and the ruling class needed only to nurture and reward labor leaders' commitments to class collaborationism to shape the labor movement into an institution which can harmlessly fit into the power structure.

Much of the work involved in taming the radical tendencies in the labor movement was accomplished by forces within the movement itself. Of course, the ruling class encouraged the purging, red-baiting, and blackballing perpetrated against left-wing unionists by labor's class-collaborationist leaders. Institutions of the power structure suited for violence, the police, private security forces, and military, were unleashed upon militant workers and unionists when the ruling class deemed it necessary. The internal struggles within the movement which favored labor's right-wing and the brutality inflicted upon labor's left by the ruling class mixed to create a venomous potion. Thus, it was not so much a process of co-optation, but rather a combination of the collaboration between conservative labor leaders, the state, and employers and outright violence against labor's progressive wing which, in my view, contributed the most to the transformation of the labor movement.

This book also differs from the thesis that preceded it in that it includes an examination of the participation of labor's dominant federations in international clandestine operations conducted by the U.S. government (specifically the CIA). The primary point which I hope to have made clear through this examination is that U.S. labor's collaboration with the state and the capitalist class in undermining the left and militant unionism (at home and abroad) precipitated the advancement of global capitalism and neoliberalism. Therefore, the U.S. labor bureaucracy is partly responsible for disastrous impacts of the neoliberal paradigm on the global working class.

Today, the AFL-CIO remains connected to the U.S. government in a similar manner. The AFL-CIO-affiliated Solidarity Center, established after the end of the American Institute for Free Labor Development (AIFLD), is predominantly funded by the United States Agency for International Development (USAID) and the National Endowment for Democracy (NED). Like AIFLD, Solidarity Center's operations are focused on supporting labor unions and federations abroad that are sympathetic to Washington's aims. For instance, Solidarity Center has close ties to the Confederación de Trabajadores de Venezuela (Confederation of Workers of Venezuela) (CTV). CTV's former leader, Carlos Ortega, was a major figure in the 2002 attempted coup against Hugo Chavez.

Global capitalism and the neoliberal project have made it impossible for labor movements to avoid an internationalist perspective. The AFL-CIO's international affairs reflect the federation's status as an institution of the power structure. In order to combat the destructive agendas of transnational corporations and the authoritarian political structures which advance them (even if they do not outwardly promote them), a new labor movement is necessary. It is hoped that this book will assist this project in some fashion.

Developing and writing this book has been both difficult and exciting, particularly because of the moment in time in which it is being produced. A significant hardship, albeit a welcome one, has been keeping track of all of the developments in the labor movement which every day seem to compound into a greater current. Recently, railroad workers across the country were on the verge of a nationwide strike, nearly 300 workers at a Home Depot in Philadelphia filed for recognition as an independent union, teachers in Seattle ended a week-long strike, and telecommunications workers in California struck for improvements in workplace safety. There have been numerous other recent labor events in addition to those mentioned above, and the point is that chronicling the state of U.S. labor today has been a joyously dizzying affair. After documenting one union victory or demonstration of worker-led action, another pops up demanding to be recognized in writing as well, and so on. With all of this electricity and excitement buzzing in the labor movement, I can think of no better time than the present for this book to be written.

I would like to thank Dr. Clayton Peoples from the Sociology Department of the University of Nevada, Reno, for his guidance while I crafted the thesis which provided the foundation for this book. I thank Dr. Berch Berberoglu, also from UNR's Sociology Department, for his editorial support and assistance. I would also like to thank my mother, Teresa, for her help in painstakingly reviewing this book's contents. Most of all, I would like to thank my wife, Kailey, for putting up with me during the process of researching and writing this book. It has been a long, difficult project, and I could not have completed it without her help.

Cleveland, OH, USA Adam Barrington

Contents

CHAPTER 1

Introduction

This book was originally conceived as an analysis of social movement co-optation using the U.S. labor movement as an historical case study. Through a critical and comprehensive examination of U.S. labor's transformation from a radical force which challenged the political and economic power structure into an institutionalized, bureaucratic tool for the regulation of workers, I had hoped to uncover not only why and how this transformation took place, but also what could be done to reverse it. The truth, however, is that co-optation no longer serves as a complete or coherent explanation for the current state of the U.S. labor movement. The story is much more complex.

U.S. labor history is particularly brutal (Cochran 1977:29). Workers organizing themselves into class-conscious associations were met with violence and terror in numerous forms and at varying degrees of intensity from the earliest days of the labor movement. Yet, despite the bloodshed, lynching, bombing, imprisonment, slander, and humiliation which greeted the movement throughout its history (particularly during moments of reactionary hysteria), there always emerged from the rubble another challenge to the ruling class prepared to carry the movement further. This spirit of defiance and optimism is responsible for the continuity of the labor movement perhaps more than anything else. Certainly, this spirit has waxed and waned over the course of the U.S. labor movement's history, the beginnings of which can be found a few decades after the American

A. Barrington, *The U.S. Labor Movement in the 20th and Early 21st Century*, Social Movements and Transformation,
https://doi.org/10.1007/978-3-031-30077-6_1

Revolution (Lens 1961:30). However, it can and should be argued that the movement has always been propelled by the idea that it is possible to live in a different manner, to discover more liberating and egalitarian ways for human beings to relate to each other.

It is the stubborn conviction that another, better world is possible combined with labor's unique (albeit not always embraced) ability to transcend perceived identity barriers (race, sex, etc.) that gives the labor movement its strength and durability. It is also what makes the labor movement, at least when it is at its most militant and class-conscious stage, intolerable to the ruling class. While there is room in the power structure for social movements that do not directly challenge the system, the very engine of the labor movement, class conflict, places it in a uniquely confrontational position in relation to the interests of capital and the ruling class. For this reason, organized labor in the United States has been exposed to various forms of state- and business-sponsored aggression, some being more effective than others in crushing the revolutionary potential of the labor movement.

When the first organizations resembling labor unions formed in the United States, they were established by skilled craftsmen who sought to protect their livelihoods. There was not much about them that could be called revolutionary, although at the time (late 1700s) such associations, despite their primitiveness, could be perceived as radical. However, as the years passed, early unionists and their organizations would indeed begin to articulate their aims in the language of revolution. By 1825, when the United States was in the throes of the later stages of its industrial revolution, workers' organizations began calling themselves 'unions'. Only a few years thereafter, in 1828 and 1829, the early U.S. labor unions had formed their own political parties (Davis 2018:3). These political parties, such as the New York Workingmen's Party, made demands which even in today's political climate would be considered revolutionary, if not outright communistic. They opposed private property and the inheritance of wealth. They called for equal citizenship and equal education rights through a free public school system. They demanded an end to debtors' prisons and the militia. At the root of these radical demands was their conviction that there are haves and have nots, autocrats and democrats, rich and poor—conflicting groups with irreconcilable interests.

This conviction would later manifest itself in the form of the Industrial Workers of the World (IWW) in 1905, which challenged the conservatism and exclusivity of the American Federation of Labor (AFL), the dominant union federation in the United States at the time. The IWW, or 'Wobblies', organized workers regardless of race, sex, national origin, or skill level. The Wobbly philosophy of industrial unionism also differed from that of the craft-unionist AFL in that the IWW did not seek mere wage increases or a shortened workday: they called for the end of capitalism and demanded worker ownership and control of the means of production (Savage 1922:4).

The IWW's radicalism and militancy made it a target of state terror, which was exacerbated by the first Red Scare and anti-Bolshevik hysteria of WWI. Violent attacks on IWW members by police and vigilante groups, in addition to mass arrests, trials, and convictions of Wobblies under the Espionage Act (1917) and anti-syndicalist state and municipal laws dramatically hindered the IWW's ability to continue its mission. The assaults suffered by the IWW at the hands of the state, vigilantes, and thugs hired by employers made raiding (plundering of members) by more established unions easier, which further diminished the Wobblies' influence and capacity to organize and mobilize workers. While the IWW was never dealt a truly fatal blow (it would gain new life with the radicalism of the 1960s and still exists today), by the 1930s, it was no longer the dominant vehicle of militant labor activism.

When the Congress of Industrial Organizations (CIO) split from the AFL in 1938, it signaled the birth of a new era in the U.S. labor movement (Glaberman 1952:11). The CIO was formed as a committee within the AFL in 1935 under the name Committee for Industrial Organization. The purpose of the committee, founded by John L. Lewis of the United Mine Workers (UMW), was to organize unskilled workers in industrial workplaces (something the AFL was not accustomed to nor particularly interested in). Lewis was no radical, but a series of successful strikes in the early 1930s, led by workers with left-wing proclivities, made it apparent to Lewis and other labor leaders dissatisfied with the AFL's conservative, conciliatory approach to labor organizing that the future of the labor movement was dependent on its ability to reach unskilled industrial workers.

It must be emphasized that the CIO's unprecedented organizing campaigns and strikes, along with its more progressive tendencies (racial equality, etc.) were not part of a program established by labor bureaucrats, but by rank-and-file militant workers. These workers and organizers (many of whom were members of the Communist Party or leftists of another type) are responsible for the largest union organizing drive in U.S. history, not Lewis or any other cautious and politically amorphous labor bureaucrats. In fact, many of the militant worker struggles in the 1930s, organized from below and reliant on strikes and other forms of direct action, occurred before the CIO was even founded (Lynd 2015:52).

After WWII, the hysteria which characterized the first Red Scare resurfaced and again targeted the labor movement. The Taft-Hartley Act (1947) ordered labor unions to purge communists from their ranks. The second Red Scare, embraced by both major U.S. political parties, culminated in a delirious witch hunt which impacted the lives of millions of Americans who were targeted, interrogated, slandered, harassed, and blacklisted for being even suspected of having ties to the Communist Party or other left-wing organizations. The CIO, which had long been ridiculed by conservatives as being overrun with communists, was deeply wounded by the Red Scare, Taft-Hartley, and other exhibitions of rabid anticommunism. While a few CIO unions refused to engage in the purges, the majority did, and chased from their ranks their most passionate, idealistic organizers. The CIO would not survive as an independent federation long thereafter.

The second Red Scare and anti-union legislation of the post-WWII United States did considerable damage to the U.S. labor movement as well as the political left in the U.S. as a whole. However, perhaps more devastating to the labor movement's class-conscious tenacity was the contract it made with the Democratic Party during the presidency of Franklin Delano Roosevelt (FDR). Roosevelt's New Deal, with all of its shortcomings and blemishes, was a godsend for many working-class Americans. For this reason, it was only to be expected that workers and the labor unions representing them would see an ally in FDR, and a political home in the Democratic Party. This is when the Democratic Party, suddenly finding the credibility to do so, adopted its reputation as the 'workingman's party'.

Labor's alignment with a mainstream political party brought about a decline in radical, organic working-class politics (Lynd 2015:59–60). Prospects for a new revolutionary labor party resembling perhaps those formed by militant American workers in the 1820s withered away. There were, to be sure, left-wing workers who decried any sort of bargain between labor and either of the capitalist political parties, but their firm radicalism (which was not always expressed in the most effective manner) did more to isolate them from their fellow workers than encourage revolutionary fervor.

In 1955, the AFL and CIO merged to become the AFL-CIO. Since then, the U.S. labor movement has witnessed a near consistent decline in union membership and participation in workplace organizing. While labor unions in the United States remained influential following WWII, the radicalism and militancy that had defined the movement's past had dissipated. In its place emerged a form of unionism which, although generally cautious and predominantly focused on matters of wages, working conditions, and benefits for its membership, does embrace social struggles to a degree when enough pressure is applied to labor, and when it is convenient for the labor bureaucracy. In many ways, the labor movement, with the exception of the radically egalitarian industrial unions, had to be dragged kicking and screaming into supporting the human rights of 'non-white' workers, and the persistent racism which pervaded the 'white' industrial working class played a significant role in the undoing of radical labor's attempts to transform U.S. politics (Davis 2018:85).

The business unionism of the AFL, the philosophy which dominated it since the time of Samuel Gompers, combined with the more class-conscious philosophy of the CIO, and the result was a *social unionism* which is neither radical nor completely conservative (although it tends to lean in the direction of conservatism in that it does not question the legitimacy of the capitalist power structure as a whole). The U.S. labor movement, through the AFL-CIO, has largely adopted the 'third way' politics of the Democratic Party—that is, it may support struggles based in identity politics or promote improved bargaining contracts, but maintains that capitalist relations of production are more or less legitimate and beyond scrutiny.

The politics of the AFL-CIO is determined by unelected bureaucrats, often linked to the Democratic Party, with the expectation that it will be followed by local unions at lower administrative levels (Yates 2009:118). The U.S. labor movement's marriage to the Democratic Party has stifled political independence and worker militancy. Whatever bouts of 'progressivism' the labor movement has shown since 1955, the anti-capitalist idealism which fueled the largest union organizing drive in U.S. history had been thoroughly extinguished by the time the AFL-CIO was established.

The U.S. labor movement's reluctance and/or inability to organically connect itself with the Black liberation struggle and Civil Rights movement significantly diminished any chance of a radical, class-conscious labor movement in the United States. In 1923, Ben Fletcher, the renowned Wobbly organizer who helped found and lead Local 8 of the IWW's

Marine Transport Workers Industrial Union on the Philadelphia waterfront, wrote that "No genuine attempt by Organized Labor to wrest any worthwhile and lasting concessions from the Employing Class can succeed as long as Organized Labor for the most part is indifferent and in opposition to the fate of Negro Labor" (Fletcher 2021 [1923]:194). As a Black Wobbly organizing at a time when the mainstream of the U.S. labor movement (embodied by the AFL) was openly hostile towards Black workers even to the point of refusing to organize them, Fletcher was certainly in a position to speak from experience about the racism and exclusionary tendencies of U.S. labor. Fletcher continues: "The secret of Employing Class rule and Industry's control, is the division and lack of cohesion existing in the ranks of Labor" (Fletcher 2021 [1923]:194).

Fletcher's words are as true today as they were when he first put them to paper. There is little hope for the labor movement if it cannot build meaningful, organic alliances with today's Black liberation activists and organizations. Similarly, U.S. labor's failure to forge coalitions with progressive organizations representing the interests of Latino/a, Asian American, Indigenous, and LGBTQA+ workers, as well as environmentalist groups, has maintained a troubling disconnect between social justice activism and labor unions.

The institutionalization of the U.S. labor movement is particularly visible in the manner in which unions have adopted the capitalist model of employment in their own operations. Union organizers used to carry out their important work as militants, oftentimes risking their lives in what they perceived as a project for the liberation of the working class. Today, union organizers are paid professionals and, along with the lobbyists in Washington, D.C., are to a significant degree separated from the rank and file (Cochran 1977:128).

The purges and raiding of 'red' unions (unions with communist or left-wing sympathies) after Taft-Hartley and the intensity of the second Red Scare ensured that organized labor's potential as a revolutionary and dynamic movement was severely marred. As the Cold War evolved and grew in magnitude, the AFL-CIO's devotion to the preservation of capitalist social and economic relations in the United States was extended to other nations (Morris 1967:34). Having proved its credentials as an anti-communist organization to the U.S. government, the AFL-CIO, through partnerships with U.S. intelligence agencies, became an instrument for surveillance of workers and combating radicalism in labor movements abroad (Yates 2009:127).

The dominant labor federation has operated since the 1955 merger as a mechanism not for building and mobilizing worker militancy and power, but preserving capitalist relations in production and neutralizing worker-led efforts that challenge capital. This modus operandi adopted by the AFL-CIO in the United States following WWII was expanded to allow for interference on an international scale in the form of the American Institute for Free Labor Development (AIFLD). Even before the 1955 merger, however, the AFL supported the interests of U.S. capital abroad through the Free Trade Union Committee (FTUC), the sole purpose of which was to prevent and combat communist influence in international labor unions. AIFLD was therefore an acceleration of a political program which had already been embraced by U.S. labor's conservative bureaucracy.

Today, the AFL-CIO, through its non-profit Solidarity Center, operates abroad with the same goals as when it managed FTUC and AIFLD. Solidarity Center is funded by the National Endowment for Democracy (NED)—an organization founded in 1983 which promotes U.S. political and economic interests abroad and often works in tandem with the Central Intelligence Agency (CIA). The AFL-CIO, with the support and guidance of the CIA, has assisted U.S. capital in maintaining its international dominance for decades through attacking and dismembering unions associated with Communist or other left-wing parties, and even meddling in political elections.

The AFL-CIO's commitment to preserving the power structure in the United States and bolstering U.S. corporate interests abroad has not generated fruitful results for the federation nor the U.S. labor movement. On the contrary, union power and membership in the United States have been in a consistent state of decline, the intensity of which varies from decade to decade, since the 1955 merger of the AFL and CIO and the institutionalization of the U.S. labor movement.

The snuffing out of left-wing, militant unionism, first in the United States and then internationally at the behest of the U.S. state and corporate interests, has proved disastrous socially, economically, and politically on a global scale. The rise of right-wing authoritarianism, pseudo-populism, reactionary militias, the widespread influence of conspiracy theory, chauvinist nationalism, racism, xenophobia, and diminished standards of living can all be traced to the annihilation of formidable left-wing or progressive challenges to neoliberalism and global capitalist hegemony. Labor movements in particular have stood in the way of the expansion of this hegemony, and so had (and have) to be dealt with ferociously and intensively. The business-friendly wing of the U.S. labor movement, first in the form of the AFL and now the AFL-CIO, materialized as the ideal instrument for the fulfillment of this aim.

Anti-union laws in the United States, including Taft-Hartley, 'right-to-work', and the National Labor Relations Board (NLRB) regulations pertaining to union organizing, elections, and representation have done considerable damage to the labor movement. It can be argued that the AFL-CIO's institutionalized approach is a desperate attempt to remain relevant and respectable through coexistence with these laws rather than risk further disintegration through combating them. It is true that the socioeconomic and political domains in the United States have left labor meek and cautious to the point of impotence. However, recent developments offer some indication that U.S. labor's dynamism, appeal, and potential as an insurgent movement have not been lost completely.

The wildcat strikes led by teachers across the country in 2018 and 2019 showed worker militancy that had been unseen for decades. These strikes inspired workers in other sectors and industries to take similar actions. Roughly 2000 strikes have been reported in the United States since March 2020, the beginning of the COVID-19 pandemic. On April 1, 2022, the Amazon Labor Union (ALU), without the backing of an already existing labor union or the AFL-CIO, became the first union to successfully organize a U.S. Amazon warehouse and win a union election. Independent unionism has spread recently in other workplaces and sectors, indicating a turn towards a unionism which contrasts from the cautious, conservative unionism of the AFL-CIO.

There are various reasons to believe something of a labor renaissance is underway in the United States, especially when considering that the popularity of unions reached its highest point in 50 years and NLRB petitions for union elections increased 57% in the first half of the 2021 fiscal year alone (NLRB 2022). Whether these signs of a revitalized, militant U.S. unionism will develop into a durable, coherent movement powerful enough to challenge both capital and the dominance of the AFL-CIO is yet to be seen. A new labor movement capable of challenging the legitimacy of the labor bureaucracy while also building a mass movement with the strength, discipline, and creativity necessary to disrupt and eventually transform the power structure will need to develop close ties with progressive activists and organizations. Forging radical, collaborative relationships with workers and revolutionary labor organizations around the world will also be of supreme importance for a new U.S. labor movement. Just as capitalism has become globalized and 'without a country', so too should a coherent, militant, and disciplined new labor movement.

The future of the U.S. labor movement will depend on today's labor organizers and activists being capable of studying U.S. labor's past, learning from its mistakes, mapping out the pitfalls and traps which mangled and bastardized it before, and exercising the creativity, discipline, and rugged optimism necessary to bring to life a new labor movement (and a new world) from the ashes of the old.

References

Cochran, Bert. 1977. *Labor and Communism: The Conflict that Shaped Labor Unions*. Princeton, NJ: Princeton University Press.

Davis, Mike. 2018. *Prisoners of the American Dream: Politics and Economy in the History of the U.S. Working Class*. London, England: Verso Books.

Fletcher, Ben. 2021. The Negro and Organized Labor. In *Ben Fletcher: The Life and Times of a Black Wobbly*, ed. Peter Cole. Oakland, CA: PM Press.

Glaberman, Martin. 1952. *Punching Out*. Edmonton, Alberta: Thought Crime.

Lens, Sidney. 1961. *The Crisis of American Labor*. Beaminster, England: Barnes.

Lynd, Staughton. 2015. *Solidarity Unionism: Rebuilding the Labor Movement from Below*. 2nd ed. Oakland, CA: PM Press.

Morris, George. 1967. *CIA and American Labor: The Subversion of the AFL-CIO's Foreign Policy*. New York, NY: International Publishers.

NLRB. 2022. Union Election Petitions Increase 57% in First Half of Fiscal Year 2022. *National Labor Relations Board*. https://www.nlrb.gov/news-outreach/news-story/union-election-petitions-increase-57-in-first-half-of-fiscal-year-2022.

Savage, Marion Dutton. 1922. *Industrial Unionism in America*. New York, NY: The Roland Press Company.

Yates, Michael. 2009. *Why Unions Matter*. New York, NY: Monthly Review Press.

CHAPTER 2

What Happened to the U.S. Labor Movement?

Looking at the state of the U.S. labor movement today, one may find it surprising that Marx and Engels viewed the working class in the United States as uniquely positioned to develop class consciousness and articulate it through political struggle with the capitalist class. In a July 25, 1877 letter to Engels, Marx suggested that, following the Civil War, the working class in the United States seemed to be on its way to forming a labor party, and even suggested that the International Workingmen's Association should have made the U.S. its headquarters (Marx 1877). In the preface to the 1887 American edition of *The Condition of the Working Class in England*, Engels writes that while the European working classes required years to develop class consciousness and begin the formation of their own political institutions (labor parties, etc.), the working class in the United States accomplished this feat in ten months (Engels 1887). Obviously, the optimism that Marx and Engels felt toward the U.S. working class appears to have been unwarranted. The first portion of the task at hand is thus to determine why the working class in the United States, with all of its apparent revolutionary potential, has failed to meaningfully challenge the capitalist power structure.

In order to understand the U.S. labor movement's transformation from a dynamic, militant force against the domination of capital into a compromised, bureaucratic machine, one must examine the purposes of institutionalization in the maintenance of the power structure. Here,

A. Barrington, *The U.S. Labor Movement in the 20th and Early 21st Century*, Social Movements and Transformation,
https://doi.org/10.1007/978-3-031-30077-6_2

power structure is defined as the framework upon which ideological control systems are built and operate as a network. Specifically, one must pay attention to the connections which exist between the ruling class and its institutions and the ways in which they relate to the state apparatus. The power structure is comprised of various institutions which create and preserve a dominant ideology, one which permeates society and influences the perspectives, assumptions, and beliefs of the people within society.

The reason the U.S. labor movement was able to become institutionalized is that the germs of conservatism, bureaucracy, and class collaborationism were present early on in the movement's history. It is true the U.S. labor movement has been home to radical unions led by rank-and-file leaders who want to fundamentally change society for the benefit of the working class. However, business-friendly union leaders such as Samuel Gompers, quick to forge alliances with employers and the state to the detriment of the working class and working-class radicalism, have also been a consistent and dominant presence in U.S. labor (Davis 2018:37–38). This second trend has played a significant role in determining the course of the movement and is largely responsible for where unions in the U.S. are today.

In capitalist society, consumption is primarily the way in which people are encouraged to express themselves. The commodities which are produced therefore offer a limited scope for human expression within capitalism, even as everything (including people) becomes commodified. For social movements, commodification occurs through a process of co-optation and institutionalization which entails a social movement, assumed to be a challenge to at least some aspect of the power structure, becoming integrated into the fabric of the power structure and bled of its ability to challenge the ruling class.

The end result is that the movement becomes a consumable (and preferably profitable), non-threatening entity that does not challenge the interests of the ruling class (Dauvergne and LeBaron 2014:83–84). One is free to participate in this or that movement, join this or that 'progressive' organization, become involved in acts of protest or in some level of apparently subversive behavior, and this is the extent of their participation—the power structure remains intact, and the participant is able to feel as though they have *done something*. This approach is beneficial to the ruling class in at least two ways: (1) the ruling class gains legitimacy in the eyes of society for tolerating, or even embracing, challenges, and (2) the ruling class obtains control over the social movement and thus can prevent any truly competent challenge from emerging.

This process, in the eyes of the public, has made calls for radical change obsolete in that a system which seemingly welcomes challenges and is quick to adjust itself accordingly (on a superficial level) cannot be illegitimate. The capitalist power structure's ability to absorb challenges to its dominance is imperative for its survival and expansion. The illusion of the 'open society' that is generated by institutionalization and co-optation safeguards the power structure and the dominant ideology of the ruling class. If the ruling class in the United States still embraced the violence and terror it once did when confronting challenges to its dominance, it would lose legitimacy, and therefore would be vulnerable to organizations and movements demanding an alternative socioeconomic structure. By creating the illusion that the power structure is open and tolerant of challenges, calls for dismantling the power structure are more suited for ridicule and can be isolated from 'reasonable' politics in the popular arena.

Even today in the United States, one finds revolutionary, anti-capitalist politics only on the fringes—the furthest 'left' one can get, if they are to be considered 'reasonable' enough for a visible platform, is the moderate 'progressivism' espoused by figures who are still tightly controlled by the right-wing of the Democratic Party. This is not because the ruling class continues to respond to the left with the violence or coercion which it used against left-wing and working-class movements in the past. It is because, through violence, intimidation, incarceration, and other forms of harassment, the left in the United States was chased to the periphery of politics and social discourse, and its position is now maintained through the institutionalization and co-optation of social movements.

The labor movement in the United States stands as the preeminent example of how a challenge to the power structure becomes institutionalized by the ruling class. While the movement has long been under the control of conservative and moderate bureaucrats, it truly became institutionalized when it adopted the practices associated with business—it placed monetary concerns over the wellbeing of workers. It hired its own employees, and being a union organizer became a profession. Its leaders rubbed elbows with politicians and made backroom deals with employers, often to the detriment of union members (Lens 1961:74). It endorsed the Cold War hostility toward the communist project and participated in U.S. intelligence operations abroad, and it continues to bolster an economic and political arrangement which denounces class conflict and envisions a world in which capitalism offers the best possible outcome for humanity.

The professionalization of roles within organized labor which had previously been volunteer positions taken up by rank-and-file unionists in addition to their duties on the job has had a significant impact on the movement. Unions now hire paid staff organizers to do the work that had previously been done by the workers themselves. These paid organizers, along with paid stewards, coordinators, and other staff, are detached from the rank-and-file. They are concerned not so much with building worker power but with hitting quotas, securing deals with management, and, most importantly, with their paychecks (Yates 2009:95). With the hiring of staff to do the heavy lifting of organizing, unions have shown their adoption of the business model. Executive boards oversee the staff, reprimand them for not meeting expectations, give them raises for doing a good job, and fire them when they feel the need. It is also worth noting that, especially on the local level, union staff is typically not represented by a union, and many of the workers are at-will (able to be fired without reason at any time during their employment).

It must be noted that the U.S. labor movement prior to the merger of the AFL and CIO should not and cannot be viewed through a lens which glorifies its progressive, radical aspects but ignores its shortcomings. It is true that the U.S. labor movement was radical, egalitarian, and socially progressive at various periods in its history. However, the philosophy of a working-class solidarity that transcended identities of race, sex, and national origin was not shared across the labor movement as a whole at any point in its history (Moody 1993:22–23). There has always been a conservative tendency in the U.S. labor movement which has more or less anchored it to the power structure, and has adapted to the evolution of the power structure as time has passed. It was only natural for this conservativism in labor to mimic the business model in an attempt to coexist with capitalist relations rather than combat them. As it turns out, the capitalist power structure found it more beneficial to coexist with business unionism rather than risk the emergence of a militant, anti-capitalist unionism which might undermine the ruling class entirely. This is the root of labor's vulnerability to institutionalization and co-optation, which will be explored in more detail in the pages that follow.

After WWII

Throughout its history, but particularly in the twentieth century, the U.S. labor movement was confronted with violence and state terror (Cochran 1977:29). Its radical tendencies in particular, which espoused opposition to existing socioeconomic relations and called for egalitarianism and shared ownership of property, were viewed as threats to the ruling class and its interests. Thus, this wing of the movement had to be crushed with swiftness and severity, and the ruling class had no qualms using whatever methods were available to eradicate the threat. This included lynching, brutalization and murder by police and hired thugs, bombing, and, in the case of the Battle of Blair Mountain, the largest labor uprising in U.S. history, the weight of the U.S. Army. However, following WWII, this relationship changed.

Labor played an integral part in maintaining the U.S. war machine, with many unions signing no-strike pledges to show their commitment to the fight against the Axis powers (Murolo and Chitty 2018:193–194). During this time, the influence of the Communist Party in the United States was still strong in the labor movement, and although there was some initial hesitancy in whether to support the war, the Communists eventually came to view the fight against fascism as compatible with their principles, and so put their revolutionary aims at home on hold. A 'Popular Front' coalition was established between left-wing unionists and the Roosevelt Administration, which had previously come under scrutiny and harsh criticism from the left for its attempt to 'save capitalism' through the New Deal, which was viewed as problematic by revolutionaries.

The coalition between the liberal adherents of FDR and the communists would last roughly until the 1948 presidential election, during which the communists pushed for Henry Wallace of the Progressive Party (who had served as vice president during FDR's presidency) against Truman and the Democrats. This produced a conflict between the communists and the politically mainstream unionism which at the time was entering its romance with the Democratic Party. Roosevelt's New Deal, which offered working-class Americans relief in the midst of economic turmoil, was just progressive enough to convince workers that the overthrow of the capitalist power structure in its entirety was not necessary, and that they had a political home in the Democratic Party. Following the New Deal, millions of workers, many of whom led and participated in strikes and conflicts with police and the military that reached almost insurrectionary proportions, found themselves falling in line behind a political program designed to protect the interests of the ruling class and the capitalist power structure (Davis 2018:6).

The disappearance of viable left-wing movements and parties in the U.S. political arena has directly impacted union density and the labor movement as a whole. This disappearance was not caused by any specific or peculiar feature of U.S. political culture, but resulted from various events and reactions from the ruling class which made left-wing political activists and organizations (including radical unions) targets of state aggression. One must consider, for example, the New Deal, the Taft-Hartley Act, and the jingoist hysteria that swept the United States during WWI and WWII, which culminated in two Red Scares. All of these factors, among others, contributed to the obliteration of once influential radical and militant progressive groups and unions, and effectively decapitated labor as a revolutionary movement.

Labor and Politics

Labor and political culture are directly intertwined, and the weakness of organized labor in the United States helps discern why there is no competent left-wing political party in the United States (Lipset 1998:123). Conversely, the absence of a competent left-wing political party in the United States largely explains why the U.S. labor movement is weak. Unions in the United States are institutionalized, part of the mainstream sociopolitical machinery, and are thus at the mercy of ruling class institutions that are hostile to worker militancy and organization. For example, in other countries with stronger labor movements, one finds no institutions similar to the National Labor Relations Board found in the United States, which moderates negotiations between employers and workers and determines which unions can be deemed legitimate. Mainstream unions in the United States are docile and meek, while elsewhere they have retained a radicalism which directly puts them in confrontation with the state and the capitalist class.

Political independence of unions is of the utmost importance. Unions associated with leftist politics are stronger and more influential than conservative business unions, and union density is directly impacted by the presence or absence of effective left-wing political movements and parties. In the United States, this historical correlation is quite noticeable: union density grows when popular votes for left-wing political parties increase;

when votes for Communist or socialist parties decrease, union density declines (Stepan-Norris and Southworth 2010:242). During the first Red Scare (1917–1920), political radicals, militant unions, and immigrants were heavily targeted by the U.S. government, and there was a consequent lull in union activity. Then, in 1920, when Eugene Debs ran for president from a prison cell, there was a bump in union organizing and labor activity (it is also worth noting that Debs had garnered 6% of the vote with his 1912 run for the presidency and 3.4% in 1920).

The second Red Scare (1947–1957) coincided with the passage of Taft-Hartley, which outlawed communists (and those accused of being communists) from being members of the American Federation of Labor and the Congress of Industrial Organizations, at the time the two largest labor federations in the country. The second Red Scare inflicted humiliation, invasive and repressive legislation, and a brutal inquisition upon the U.S. labor movement, and saw to it that the best organizers in labor, the radicals, were removed from any positions of influence. U.S. political culture was also deeply impacted by the second Red Scare, as assaults on the New Deal (which was flimsy to begin with) and progressive politics increased, and labor militants were excluded from mainstream political spheres.

Not all blame can be placed on Taft-Hartley or even the two Red Scares, however. The ways in which the Wagner Act, widely viewed as pro-labor legislation, has impacted the U.S. labor movement is worth consideration as well. The U.S.'s unique labor policies have done quite a bit to diminish labor radicalism and militancy without directly attacking unions. For example, exclusive representation, which requires one union act as the representative for workers in a workplace, eliminating competition between unions, has been detrimental to union density and labor militancy.

Competition between unions had historically been a common occurrence in the U.S. labor movement, with unions vying for members by showing their militancy and devotion to the interests of workers. However, when exclusive representation became 'the law of the land' with the Wagner (National Labor Relations) Act, the more conservative and boss-friendly unions were able to secure representative positions through their political and financial resources and backroom deals with management. Rivalries between unions and internal struggles in labor fed worker militancy, encouraged democracy in unions, and increased the odds of solid collective bargaining contracts—precisely what U.S. labor legislation seeks to prevent. Conservative business unions were rewarded for their adherence to the values of the capitalist power structure, and left-wing unions were extirpated from their positions of influence in the workplaces they sought to represent.

In addition to the outright brutality that militant workers have suffered historically at the hands of the ruling class, conservatism, bureaucracy, compositional shifts in the labor force and the foundations of U.S. labor law are all responsible for the dismal state of the U.S. labor movement. The United States is somewhat unique for its conservative mobilization biases (right-wing movements are tolerated while left-wing movements are not) which determined the cautious and conservative development of U.S. labor as an institutional force. Institutional models in the United States practically guaranteed that the labor movement would embrace conservatism and the ideology of the ruling class rather than continue its trajectory of radicalism and political engagement (Godard 2009:87).

Although there are a few examples of the dominant labor federation of the United States, the AFL-CIO, supporting progressive causes, the unions within the federation engage in such political struggles as appendages of the Democratic Party rather than as independent, militant organizations with organic sociopolitical goals. Even 'pro-labor' legislation such as the Wagner Act rendered the labor movement vulnerable to co-optation and institutionalization, and there is good reason to suspect this was the main purpose of introducing such legislation (Mills 1948:231–232). While the New Deal, as sloppy as it was, and the help from above that labor received during the Roosevelt years, did benefit union density growth to a degree, it was not sufficient to sustain a militant, independent, and radical labor movement capable of organizing American workers and meaningfully challenging the interests of the ruling class.

After the AFL and CIO combined and became an ally to mainstream, capitalist politics, it assisted the ruling class and U.S. state in undermining radical labor unions abroad. Through the American Institute for Free Labor Development (AIFLD), the AFL-CIO, in collaboration with the CIA, assisted in the overthrow of democratically elected, progressive regimes abroad, aiding U.S. imperialism and advancing the interests of U.S. corporations. This signifies, perhaps more than anything else, the complete institutionalization of the U.S. labor movement (or at least its dominant federation) by the power structure.

Exclusive Representation and Systemic Restraints

The U.S. labor system is uniquely rigid, much to the benefit of employers. For example, it involves what is called 'exclusive representation,' which is a feature of the system that promotes and maintains the institutionalization of the labor movement. Exclusive representation means that one union will oversee an entire workforce, eliminating competition between unions. This has historically led to the displacement of more radical unions in favor of boss-friendly business unions, and the imposition of an obligatory political task for union bureaucrats to defend every contract as 'the best we could get', even when concessions are given and/or worker power is diminished. Docile, boss-friendly unions are rewarded with guaranteed rights of representation in workplaces, and employers are given unconditional control over workplace operations through no-strike clauses and management prerogative agreements. Rank-and-file grievances and frustrations are subdued by union leaders in order to preserve cohesion and agreeable relations with employers.

Before this system was introduced following the New Deal, unions competed for representation rights and members in workplaces, and this competition brought positive results for both collective bargaining and union democracy (Stepan-Norris and Southworth 2010:228). Furthermore, despite claims to the contrary, direct competition and rival unionism did not distract workers or curtail organizing efforts, but in fact increased union density and worker leverage against their employers. Prior to the restrictions introduced by exclusive representation, unions could garner support by appearing as the most radical option, making bolder demands than their competitors, and engaging in direct action to show their willingness to confront the boss (Richman 2018:3).

The uncertainty that thrived in this environment led to some of the most significant moments of worker militancy in U.S. history. The 'one-upmanship' between rival syndicalist and industrial unions, many led by anarchists or communists, along with numerous craft unions, produced multiple industry-wide strikes between 1911 and 1934. This changed during WWII, when unions agreed to sign pledges not to strike in order to maintain defense production.

Solidarity and Direct Action

The story of the labor movement in the United States clearly shows the pitfalls social movements face in an environment designed to keep them restricted, incoherent, and feeble. However, the story also shows an alternative path that can be taken, and indeed was taken in labor's most militant periods, often in extreme and dangerous circumstances. The U.S. labor movement at its most ferocious and radical posture provides a blueprint for social movements that seek to effectively challenge the power structure, even under extremely hostile conditions.

Unions are an effective vehicle for social change because they draw upon the preexisting identities, relationships, and experiences shared by individual participants (Dixon et al. 2004:6). While some social movements must establish identities for participants and produce frames in order to sustain those identities, unions (and effective class-conscious organizations in general) are able to organize and mobilize people by building on foundations that already exist in economic, political, and social environments. Social affiliations, friendships, and shared experiences are often the filters through which calculations and decisions regarding participation in a movement are determined, and unions have the benefit of developing and organizing along these lines. Thus, unions are a particularly organic example of social movement organization wherein identities and frames are not created but are rather recognized and articulated through participation in the organization.

Another benefit of unions is that assertive labor action has a tendency to foster worker militancy and encourage strike activity. Militant unions and worker organizations, therefore, have the ability to both produce and sustain worker militancy through direct action. Because of the way in which strikes, walkouts, shutdowns, sabotage, and other forms of militant worker action promote further action, unions and union activity significantly influence worker mobilization and have the capacity to maintain and escalate tactics so long as the participants deem them effective and necessary (Dixon et al. 2004:6). There is also some evidence that suggests that loose, unbureaucratic union organization leads to greater worker mobilization, with worker solidarity and actions buttressed by shared experiences and practices that are brought into conflict with common grievances. In reviewing the history of the U.S. labor movement, this seems to be the case, as the more conservative, bureaucratic craft unions were far less militant and mobilized than the diverse, radical, flexible industrial unions.

There is an observable reciprocation in coaction between unions and worker solidarity. Workers weigh the level of organizational support and degree of clout they have in their workplace and engage in collaborative action and risk-taking according to the potential gains which might be won. In this process lies the ingredient that makes unions durable vehicles of social movement activity: the worker determines how their identity relates to the workplace as a habitat (Lynd 2015:54–55). The workers realize their relationship to the environment and to their fellow workers, and this compels their decision to embrace a collective, class-conscious identity. Thus, unions and worker organizations become the vessels for engaging in actions which accommodate and articulate the shared experiences and interests of their members.

Labor activism in the past produced greater results in organizing and mobilizing when its messages reiterated the perceptions and convictions of workers' preexisting solidarities and shared cultural practices. For example, much has been written on the way in which labor organizations with drastically differing political philosophies, including even some unions associated with the AFL, eventually embraced militant direct action and syndicalist tactics because such strategies were more consistent with workers' indigenous solidarities and experiences. Such action was also significantly more successful in obtaining the goals of the workers.

This illustrates the point that the militant, radical, unbureaucratic industrial unions (such as the IWW and later the CIO's more radical affiliates) were more successful in their selection of tactics, so successful in fact that their conservative and moderate rivals were forced to emulate, at least to some degree, their example. While craft unionism is characterized by exclusivity, political conservatism, and membership homogeneity, industrial unionism developed worker power through mass organizing, inclusivity, and militancy. The various radical philosophies espoused by industrial unions spoke to the needs and interests of the workers beyond the workplace. Whereas the craft unions and reformist labor leaders of the AFL made only basic economic demands, the radical industrial unions such as the IWW called the legitimacy of the capitalist system as a whole into question (Kolin 2019:124).

As stated above, the more militant, syndicalist-style of action practiced and promoted by industrial unionists was eventually adopted (to some degree) by the more conservative craft unionists, as the tactics of the industrial unionists proved more effective. It is also worth noting that industrial unions tended to be organized along preexisting networks between workers rather than craftsmanship and skill, as was the case for the conservative craft unions. Because industrial unions were open to all people regardless of race, sex, religion, or national origin, members were able to organize both along the lines of existing networks as well as in a way that transcended their preexisting identities and united them under the banner of their shared working-class experiences and interests (Savage 1922:308–309).

The industrial unions tended to have a stronger sense of solidarity between members because industrial unionism bolstered workers' preexisting solidarities and relationships and sharpened worker solidarity through direct action at the point of production. Workers engaged in the sharing of grievances, confrontations with management, group-building exercises outside of the workplace, and other activities which developed a shared vision of fairness and justice. The shared understanding of justice and fairness established in the industrial union setting could be seen in the form of workers defending each other when confronted with abuse from management.

Workers risking their livelihoods for their fellow workers by resisting management not only presented a challenge to the interests of the employer, but also strengthened the bond of solidarity between the workers. The willingness to put oneself in harm's way for a fellow worker, to risk losing a job in the name of solidarity, is what made industrial unionist tactics effective in building trust and unity between workers. Thus, the act of confronting an abusive boss or engaging in direct action to support a persecuted worker, of putting into practice the old slogan "an injury to one is an injury to all", has a way of both demonstrating and encouraging worker solidarity and union activity. The militant tactics and resolute solidarity of the industrial unions forged worker power through a relationship of mutual reinforcement: the more solidarity, the more direct action and the more direct action, the more solidarity between workers.

Despite industrial unionism's philosophical opposition to bureaucracy, sustained activity is dependent on a militant and accountable cadre to call upon workers for their participation. For example, the Industrial Workers of the World (IWW) does not have presidents or bureaucratic executive boards, but it does have elected delegates and organizing committees. In order for intrinsic worker solidarities to develop into sustained direct action in the workplace, conscious leadership and mutual defense practices are of the utmost importance. Group leadership, if it is effective, provides a foundation for direct action, increased participation, and building collective identities. Leadership in industrial unions functions as a skeleton upon which the muscle of the movement is grown. The class consciousness of responsible leaders in the industrial unions entrenches them in the labor movement, the vehicle of the working class for the pursuit and attainment of its goals. Through the responsive, accountable leadership of 'organic intellectuals' (to borrow a term from Gramsci) *within* the working class, class consciousness can be introduced to and acquired by workers and weaponized against the power structure (Gramsci 1971:60–61).

Workers may engage in direct action if they perceive the benefits outweigh the risks, if the proper support is behind them, and if they feel they have enough leverage in the workplace. However, workers may also participate in direct action if there is a legacy of such action in their workplace, or if such action resonates with their shared experiences and interests. If a group of workers toil together in a sector known for instances of worker protest action, they are more likely to engage in protest action, as are workers who have recognized the social and economic patterns in the experiences they share with their fellow workers. There is an organic support system based on class consciousness and a history of action that paves the way for organized, militant worker activity, with unions providing organizational resources and structure. The organization and resources supplied by unions combined with militant worker solidarity significantly impacts the potential for worker actions (strikes, shutdowns, sabotage, etc.) and their success.

Industrial unionism, in contrast to craft unionism, has an observable positive connection to strike action, and this is largely due to direct action's mutually reinforcing relationship with worker solidarity. Industrial unions are capable of nurturing preexisting relationships and identities while also building class consciousness and worker solidarity, effectively promoting a combination of union organization and visceral worker solidarities, which makes industrial unionism more likely to successfully advance collective direct action. There was, however, a major discrepancy between labor bureaucrats and rank-and-file industrial unionists in terms of favored tactics. The leadership of the CIO, for example, favored legally binding collective bargaining contracts as a means to gain equal footing with employers. The rank-and-file of the industrial unions, on the other hand, fought their bosses with sustained direct action and militant worker solidarity (Lynd 2015:52).

Meaningful labor action, the primary example of which is the strike, is produced by, and also has the ability to bolster and expand, worker solidarity. Participation in a strike or other form of worker activism has a radicalizing effect, one which increases the militancy of the worker and builds class consciousness. While mainstream labor unions are often non-confrontational, and the union bosses usually do their best to *prevent* rank-and-file action, the passion and power which derives from collective action, when embraced by a union, reinforces the legitimacy of the labor organization, builds worker solidarity, and places class consciousness at the forefront of the struggle between the employers and the workers.

Violence Against Labor

Today the continued class war against workers and the labor movement is not conducted in explicitly violent forms, but the history of the U.S. labor movement is spangled with bloodshed. The ruling class, comprised of business magnates and their pet politicians, has time and again used the might of the state and private police forces (the Pinkertons, etc.) to violently subdue the working class when it got out of line. In such moments when the ruling class felt threatened by the potential of societal upheaval, the capitalists who were typically in competition with one another came to agree that the true battle was not between masters of industry but between employers and workers who were dissatisfied with their lot. In this sense, the ruling class has been for quite some time deeply class conscious.

In May 1886, the capitalists were so concerned about the mobilization of workers in Chicago that they deemed it necessary to exert the full might of the state, including the military, to impose their dominance and enforce the law of the market (Green 2007:178). When a mass meeting of workers held in Haymarket Square was disturbed by an explosion of unknown origin, the police, who had gathered around the workers prior to the blast, opened fire on the crowd. At least 4 but possibly as many as 8 civilians were killed, and 30 to 40 were wounded (Avrich 1984:210). Following the attack on the meeting, employers regained control over their workforces, and the workers' demand of an eight-hour day had been smothered. Much of the public, fed hefty doses of anti-union propaganda through newspapers, sided with the police and grew increasingly antipathetic toward the left, particularly anarchists, who were portrayed as crazed, anti-American bomb-throwers.

The Haymarket Affair is but one instance of brutality contained within a larger historical pattern of anti-union and anti-worker violence which characterized the traditional response of the ruling class to the labor movement in the United States. The first recorded fatalities of striking workers in U.S. history were those of two tailors in 1850 who were killed by police during a demonstration in New York City (Selcer 2006:88). Violent attacks against workers and organizers have often involved police (both state and private) employed to protect the interests of business owners. Occasionally the military has been sent in to crush working class uprisings, perhaps the most famous example being the 1921 Battle of Blair Mountain, during which roughly 100 miners were killed in battle with state police and the West Virginia National Guard. President Harding even threatened to send Army planes to drop bombs on the miners, and private planes were indeed used to drop homemade explosives in addition to poison gas and bombs leftover from WWI on several locations where the miners had established bases.

In September 1917, in the lead up to the first Red Scare, IWW offices across the United States as well as the homes of Wobbly leaders were raided by Justice Department agents and local police. Materials including typewriters, meeting minutes, correspondence notes, and even paperclips and rubber bands were seized by the agents and police, who confiscated over five tons of material from the IWW's Chicago headquarters alone (Dubofsky 1969:406). The IWW had by then already been well acquainted with violent harassment by the state, as well as by vigilantes and right-wing citizens' organizations. In November 1916, at least five but as many as 12 IWW members were killed by police and vigilantes in the Everett Massacre in Everett, Washington. In August 1917, a month before the Justice Department raids of the IWW offices took place, Wobbly organizer Frank Little was wrestled from his bed by six masked men in Butte, Montana. Little was tied to the bumper of a car by the men and dragged over the street's granite blocks before being beaten and hanged from a railroad trestle on the Milwaukee Bridge.

These are but a few examples of the violent acts committed against the Wobblies. How the union might have grown and developed if left unhindered by such assaults is an unfortunate question to which there is no answer. The IWW was targeted by the state and right-wing vigilantes because of its radicalism, but the violence against labor did not cease with the near obliteration of the Wobblies. Throughout the 1930s, unions and labor activists across the country battled police and occasionally the military in bloody conflicts, including the nearly decade-long Harlan County War (1931–1939) in Kentucky, the Chiquola Mill Massacre (1934) in South Carolina, and the Memorial Day Massacre (1937) in Chicago, Illinois.

An entire volume, and likely more, could be devoted to chronicling the barbarism unleashed upon workers and unions by the state and the ruling class of the United States. The point here, however, is to place historical violence against labor in the larger context of an explanation for where U.S. labor is today and how it got there. It is worth remembering while reviewing this history of anti-union violence that when the Wobblies or other militant unions and labor activists were being brutalized the class collaborationists steering the AFL did not side with the attacked workers but with the state and the capitalist ruling class. The conservative labor bureaucracy was as eager to expel radicals and militants from labor's ranks as were the capitalist employers, and this was made especially clear during the first and second Red Scares.

The Cold War and Institutionalization

During WWII, CIO affiliates (though not all of them) agreed to sign no-strike pledges in order to prevent disruption of wartime manufacturing. Prior to U.S. involvement in the war (especially in the 1930s), militant workers were at the forefront of a massive nationwide unionization drive, and strikes were a major component of their organizing strategy (Lynd 2015:52). The CIO harnessed this philosophy of industrial unionism, which brought it into conflict with the still craft-focused AFL. However, WWII had a way of disciplining labor. With few exceptions, unions and militant workers who had previously been engaged in confrontations with the state and employers found themselves in lockstep with the government and the labor bureaucracy in support of the war effort.

Labor unions, particularly the conservative craft unions affiliated with the AFL, had already garnered much experience in making deals with employers and the government by this time. Labor bureaucrats, bosses, and the state shared a common goal, that of amputating labor's radical wing and making unions a tame, moderating force in the power structure. The no-strike pledges and participation of union labor in wartime agreements with the state and employers made this project wider in scale. During the war, workers who may have engaged in strikes or other forms of direct action were prohibited from doing so. Labor became a part of the state-business machinery. Following the war, anti-union legislation and the second Red Scare destroyed much of what was left of labor's revolutionary potential.

As the U.S. government's focus shifted from the Axis powers to its former wartime ally, the Soviet Union, anticommunism again emerged as the hysterical religion of the ruling class. The U.S. government's anticommunist agenda following WWII effectively 'purified' U.S. society by targeting and harassing perceived subversives and eliminating the livelihoods of anyone thought to be sympathetic to communism or the political left in general (Blackstock 2000:35). The labor bureaucracy followed along obediently. Communists and suspected communists were purged from labor unions, blacklisted, interrogated, publicly humiliated, and put under intense surveillance. Labor's left-wing was effectively expelled from the movement with the help of labor bureaucrats. Having proved its devotion to the ruling class's program of anticommunism at the domestic level, U.S. labor would be tasked with providing similar assistance to the U.S. government and capitalist class internationally.

After WWII, Communist parties around the world gained popularity and respectability for their commitment to anti-fascism, which had been put on full display during the war. Communists had been, after all, among the first to warn of the dangers of Nazism and fascism, and during the war, they had organized partisan militias to combat the Axis powers. In countries such as Greece, Italy, and France, it appeared that communism would rise to power through popular and democratic means. This was deeply concerning to the ruling class in the United States.

In Latin America, the situation was similar. Left-wing political organizations and labor unions gained popular support with demands for land reform, democracy, literacy campaigns, and other measures which jeopardized U.S. business interests south of the border. The U.S. government supported reactionary military leaders and anticommunist militias, and hoped to crush any movements which might inspire further left-wing or progressive movements. Labor leaders in the U.S. were enlisted to diminish the influence of communism and other left-wing political ideologies in labor movements abroad (Davis 2018:194). In collaboration with the Central Intelligence Agency (CIA), the AFL and CIO, and then AFL-CIO after their merger in 1955, established 'schools' for educating international labor leaders and unionists in anticommunism and capitalist ideology. Through the Free Trade Union Committee (FTUC) and later the American Institute for Free Labor Development (AIFLD), the U.S. labor bureaucracy did its part in making the world safe for capitalism. Today, the working class in the United States and workers around the world are living with the consequences of the global expansion of capitalism.

In short, institutionalization means that the labor movement in the United States, or at least U.S. labor's dominant federation, the AFL-CIO, functions as an appendage of the power structure. This is not to say that all of the federation's affiliates operate uniformly, or that union leaders are all beholden to the powers that be. The top-down, bureaucratic arrangement of the AFL-CIO, combined with its deference to the ruling class political machinery (mostly through the Democratic Party), has resulted in a gulf between the labor bureaucracy and millions of workers who are daily sinking further into precariousness. Labor leaders at the top of the AFL-CIO pyramid rub elbows with politicians, shake hands with elites and employers, attend conferences and expensive dinners alongside representatives of the ruling class—in a word, they continue to engage in class collaborationism instead of building consciousness and power in the working class (Moody 1993:347).

No single person can be blamed for the state of affairs in U.S. labor today, nor can the situation be fully explained by theories of co-optation. The conditions which produced the labor bureaucracy and gutted the U.S. labor movement of radicalism are the same which have elsewhere maintained and expanded the functionality of the power structure within the system. The labor movement cannot be said to have been co-opted by the ruling class because a significant portion of its leadership, past and present, has aligned with the ruling class and pursued legitimacy within the power structure rather than advocating structural change. On the other side of the coin one finds the revolutionary movement—the Wobblies, the radical industrial unions, the unionists who embraced progressive political ideologies, civil rights, feminism, and egalitarianism. The labor movement's predicament today is not so much the result of co-optation as it is the result of the forced collapse of its militant wing.

In order to develop a better understanding of where the U.S. labor movement is today and where it might be headed, it is necessary to examine its history. One will not find a definitive moment when the movement changed its face. Rather, it will become apparent that the labor movement itself has acted as a battlefield for competing perspectives and aims. It is hoped that this investigation will inspire further discussion and debate, and perhaps aid in the resurrection of the ideas and convictions which guided the U.S. labor movement at its most militant and optimistic points.

References

Avrich, Paul. 1984. *The Haymarket Tragedy*. Princeton, NJ: Princeton University Press.

Blackstock, Nelson. 2000. *Cointelpro: The FBI's War on Political Freedom*. 3rd ed. New York, NY: Pathfinder Books.

Cochran, Bert. 1977. *Labor and Communism: The Conflict that Shaped Labor Unions*. Princeton, NJ: Princeton University Press.

Dauvergne, Peter, and Genevieve LeBaron. 2014. *Protest Inc: The Corporatization of Activism*. Oxford, England: Polity Press.

Davis, Mike. 2018. *Prisoners of the American Dream: Politics and Economy in the History of the U.S. Working Class*. London, England: Verso Books.

Dixon, M., V.J. Roscigno, and R. Hodson. 2004. Unions, Solidarity, and Striking. *Social Forces; a Scientific Medium of Social Study and Interpretation* 83 (1): 3–33. https://doi.org/10.1353/sof.2004.0107.

Dubofsky, Melvyn. 1969. *We Shall Be All: A History of the Industrial Workers of the World*. Chicago, IL: Quadrangle Books.

Engels, Friedrich. 1887. *The Condition of the Working Class in England*. Stanford University Press. https://www.marxists.org/archive/marx/works/1887/01/26.htm.

Godard, John. 2009. The Exceptional Decline of the American Labor Movement. *Industrial & Labor Relations Review* 63 (1): 82–108. https://doi.org/10.1177/001979390906300105.

Gramsci, Antonio. 1971. *Selections from the Prison Notebooks of Antonio Gramsci*. New York, NY: International.

Green, James. 2007. *Death in the Haymarket*. New York, NY: Anchor Books.

Kolin, Andrew. 2019. Repression, Resistance, and Development of the Labor Movement in the United States. In *The Palgrave Handbook of Social Movements, Revolution, and Social Transformation*, ed. Berch Berberoglu. New York, NY: Palgrave Macmillan.

Lens, Sidney. 1961. *The Crisis of American Labor*. Beaminster, England: Barnes.

Lipset, Seymour Martin. 1998. American Union Density in Comparative Perspective. *Contemporary Sociology* 27 (2): 123. https://doi.org/10.2307/2654769.

Lynd, Staughton. 2015. *Solidarity Unionism: Rebuilding the Labor Movement from Below*. 2nd ed. Oakland, CA: PM Press.

Marx, Karl. 1877. *Letters: Marx-Engels Correspondence 1877*. https://www.marxists.org/archive/marx/works/1877/letters/77_07_25.htm.

Mills, C. Wright. 1948. *The New Men of Power: America's Labor Leaders*. London, England: Harcourt, Brace & Co.

Moody, Kim. 1993. *An Injury to All: The Decline of American Unions*. New York, NY: Verso Press.

Murolo, Priscilla, and A.B. Chitty. 2018. *From the Folks Who Brought You the Weekend: A Short, Illustrated History of Labor in the United States*. New York, NY: New Press.

Richman, Shaun. 2018. The West Virginia Teachers' Strike Has Activists Asking: Should We Revive the Wildcat? *In These Times*. Retrieved http://inthesetimes.com/working/entry/20987/west_virginia_teachers_strike_wildcat_janus.

Savage, Marion Dutton. 1922. *Industrial Unionism in America*. New York, NY: The Roland Press Company.

Selcer, Richard F. 2006. *Civil War America, 1850 to 1875*. New York, NY: Facts On File.

Stepan-Norris, Judith, and Caleb Southworth. 2010. Rival Unionism and Membership Growth in the United States, 1900 to 2005: A Special Case of Inter-Organizational Competition. *American Sociological Review* 75 (2): 227–251. https://doi.org/10.1177/0003122410365308.

Yates, Michael. 2009. *Why Unions Matter*. New York, NY: Monthly Review Press.

CHAPTER 3

The Early U.S. Labor Movement

In the late 1700s and early 1800s, worker associations in the United States, before they called themselves 'unions', expressed their frustrations with mutinies, walk-offs, violence, and other forms of action which on their own did not build anything like a movement, but did require coordinated participation and solidarity. The workers who led these spontaneous actions did not establish lasting organizations and there was no continuous participation in labor activism until the 1820s. Despite being less sturdy and enduring than the unions that would develop later, worker organizations during this period were class conscious, radical, and political.

Workers established their own political parties, such as the Workingmen's party in New York, which secured 6000 votes out of 21,000 in 1829 (Lens 1961:30). Newspapers of the time even suggested these working-class parties signaled the coming of another American Revolution. Although the political parties of the early U.S. labor movement would prove short-lived, their calls for egalitarianism, cooperatives, and free land, in addition to their opposition to private property, influenced the undoubtedly socialist character of the labor unions in the United States that came after and carried the workers' struggle forward. Such radical values were essential for the Industrial Workers of the World (IWW), which declared at its 1905 founding convention in Chicago: "The working class and the employing class have nothing in common," and "The army of production must be organized, not only for everyday

A. Barrington, *The U.S. Labor Movement in the 20th and Early 21st Century*, Social Movements and Transformation,
https://doi.org/10.1007/978-3-031-30077-6_3

struggle with capitalists, but also to carry on production when capitalism shall have been overthrown" (IWW 1905).

The U.S. labor movement has never been driven by a single vision, nor guided by a single voice. Its history is one of internal struggle, contradiction, and conflict. The U.S. labor movement has evolved over time with developments in socioeconomic and political conditions. Confronted with major questions involving the ideological assumptions and prejudices of U.S. society, the house of labor has been throughout its existence unmistakably divided. This division is best understood in the context of the historical competition between U.S. labor's two dominant factions: the craft unionists and the industrial unionists.

Beginning

In the decades following the 1776 revolution, labor in the United States was beginning to take its form as a movement. At this time, labor was not concerned with mere wage increases or the length of the workday. It was focused on building cooperatives, agitating for free land, and building a new way of life which offered some level of comfort for workers living in the midst of frightening economic instability. Between 1790 and 1845, one million immigrants, many of whom harbored radical political values, came to the United States and nurtured the bond between U.S. labor and socialistic politics. Immigrant workers would continue to play a significant role in building class-conscious unionism well into the 1900s, with foreign-born workers making up a large percentage of the IWW's membership as well as that of the Communist Party in the U.S. (Cochran 1977:7).

Working-class organizations grew in the city centers, and workers engaged in political organizing and coordinated strike strategies. The leaders of these early unions were men who participated in union activity in their spare time, organizing and mobilizing workers after working long days at their craft benches. This type of leadership contrasts starkly from that of the professional union leader and paid labor organizer who will emerge further down the road.

The city-central body, comprised of various unions representing different crafts, operated as the core of the early U.S. labor movement. The unions did not attempt to create a national union. Rather, each city-central body developed in accordance with the unique characteristics, perspectives, needs, and ideals of the workers who built them. Even the National

Trades' Union, established in 1834, was not a national union, but a representative organization consisting of the unions of seven city-central bodies (Lens 1961:33). The local quality of the city-central body as the hub for fledgling unions is of considerable importance. It allowed unions and labor organizations to develop in accordance with the interests of the rank-and-file workers living in the areas in which they surfaced. The city-central bodies brought workers in close proximity to the early labor movement, and the organizations the workers built were organic creations designed to provide real, audacious representation of their class interests. Today, the local unions that serve as secondary legislative accessories for the larger national unions cannot boast this much.

The years leading up to the Civil War saw the conflict between the northern and southern ruling classes ripen, and it became apparent a confrontation would erupt. The North viewed the South's slave economy as a hindrance to the United States achieving industrialization, which was necessary if the U.S. was to become a true competitor on an international scale. While the abolition of slavery served as the cause which gave the war against the South its appearance as a moral crusade, the dominant motivation for the northern elite was not so much the humanity and wellbeing of the enslaved, but rather economic interests which demanded industrialization and competition with Europe. The South's slave economy stood in the way of the United States' evolution from mercantilism to industrial capitalism, and this is the primary reason for the war between the States. The ramifications if the Civil War were felt by both labor and industry. Between 1859 and 1899, the number of industrial plants and wage workers soared to new heights as invested capital grew to nine times its former amount. Following the war, the United States, rich with new wealth unearthed in the West and with millions of immigrants, was able to grow to proportions which made it capable of economically challenging the nations of Europe (Lens 1961:34).

The period following the American Civil War was one of precariousness for the working class. During the two decades that followed the war, union activists and workers took up the task of organizing, fighting for better wages and conditions in their workplaces, while simultaneously aspiring to elevate the interests of the entire working class. The economic crisis between 1873 and 1897 exacerbated the conflict between workers and employers. Despite the limited success enjoyed by workers in their efforts to unite in the midst of this conflict, the solidarities they established in their neighborhoods and workplaces presented a substantial challenge to the interests of the capitalist class.

With the emergence of the twentieth century came the 'scientific management' pioneered by Frederick W. Taylor, which quickly became popular with industrialists with its religion of efficiency and predictability. Taylorism, with its 'deskilling' impact on the labor force, made it easier for employers to replace workers and eventually allowed capital to move more freely to avoid regions with strong unions (Yates 2009:195). The dawn of the new century also changed the function of the state, which in the preceding period of laissez-faire acted solely as a bludgeon against obstinate labor activists at the behest of employers. The state in the new age of Taylorism retained its role as the guardian of capital, but was less inclined to simply crush opposition (although it continued to do so when it was deemed necessary). Instead, it sought political solutions to the problem of class conflict.

While industry and state were undergoing transformation, the U.S. labor movement was transforming as well. Union membership in the United States quadrupled between 1897 and 1903, and the American Federation of Labor (AFL) established itself as the movement's dominant agent. The AFL was not, however, viewed by all working people as the legitimate representative for the working class (Savage 1922:49). Other unions continued to organize and operate outside of the AFL, and in 1905, the Industrial Workers of the World openly challenged the AFL's position as the face of labor (Kimeldorf 1999:2). Regardless, the size and influence of the AFL led to its being recognized by a majority of union activists as the legitimate house of labor. The political philosophies of working people in the United States at the time were, however, anything but uniform. For every disciple of Samuel Gompers' conservative 'pure and simple unionism' one could find a socialist, syndicalist, or anarchist. Although a majority of the officials in the various unions that comprised the house of labor prior to the 1920s endorsed Gompers' business-friendly unionism, the ranks of the labor movement swelled with socialists, anarchists, and other types of radicals.

Regardless of their political or philosophical differences, workers agreed that their greatest hope of reforming the United States into a republic of the working class was through organizing and mobilizing workers into their own labor federation. There was, however, some disagreement about how this might best be put into practice, as the more class-conscious union activists found the conservatism of the craft unions a serious impediment to organizing workers. This divide between the cautious, conservative craft unionists and the radical industrial unionists would become the foundation of an internal struggle within labor which would bring significant consequences in years to come.

A House Divided

The conflict between the more conservative and homogenous craft unions and the militant industrial unions is a centerpiece of the U.S. labor movement's history. While the AFL's craft unions largely excluded black workers, women, unskilled laborers, and immigrants from membership, the industrial unions, chief among them the IWW, proudly held a philosophy of inclusion, allowing all workers regardless of race, sex, nationality, religion, or skill level to join (Dubofsky 1969:9). A key point to understand here in terms of this conflict within labor is that, while choosing between the two species of union, bosses viewed the conservative craft unions as the obvious favorable choice. Though they would have preferred not to have had to deal with any union at all, the next best thing to a non-union shop, as far as the bosses were concerned, was a shop unionized by a business-friendly association rather than a radical industrial union.

The conservative craft unions sought to protect the interests of a small, skilled portion of the working class. The industrial unions, on the other hand, sought to organize the whole of the working class, and the more radical of the industrial unionists called for the fundamental transformation of the economic and social structure. As Marxist union organizer and co-founder of the Industrial Workers of the World Daniel De Leon said, summarizing the revolutionary perspective of industrial unionism, "the Industrial Union is at once the battering ram with which to pound down the fortress of Capitalism, and the successor of the capitalist social structure itself" (De Leon 1913). Industrial unionism, De Leon said, "is the Socialist Republic in the making; and the goal once reached, the Industrial Union is the Socialist Republic in operation" (De Leon 1913).

The revolutionary philosophies of the more militant industrial unions, of which the IWW is the prime example, were built on thorough and vicious critiques of the capitalist system, and developed with inspiration from the solidarities the unions nurtured among exploited workers. Their critiques did not stop at the boss. They also targeted moderate and conservative trade unions and even nominally left-wing political parties, which they viewed as impediments to the organization of the working class and the revolutionary creation of a just, egalitarian society.

At the July 7, 1905 founding convention of the Industrial Workers of the World in Chicago, delegates were summoned by a manifesto which said: "Social relations and groupings only reflect mechanical and industrial conditions", and "Universal economic evils afflicting the working class can be eradicated only by a universal working class movement". The manifesto concluded that the "movement to fulfill these conditions must consist of one great industrial union embracing all industries," a union that is "founded on the class struggle", and the "general administration" of which "must be conducted in harmony with the recognition of the irrepressible conflict between the capitalist class and the working class" (IWW, First Convention, 1905).

One can see in the lines of the manifesto quoted above the philosophical differences which distinguished labor's militant camp from the conservatism of the dominant federation. The popularity of the gospel of direct action preached by the Wobblies deeply concerned not only the business class but also the boss-friendly, Gompers-style union leadership of the AFL. As discussions about socialism, general strikes, industrial unionism, and revolution permeated pubs, eateries, lodges, and other working-class enclaves, the leadership of the AFL began to devise plans for crushing the radical challenge presented by the IWW to the legitimacy of the dominant labor federation.

The 1905 strike at the General Electric (GE) plant in Schenectady showed clearly how determined the leaders of the AFL were to crush the IWW and their radical unionism (Montgomery 1995 [1987]:314). After management at the plant fired three workers who were organizing for the IWW, the Wobblies fought back by holding a sit-down strike, and rejected anything less than the full reinstatement of the workers to their posts. The International Association of Machinists (IAM), an AFL affiliate, resolutely opposed the strike, and played a major role in its disintegration. GE replaced up to two hundred militant workers, and the Wobbly-dominated Lodge 704 was reorganized and placed under the control of IAM. Thus, even in the IWW's first year, the forces of capital and business unionism recognized the threat posed by militant, organized, class-conscious workers and, for the preservation of their shared interests, joined together to trample radical, worker-led labor activism.

Despite the efforts of the ruling class and the labor aristocracy of the AFL, both seeking to eradicate the radical working-class movement that emerged in the form of the IWW and industrial unionism, the concept of the One Big Union remained popular, and the revolutionary potential of organized labor was being discussed by workers in various industries. Marxists and other radicals engaged in spirited debate regarding the importance of strikes and the role of workplace organizing in combating the capitalist power structure and building the revolutionary potential of the working class. The industrial unions were calling for more than better wages and working conditions: they were demanding drastic changes to the socioeconomic structure as a whole, and an end to the exploitation of workers by bosses and the capitalist system (Savage 1922:4). Industrial unions were thus more than associations representing workers in this or that workplace—they were vehicles for spreading class-consciousness and socialist values among the working class.

The power of industrial unions, and the source of their appeal to the working class, was that they organized and initiated direct attacks against capital. However, even in the industrial unions there were significant philosophical disagreements among workers. For example, the socialists who engaged in debates regarding the relevance of the industrial union in the class struggle did not share the view held by their anarcho-syndicalist comrades that participation in the political arena was wasteful or harmful to the movement. Despite the differences in their perspectives, the radical workers, whether socialist, anarchist, or somewhere in between, could agree that the union held as much significance in their movement as the political party, and therefore deserved their energy and attention. The revolutionary potential of the union presented the key to organizing the workplace for worker control.

World War and Class War

The labor movement in the United States after 1909 was full of energy and radical fervor. With a substantial increase in strikes and labor activism came rapid growth in union membership, both within and without the AFL. The outbreak of WWI exacerbated tensions in and around the dominant labor federation, and the shift toward a war economy further linked industry and the state. Class-conscious activists in the labor movement resisted the war. Eugene V. Debs, socialist, labor leader, and founding member of the IWW, was arrested and charged with sedition after encouraging resistance to the draft in a 1918 speech in Canton, Ohio. Debs is also notable for his numerous presidential campaigns on the Socialist ticket. When Debs ran for president from his prison cell in 1920, he garnered nearly a million votes. It was the most successful presidential campaign for the Socialist Party and would be the party's high-water mark.

Despite the hardships that were magnified by the war, workers across industries discovered a new sense of power in their ability to fight capital, win strikes, and fundamentally change the conditions in their workplaces. The new methods of organizing developed by radical unionists challenged the scientific management of Taylorism and simultaneously tested the legitimacy of the AFL's business unionism. The bosses and the conservative leadership of the AFL once again understood their common interests were under attack, as strike participation in the years between 1916 and 1922 swelled far beyond those of any other period. Between 1919 and 1922 alone, there were more than 10,000 strikes across the country involving over 8 million workers (Murolo and Chitty 2018:137).

The demands of the workers overwhelmed the AFL leadership and frightened business owners and the state. Whereas the labor bureaucrats at the helm of the AFL sought to reconcile the interests of the federation with those of the state and employers, the rank and file called for the release of political prisoners, public ownership of industries, and other radical reforms. This period also saw violent conflicts erupt between workers, capitalists, and the state. In 1921, striking mine workers in West Virginia engaged in the largest labor uprising in U.S. history, the Battle of Blair Mountain, during which the miners fought for the right to unionize in battles not only with police and strikebreakers but also with the West Virginia National Guard.

The first 'Red Scare' (1917–1920) erupted in response to the series of world revolutions (including the Russian Revolution of 1917) and various strikes (including the massive Seattle General Strike of 1919) which took place during, and in the aftermath of, WWI. During this time, the Justice Department and Labor Department prioritized neutralizing radicals through deportation and imprisonment. The ruling class, shaken by what was happening in the United States and around the world, responded with violent crackdowns on 'reds,' people perceived as having left-wing political sympathies. Legislation was introduced which restricted freedom of expression and specifically targeted leftists (Sedition Act of 1918—an extension of the Espionage Act of 1917). The Palmer Raids, named after Attorney General A. Mitchell Palmer, were direct attacks on labor unions and immigrants by the Justice Department which involved the targeting and capturing of individuals suspected of having ties to communism or anarchism. The IWW in particular was targeted during this time by both the state and U.S. citizens swept up in the patriotic hysteria of WWI. Frank Little, a Wobbly organizer, was lynched in Butte, Montana, in 1917. In 1918, over one hundred Wobblies were put on trial *en masse*. All were convicted and given extreme sentences of up to 20 years in prison.

The U.S. ruling class weaponized the xenophobia and anticommunist hysteria of the war period to unleash violence upon the IWW. In 1917, 1186 striking copper miners from Bisbee, Arizona, were deported. Wobbly organizers were beaten and lynched. Sailors and soldiers attacked IWW members and demolished their labor halls. Mob violence, vigilantism, and state terror combined in an effort to crush the IWW. Even after the Palmer Raids, the Immigration Bureau of the Department of Labor routinely worked with employers and police to scrutinize and intimidate workers, especially those who were foreign-born. The result of this period of violence and hostility toward leftists, immigrants, and progressive unions was a decline in participation in labor organizations and union activism. One can only speculate as to what the U.S. labor movement would look like today had this brutality against the IWW, immigrants, and labor activists not occurred.

At the close of 1922, there was a significant deflation in the militancy of the U.S. working class, as trade unions were largely excluded from corporate enterprises and the left-wing of the labor movement was isolated from positions of influence. The AFL experienced a decline in membership between 1920 and 1923, although it retained a larger membership than it had prior to the war. The degree to which labor was subdued and fractured by the end of WWI placed the U.S. capitalist class "perhaps a generation ahead of its European competitors" (Davis 2018:53).

The dominant federation emerged from the wartime period more conservative than it had been previously. Demands which had been at least entertained by the AFL (despite being unpopular with Gompers), including nationalization of industries, a labor party, a shortened workday, and federally guaranteed union rights, completely vanished from the federation. Any remaining hopes held by progressives within the federation were crushed in 1923 during the AFL's convention in Portland. At the convention, AFL leaders praised and celebrated capitalism while calling for the expulsion of radicals and leftists from union ranks. By that time, union density in the United States had plummeted 25% since its peak in 1920.

The decade following 1923 was one of stagnation and regression for the labor movement. Militant labor activism shriveled, and strike activity descended to its lowest point. The union activists and workers who had been radicalized during the war found themselves detached from the labor movement in the reactionary political landscape of the post-WWI United States. As workers shifted their interests inward toward family and ethnic ties, radical unionists lost their ability to organize and mobilize to the extent they had previously. At this point, it appeared to the union activists that life in the United States was securely under the control of corporate interests and the ruling class. The reformist leaders of the AFL, perhaps unaware of the role that their conservatism played in the damage inflicted upon the labor movement, believed that the only answer was to wait for a more agreeable political atmosphere to develop before the labor movement could rebound. As it so happens, when that atmosphere arrived, "the petrified house of labor split in two" (Montgomery 1995 [1987]:7).

The Rise of the CIO: Organizing the Unorganized

"The most famous punch in US history wasn't thrown by the Manassas Mauler or the Brown Bomber," writes Mike Davis in his essay "Punch-Out Time", "but by labor leader John L. Lewis," the "irascible bushy-eyebrowed president of the United Mine Workers" (Davis 2007:295). The target of the punch delivered by Lewis was United Brotherhood of Carpenters and Joiners of America president William Hutcheson, who had exchanged harsh words with Lewis at the 1935 AFL convention in Atlantic City.

"Bitter personal animosities engendered by the rivalry between industrial and craft unionists broke out on the floor of the American Federation of Labor Convention today," the New York Times reported in October 1935, "resulting in a fist fight between John L. Lewis, president of the United Mine Workers of America, and William S. Hutcheson, president of the United Brotherhood of Carpenters and Joiners of America" (Stark 1935:22). The 'left hook' which came to symbolize the rebellion of the industrial unions against the leadership of the AFL "was Lewis's way of saying goodbye to the American Federation of Labor (AFL) and the conservative, often nativist, craft unions that dominated it" (Davis 2007:295).

Prior to the 1935 AFL convention which acted as the stage for the infamous brawl between Lewis and Hutcheson, Lewis had already made a name for himself in the U.S. labor movement. Lewis had been a mine worker in Iowa and Illinois before he became a full-time organizer for the AFL in 1911. In 1921, he was elected president of the United Mine

Workers. That same year, Lewis attempted to unseat Gompers at the AFL convention.

The 1921 AFL convention was unique in that "the progressive bloc" of the AFL included several of the federation's leaders with the largest numbers of votes to cast. Shared among the union delegates were predictions of coal, railroad, and metal workers building a coalition to seize control of the AFL and promoting an agenda of public ownership of U.S. industry. Lewis sought support from these delegates in his bid to unseat Gompers, and declared at the convention his support for nationalization, health insurance, unemployment compensation, and other progressive legislation. In response, Gompers and his supporters attacked Lewis, calling him, among other things, an IWW agent, a pawn of yellow journalism publisher William Randolph Hearst, and a coward. Despite the incoherence of the attacks hurled at Lewis, Gompers was successful in dividing the delegates of the railroad and metal unions (Gompers had also promised them seats on the Executive Council). By retaining the support of the building trades (with the exception of the carpenters) and dividing the pro-Lewis blocs, Gompers "was reelected by a margin of 25,022 to 12,324" (Montgomery 1995 [1987]:406).

Just three weeks after Lewis struck Hutcheson at the 1935 AFL convention, another convention took place: that of the Committee for Industrial Organization. Frustrated by the refusal of the AFL's leadership to support the organizing efforts of fledgling industrial unions, Lewis summoned the leadership of other unions within the AFL to discuss the formation of a faction within the dominant federation that would focus on 'organizing the unorganized' in the spirit of industrial unionism. The Committee for Industrial Organization was formally established on November 9, 1935 with the primary objective of organizing workers in industries that were neglected by the leadership of the AFL (Stepan-Norris and Zeitlin 2002:2).

The conservative leadership of the AFL was hostile to the Committee from the start. Just a year after the founding convention of the Committee for Industrial Organization, the committee's ten international unions were suspended by the AFL and charged with 'fomenting insurrection' and 'dual unionism'. Against the expectations of the AFL's leadership, the sanctions brought the Committee the respect and sympathy of other unions, which soon severed ties with the AFL and joined Lewis and the other members of the dissident faction. Three years later, in November 1938, the Committee for Industrial Organization split with the AFL and became an independent labor federation: the Congress of Industrial Organizations (CIO).

Unlike the AFL, the CIO was open to all workers regardless of race, sex, national origin, or skill level, and was dedicated to providing marginalized communities and women representation in the labor movement (Haskins 1976:76). The CIO's goal, declared proudly in its constitution, was "to bring about the effective organization of the working men and women of America regardless of race, creed, color or nationality, and to unite them for common action into labor unions for their mutual aid and protection" (Stepan-Norris and Zeitlin 2002:3). With this radical spirit of inclusion, militancy, and class consciousness, the CIO was able to lead the largest and most sustained organizing drive by workers in U.S. history.

One Industrial Union Grand

From the moment of its founding, the Congress of Industrial Organizations was devoted to building a new vision of working-class identity and responsibility. Following in the footsteps (albeit not always openly) of the radical industrial unions which came before it, the CIO embodied the radicalism and militancy of labor's struggle against capital in the 1930s. In fact, many of the CIO's leaders and organizers had participated in earlier labor conflicts, and ingrained in the ranks of the CIO were radicals and unionists with a shared commitment to class solidarity and worker unity. Although the founders of the CIO were reluctant to acknowledge any connection to the Industrial Workers of the World, the CIO owed much of its existence to the efforts of the Wobblies (Werstein 1969:128). The legacy of the IWW could be seen explicitly in the CIO's use of direct-action tactics, especially sit-down strikes, which the CIO undoubtedly plucked from the IWW playbook.

It must be emphasized, however, that Lewis, despite some of the progressive rhetoric which occasionally burst forth from his mouth, was not a radical (although when compared to Gompers he certainly looked like one). To some of the more militant and class-conscious union workers, Lewis even seemed reactionary and despotic, and his actions occasionally affirmed their perspective. For example, in 1925, when less than half of U.S. workers in bituminous coal mines were covered by union contracts, Lewis, in an attempt to appease the bosses of the still unionized firms, cracked down on radicals in the CIO and ceased any talk regarding nationalization or shortening the workweek (Montgomery 1995 [1987]:409).

The story of the CIO, a labor federation often portrayed as infested with 'reds,' is complicated, especially in regards to the politics of the unions involved. While there is no doubt that leftists of various tendencies, most famously communists, found a home in the CIO and used it as a vehicle for class struggle, the revolutionary politics of the rank and file and the CIO organizers was not always shared by union leadership. The divisiveness which characterized the political struggle between organized workers on the 'right' and 'left' in the United States reached a peak in the ranks of the CIO (Stepan-Norris and Zeitlin 2002:4). For this reason, the accusations lobbed at the CIO, occasionally even by the political left (e.g., C. Wright Mills), characterizing it as an organization beholden to the interests of Moscow or Stalinism, are, frankly, ridiculous. There were multiple political factions operating within the CIO's various unions, some of which emphatically opposed communism.

It is also worth noting that even those workers and organizers in the CIO who were members of the Communist Party (CP) did not necessarily adhere to any dogmatic definition of 'communism,' and they certainly did not need their radical politics to be imported from elsewhere. Despite the timid loyalty of Communist Party officials to the Soviet line, which was known to change its shape at any given moment, the communist movement within the CIO was not beholden to any particular nation or state structure, but was rather the dominant popular expression of working-class radicalism at the time. Indeed, the class-conscious radical organizers and rank-and-file members of the CIO, in particular those who called themselves 'communists,' were among those workers who placed themselves at the forefront of the struggle against debasement and exploitation, and led the working class into fields of greater freedom and dignity. During the largest union organizing drive in U.S. history, led by the CIO in the 1930s, the unions created and maintained by communists and their allies were among the most progressive, antiracist, and egalitarian.

While John L. Lewis had been hostile toward radicals, even to the point of the *United Mine Workers' Journal* publishing hysterical material such as the September 1922 "Exposé of the Communist Revolutionary Movement in Effort to Seize America," he had to admit a decade later that the 'reds' knew how to organize (Montgomery 1995 [1987]:409). More importantly, the communist organizers were the only people who were willing to take on the massive task of organizing workers for low pay. What's more, after the AFL had all but snuffed out the spirit of radical, egalitarian unionism in the early 1930s, it was none other than the leftists who put themselves to work picking up the pieces and reassembling the labor movement as an organic expression of class-conscious vision and action.

Lewis was, again, not sympathetic to the views of communists or other radicals. In order to prevent any communist 'takeover' of the CIO, Lewis and the federation's other founders both used communist organizers to build CIO unions and restricted them to prevent any radicals from gaining positions of power and influence. Lewis, when warned about allowing 'reds' into the CIO and hiring communists as organizers, replied by sardonically asking "'Who gets the bird, the hunter or the dog?'" (Stepan-Norris and Zeitlin 2002:41).

Thus, while communists and other radicals were a force to be reckoned with as organizers and activists within the CIO, they were largely prevented from gaining positions in union leadership. Nevertheless, the class-conscious militants spearheaded an organizing drive which brought millions of workers into the labor movement, an astonishing accomplishment unseen before or since in the United States. Communists were even more effective in organizing when they were not CIO staff—in other words, when they did not have a CIO organizing committee obstructing their efforts.

While communists gained leadership of only 17% of the twelve international unions that were organized by a CIO committee, they garnered 61% of the 26 independently organized unions. The anticommunists, on the other hand, seized control in 42% of the international unions organized under a CIO committee, but in only 19% of the independently organized unions. Communists were able to reach workers not with simple promises of higher wages, but with radical idealism and moral authority, something that could not be achieved by those who lacked class consciousness or convictions beyond the desire for a kinder boss. This is of critical importance—it shows that class consciousness and an alternative perspective which denounces the brutality of the power structure as a whole and prioritizes unity and solidarity are key to organizing and mobilizing working people in a meaningful way.

The moral fight for the working class had been taken up by 'reds' long before Lewis recognized the legitimacy and importance of industrial unionism and broke from the AFL with the CIO. After all, 'Red Unionism' and 'industrial unionism' had been practically synonymous terms years prior to the rise of the CIO. The effort to organize the working class into 'one industrial union grand' had been a priority for the Wobblies, and later for the Trade Union Educational League (TUEL), which in 1929 became the Trade Union Unity League (TUUL).

After the suppression of the Wobblies, the communists became the dominant radical tendency in the U.S. labor movement, and were the leading bearers of the tradition of direct action and industrial unionism. Like the Wobblies, communists and other 'reds' saw the labor movement beyond the terms established by Gompers and the conservative business unionists. A union meant more than an extra dollar an hour: it meant a path to liberation, to working class ownership of the means of production. It also meant the unification of the working class through the destruction of barriers of race, sex, religion, and nationality (Savage 1922:3).

The ideas held dear by the Wobblies and later the communists who organized under the CIO were, contrary to the standard ideological perspective pushed by ruling class institutions, popular among workers who could be considered 'apolitical' or even 'conservative.' The ideas espoused by the radicals were supported by the material conditions encountered by workers, and the actions led by militant unionists brought tangible benefits to the lives of those who toiled.

The leadership of communist-led unions, including the International Longshore and Warehouse Union (ILWU) and United Electrical, Radio and Machine Workers of America (UE) (UE was even called "the Red Fortress" due to its association with communists), were guided by leaders who were as competent as those in the most successful unions, and their record of obtaining higher wages and better working conditions for workers while establishing solid collective bargaining agreements is as commendable as those of any of the exceptional unions. In other words, 'reds' delivered the goods, and were able to secure the loyalty of union members, many of whom were not communists, through their tireless engagement in labor struggles and their evident devotion to the working class.

One cannot deny the contributions of class-conscious radicals, in particular communists, in the tremendous achievements of the U.S. labor movement. This is especially true of the 1930s, when 'reds' led the largest union organizing drive in U.S. history. Millions of workers were brought into the labor movement not by disciples of Gompers or conservative business unionists, but by militant revolutionaries who viewed the labor movement as a vehicle of class struggle and a force which could be used for the liberation of the proletariat. 'Reds' did not gain the support of workers in the labor movement through infiltration or 'colonization', but through organizing the unorganized, a project which they prioritized years before the founding convention of the Congress of Industrial Organizations. Unfortunately, the years following WWII would destroy much of what had been accomplished by the 'reds' and the militant industrial unions in the U.S. labor movement.

No More Reds in the Union

The years of the New Deal (1933–1939) were among the most active and formative for the U.S. labor movement. There were several militant strikes which took place in 1934 alone: the Minneapolis General Strike, the Toledo Auto-Lite strike, and the West Coast Waterfront Strike, all of which, it should be noted, were led by both unions and militant left-wing organizations. The Minneapolis General Strike saw collaboration between the International Brotherhood of Teamsters (IBT) and the Communist League. The Toledo Auto-Lite Strike was a joint effort of a federal labor union (FLU) of the AFL and the American Workers Party. During the West Coast Waterfront Strike, the International Longshoremen's Association (IWA) fought alongside members of the Communist Party. In 1936–1937, autoworkers in Flint, Michigan, engaged in a sit-down strike at the General Motors plant, and the strike spread to Cleveland, Ohio, as the striking workers accelerated their struggle. The epidemic of labor militancy between 1936 and 1937, driven by communist organizers who were devoted to mass participation, worker solidarity, and egalitarianism, involved hundreds of thousands of workers and culminated in nearly 500 sit-down strikes (Davis 2018:64).

The successful strike, arguably one of the most important of the twentieth century, established United Auto Workers (UAW) as a major U.S. labor organization and won workers pay increases as well as the right to discuss union matters at work. It is also worth noting that many of the organizers of the strike, including Wyndham Mortimer, were members of the Communist Party or leftists of another sort. Thus, prior to the CIO split from the AFL, 'reds' were already an influential force in the labor movement, and they remained influential until the Taft-Hartley Act of 1947 and the second Red Scare with which the anti-union legislation coincided. Even before the second Red Scare and Taft-Hartley, however, one could sense the impending abandonment of radical politics in favor of partnership with the Democratic Party—the result of the New Deal's concessions to organized labor and the outbreak of WWII.

The post-WWII years of 1945 and 1946 saw the emergence of another wave of promising strikes in numerous industries. In 1946, the CIO launched 'Operation Dixie', an ambitious plan to organize southern workers which collapsed shortly thereafter due the CIO's internal feuds and anticommunism (Davis 2018:95–96). By 1947, nearly every federal government agency was involved in the persecution of radical unionists and their allies. It was not just the lunacy of a lone Senator from Wisconsin which trapped the U.S. public in an epoch of paranoia and derangement, although when the second Red Scare is discussed in U.S. pop culture outlets one gets the impression that it was all McCarthy's fault. The power structure, including the state and the business elites protected by it, simply would not tolerate an effective challenge to its legitimacy and control, and that is precisely what the ruling class saw in the 'red' labor movement.

The communists and their left-wing allies organizing in the CIO were but the most obvious victims of the second Red Scare, which began with Truman and finished with Eisenhower. In addition to genuine leftists, the anticommunist hysteria of the time deeply and painfully impacted the lives of U.S. citizens well outside of the domain of radical politics. The crazed inquisitions of the second Red Scare were carried out in conjunction with internal purges in the labor movement. The suppression of 'reds' in labor organizations was, however, largely executed by state agencies, which were intoxicated with the excitement of the Cold War. Federal government entities such as the Loyalty Review Board, the Coast Guard, Army, the FBI, the Justice Department, and the Immigration and Naturalization Service were heavily involved in the purges, as was Congress. Various pieces of legislation such as the Alien and Sedition Act (1940), Labor-Management Relations Act (1947), the Internal Security Act (1950) (which included the authorization of concentration camps for the internment of Communists), the Port Security Act (1950), the Witness Impunity Act (1954) and the Communist Control Act (1954) were introduced to subdue labor militancy and crush the left (Stepan-Norris and Zeitlin 2002:279). All of this, in addition to the Taft-Hartley Act and the fanatical House Un-American Activities Committee (HUAC), amounted to an assault on the U.S. labor movement from which it has never recovered.

Communists in the labor movement, along with their radical allies (or suspected allies) were the most heavily impacted by the Taft-Hartley Act, which exposed unions to increased NLRB scrutiny and threatened them with decertification and raiding from other unions if they did not comply with the purges. A year after Taft-Harley went into effect, 81,000 union officials belonging to both the AFL and the CIO had signed an anticommunist affidavit. Even after signing the affidavit, workers who were suspected communists or communist sympathizers were brought to trial, many of them on perjury charges, as the Justice Department sought to further discourage and frighten the unions. There were numerous labor leaders and unionists who were convicted and imprisoned as a result of these heinous trials.

The House Committee on Un-American Activities, or House Un-American Activities Committee (HUAC), along with numerous other congressional committees devoted to investigating the influence of communists in unions, inflamed the Cold War hysteria which fueled the second Red Scare. The HUAC harassed union leaders and rank-and-file members and threatened them when they refused to comply with the Committee's investigations.

In 1954, when the Communist Control Act was passed unanimously by the Senate and with only two opposing votes in the House, all labor unions, and not just their leaders, were brought under the surveillance of the Attorney General and the Subversive Activities Control Board (SACB). The U.S. government was given the unrestricted ability to target labor and besiege any unions thought to be 'communistic'.

Millions of workers in both the public and private sectors were required to undergo interrogations by roughly 200 agency loyalty boards between 1947 and 1956 alone. A conservatively estimated 1.5 million workers in the private sector encountered intense inquiries from both corporate and government surveillance programs. The goal of such private 'loyalty' programs, the National Industrial Conference Board admitted in a message to employers, was to eradicate radical agitators and make the workplace safe for profits. If ever there was a time when the connectedness of the U.S. ruling class and the state apparatus was painfully obvious, it was undoubtedly during the second Red Scare, although the first gives the second a run for its money.

It must be said, however, that the second Red Scare is not entirely responsible for the disintegration of 'red unionism' and the Communist Party's influential position in the U.S. labor movement. As brutal and authoritarian as it was, the state's extreme repression of the 'reds', occurring in conjunction with the raiding of 'red' unions by business unionists, cannot be blamed solely for the disappearance of unabashed radical, left-wing politics in U.S. labor. There is no denying that the political climate of the Cold War was terribly restrictive to the left, and following the FDR years, the Republicans were able to carry out incessant attacks on the New Deal without resistance from Truman or the Democrats in Congress. However, the Communist Party's inconsistent and incoherent political strategy contributed to its downfall in the labor movement. The contra dictions which plagued the Communist Party's political program rendered the 'reds' ineffective and often incomprehensible. The party's rigid adherence to the Soviet line did not help, either.

The Communist Party of the United States had cautiously supported the Roosevelt-Wallace coalition against Truman, but ultimately decided to push a third-party ticket. This change in the party's political strategy would turn out to be a reckless gamble, one which broke the center-left alliance the communists had built in the CIO and accelerated the anticommunist purges that followed. The Communist Party had not successfully convinced the CIO to endorse the Progressive ticket, and moderate unionists within the federation, including United Auto Workers (UAW) president Walter Reuther and president of the CIO Philip Murray, were enthusiastic about the Democratic Party and loathed Wallace, the Progressive Party, and communism.

Although the Communist Party had previously sought to prevent sectarianism within the CIO, a meeting on December 15, 1947 between Communist Party officials and CIO unionists signaled a shift in the party's political approach (Stepan-Norris and Zeitlin 2002:293). Communist Party representatives explained to the unionists that it had been determined that a third party was necessary and that they were to support Wallace's candidacy on the Progressive Party ticket. The Communist Party officials also told the unionists that, despite the potentially disastrous risks involved, they were to make every effort to win the Progressive Party the endorsement of CIO leadership. By all accounts, this announcement was met with hostility from the CIO unionists at the meeting, who did not care much for directives from the Communist Party's central committee.

When warned that the Communist Party's support of the Progressive Party would 'split the CIO down the middle,' New York State Communist Party chairman Robert Thompson responded by saying that the directive must be followed regardless. Of interest here is the reversal in the party leadership's line that resulted in their sudden wager on a third party, a strategy which they knew had the potential to divide the CIO. It was, after all, contradictory to the assertions made by party leaders earlier that any viable third party would need the backing of substantial sections of the labor movement as a precondition for its formation.

The October 1947 issue of The Daily Worker is worth consideration. In the issue, an editorial reported the formation of a new Communist Information Bureau (Cominform) and announced the Cominform's call for the development of 'united fronts from below' in opposition to the Marshall Plan. In regards to the United States, the editorial made no call for a third party, and instead urged for a coalition based on the Roosevelt-Wallace line. Regardless, the leadership of the Communist Party and its representatives in the CIO pushed for the Progressive Party and repudiated union members who would not do the same. The catastrophic results of the Communist Party's policy became evident in the CIO, and as the likelihood of a victory for Wallace dwindled and eventually disappeared, the communists went on the defensive. The moral authority which the Communist Party had built in the CIO had lost its legitimacy in the eyes of the workers, and this, along with political repression and union purges, brought about the obliteration of communist strongholds in the CIO. Thus, the class-conscious, militant industrial unionism the 'reds' had established in the labor movement, the spirit of which prompted the most significant union organizing drive in U.S. history, was demolished.

Red Unionism: An Autopsy

In the 1950s, the CIO was badly bruised by purges, government repression, and internal struggles. Progressive affiliates of the CIO, which were weakened by the Red Scare and the anti-union legislation introduced in the 1940s, were especially fragile. This turmoil from within, exacerbated by political battles in the federation, reduced the effectiveness of the federation's organizing for which it was renowned in the 1930s. In the 1940s, UE, the 'Red Fortress,' was under threat of raiding by the UAW, as well as other moderate or conservative unions, and CIO president Philip Murray did nothing to defend UE or discourage other CIO affiliates from raiding.

UE, formed by communists and militant workers, distinguished itself from bureaucratic, top-down unions with its commitment to worker control and union democracy (Kolin 2019:129). UE was one of the gutsy CIO unions which refused to sign the anticommunist affidavits, and its leaders were charged with contempt for refusing to cooperate with the HUAC. Eventually, however, UE was forced to reverse its earlier rejection of the Taft-Hartley anticommunist affidavits in order to appear on the National Labor Relations Board ballots for representation rights.

Regardless, the CIO leadership still refused to prevent or even discourage raiding of UE locals, and in response, UE boycotted the CIO's 1949 convention by withholding dues payments to the federation, terminating, in effect, its affiliation with the Congress of Industrial Organizations.

UE is worth mentioning here not only because it is one of the two 'red' unions that resigned or was expelled from the CIO, the other being ILWU, which survived the Red Scare and continues to exist today, but also because it has retained the principles of industrial unionism, principles which stand in stark contrast to the conservative, business-friendly politics of the AFL-CIO.

In UE's pamphlet titled "Member-Run Unionism: The Democratic Alternative that Works," UE gives credit to the IWW in the introduction. UE praises the Wobblies' commitment to democratic unionism and the inclusivity which drove the IWW to organize workers—women and men, skilled and unskilled—of all races and nationalities, a commitment which distinguished the IWW from the AFL, which only permitted skilled white men to participate in its unions (UE n.d.:1).

In the pamphlet, UE goes on to describe how the capitalist class, with its allies in the state and with some support from labor bureaucrats, undermined rank-and-file-led, democratic unionism in the 1940s and 1950s in favor of employer-friendly business unionism, with its backroom deals and barriers to the participation of union members (UE n.d.:1–2).

The UE pamphlet also includes a section devoted to 'Independent Political Action', which describes the one-sided partnership between the labor movement and the Democratic Party. While the working class in the United States has a long tradition of supporting the Democrats, labor parties and politically independent worker organizations were a significant force in U.S. labor history, and the Democratic Party owes much of its success to its ability to co-opt political parties and organizations to its left. After the relatively progressive legislation passed during FDR's New Deal administration, labor forged a partnership with the Democratic Party which has been to the benefit of Democratic politicians but to the detriment of organized labor and the working class (UE n.d.:17).

When the AFL and the CIO merged in 1955, it was clear that the AFL, which remained less militant and more business-friendly throughout the period of estrangement between the two federations, held the dominant position. The political turmoil within the CIO and the expulsion of its most effective organizers, the communists, had rendered the once powerful federation insecure and desperate. Various other social and political factors, including the election of Eisenhower and the deaths of AFL president William Green and CIO president Philip Murray, made the merger all the more appealing to the two labor federations (Haskins 1976:91).

The new leaders of the AFL and CIO, George Meany (AFL) and UAW's Walter Reuther (CIO), were much more attracted to the idea of a merger than their predecessors. As might be expected, after the first meeting of the reunited AFL and CIO came to a close, Meany took the presidency, and Reuther was reluctantly stuck in the less appealing position of vice president. The divergence in the labor philosophies of the AFL and CIO was, despite some softening in the period following WWII, as apparent as ever. After being elected president of the AFL-CIO, Meany boasted: "It may interest you to know that I am president of this great organization that has such tremendous power, and I never went on strike in my life, never ran a strike, never ordered anyone else to run a strike, and never had anything to do with a picket line" (Haskins 1976:92). Reuther, vexed by Meany's conservative leadership, later said of the merger: "We merged but we did not unite" (Haskins 1976:92).

The U.S. labor movement, since the end of the Civil War to the merging of the AFL and CIO in 1955, encompassed a wide variety of political philosophies, goals, strategies, and perspectives, the most radical of which demanded in some form the liberation of the working class from the chains of capital. There were, and still are, undoubtedly, conflicts within the labor movement: between conservatives, moderates, and leftists, between reformists and revolutionaries, and between those who hold a view of the union as a ticket to a better standard of living within capitalism and those who see the union as a hammer with which to smash the capitalist system to pieces. Of critical importance here is the fact that, regardless of one's politics or philosophical positions, the power of organized labor, of the unionized, class-conscious working class, is undeniable. This fact, recognized soberly by the ruling class, is the reason that the state and employers have invested so much time, energy, and money in the repression and quashing of militant workers and their unions, not only during the first and second Red Scares, but consistently throughout the history of the U.S. labor movement and into the present.

State repression, corporate consolidation of power, business union opportunism, and the incoherence of the left-wing of labor led to the disintegration of what could have been a revolutionary movement in the United States. The U.S. labor movement (or at least its mainstream sect) has, as a result of the incessant attacks on 'reds' and progressive unions from the ruling class and the business-unionist disciples of Gompers, been unable or unwilling to challenge the capitalist power structure in its entirety. Since the New Deal-era, the U.S. labor movement has been linked to the Democratic Party in a sadomasochistic relationship, and during the Cold War, it became a faithful accomplice to U.S. intelligence in surveillance operations and other efforts to make the world safe for capitalism. Labor's conservative leadership helped the state and business class muzzle worker radicalism in the U.S., and would later aid in the destabilization of left-wing governments and crushing of militant labor unions abroad.

U.S. Labor and Anticommunism

During the American Civil War, labor staunchly supported the North. The workers building the early trade unions in the United States found the institution of slavery repugnant and incompatible with the principles of their movement. Labor also voiced opposition to the Mexican-American War. The early U.S. labor movement was heavily influenced by socialist and progressive politics, and thus both the slaveocracy of the South and the doctrine of Manifest Destiny were seen as intolerable enemies and hindrances to human freedom. The labor movement viewed the Spanish-American War with similar contempt. However, the leaders of the AFL, including Samuel Gompers, supported the war when it began. They felt that, in order to prevent their patriotism from coming into question, it was necessary to support the U.S. government's first major imperialist venture (Morris 1967:35).

The AFL leadership's support of the Spanish-American War marked a turning point in the U.S. labor movement. Gompers and his associates thought it was in labor's best interest to be on good terms with the state. They had hoped that, if labor supported the government during the war, they would be rewarded with friendly domestic policies in return. The conservative leadership of the AFL had a significantly different opinion on matters of government policy than the rank-and-file unionists, who still opposed the war and U.S. imperialism in general. Gompers and his collaborators used their power and influence to silence dissenting voices and they then began using a strategy which would later be called 'red-baiting'.

With WWI and its aftermath, the AFL leadership's support for U.S. imperialism became integral to the federation's policies regarding foreign affairs. In 1917, the October Revolution in Russia frightened imperialist powers elsewhere. The United States sent troops to join European and Japanese armies in Russia in an attempt to crush the new socialist government there. The imperialist armies ultimately failed, and the emergence of a new challenge to the global dominance of capital gave rise to the first Red Scare. Gompers and his associates in the AFL, including William Green, who would succeed Gompers in 1925, adopted a view of the USSR that was arguably even more hostile than that of the U.S. government. Gompers and the other conservative labor leaders opposed diplomatic recognition of the Soviet Union, and they refused to have any kind of relationship with Soviet trade unions. The AFL aided the state and employers during the first Red Scare, labeling militant labor leaders 'reds' regardless of whether they had any formal ties to radical politics.

The savage violence, including murder, unleashed against the Great Steel Strike of 1919 was indicative of the threat perceived in the labor movement by the ruling class. Anticommunist hysteria brought further acts of brutality against workers and labor unions, including the Palmer Raids and the arrests and deportations that followed. This was all part of what was called 'the American Plan', which involved crushing militant unions and replacing them with company unions, implementing 'yellow dog' contracts (individual contracts) to prevent collective bargaining, and slandering progressive labor leaders in pro-capitalist propaganda.

While there were eruptions of labor militancy in this period, including multiple strikes in the textile industry and a strike led by coal miners that lasted for 15 months, the AFL leadership distanced themselves from such actions and denounced the unions involved as 'red' or 'communist'. The unions under conservative leadership sought to appease employers by allowing wage cuts and other concessions, making them essentially company unions. The conservative AFL leaders also voiced opposition to unemployment insurance, and only changed their stance years later when a rank-and-file-backed bill for unemployment insurance was sponsored by the FDR administration. The business-friendly, anticommunist tenets of the labor bureaucracy were not shared by the rank-and-file unionists, who remained militant and inspired by progressive and radical politics. However, the AFL leadership's right-wing values were shared by gangsters and racketeers, who would come to influence and even control many unfortunate unions through intimidation, terror, and violence.

Like the boss-friendly labor leaders, racketeers and gangsters, who saw organized labor as a lucrative investment opportunity, made deals with employers to crush 'reds' and stamp out militant unionists. The gangsters themselves viewed communism and left-wing politics with antipathy, and found common cause with employers and conservative union bureaucrats. Al Capone himself declared '"Bolshevism is knocking at our gates,"' and '"we must keep the worker away from red literature and red ruses; we must see that his mind remains healthy"' (Morris 1967:42). Employers hired thugs and gangsters to terrorize workers, break strikes, protect scabs and property, and disrupt union organizing. In addition to gangsters, business owners also employed private detective agencies, such as the Pinkertons, to spy on workers, sniff out 'reds', and brutalize any rank-and-file unionists who got out of line. The conservative labor leaders made use of goons and racketeers as well, inviting them to intimidate dissenting workers and violently suppress any perceived 'communist' influence in their unions.

In addition to anticommunism, racism was also an influential force in the labor bureaucracy, and the right-wing unions that dominated the AFL excluded black workers from their ranks. Racism played a significant role in the 'American Plan', as propagating racial prejudice and hostility in the working class was a means of keeping workers divided and subduing class consciousness. Black workers were brought in by employers to break strikes by white workers, the expectation being that the white workers would blame their black counterparts, who were often hired without being informed that they would be used as scabs, rather than direct their frustration toward the employer. The AFL made no attempts to build solidarity between black and white workers, and it would not be until the Civil Rights movement gained enough momentum in the 1960s that the labor bureaucracy would take racism seriously enough to address its presence in the labor movement, and even then, it did so reluctantly. The racism at home complemented U.S. imperialist expansion abroad, as the United States aggressively sought to dominate 'non-white' nations and pillage their resources.

The AFL leadership enthusiastically supported U.S. imperialism in the hopes that some of the plunder would flow to their federation. The rank-and-file had a much different outlook regarding Uncle Sam's adventures abroad, and so the conservative labor bureaucracy found it necessary to intensify its red-baiting campaigns against militant unions and their leaders. When William Z. Foster founded the Trade Union Educational League (TUEL) in 1921, the AFL leaders responded with heightened belligerence. TUEL advocated for solidarity between unions, organizing workers in neglected industries, union democracy, an end to class collaboration, rank-and-file control of the labor movement, and militant class struggle.

As TUEL garnered rank-and-file support and gained momentum, it adopted an openly anti-imperialist stance and called for the recognition of the USSR. The AFL responded to the growth of TUEL with red-baiting and purging progressive unions and their leaders. The federation eventually prohibited union members who it considered communist or sympathetic to communism from holding delegate positions at AFL conventions. After TUEL became the Trade Union Unity League (TUUL) in 1929, the AFL, frightened by the possibility of the progressive wing of the labor movement gaining an upper hand, introduced plans to subvert TUUL organizing drives, particularly in the south (Foner 2022:9).

The labor bureaucracy used anticommunism as a weapon against progressive currents in the rank-and-file that it felt would hinder its chances of getting on friendly terms with the government. The AFL's right-wing leaders aided employers and the state in crushing militant and left-wing tendencies in the labor movement, and would later assist U.S. intelligence in doing the same on an international scale. After 1955, the AFL-CIO collaborated with the CIA in intelligence operations abroad with the purpose of undermining left-wing labor unions and establishing toothless, business-friendly unionism, helping pave the way for U.S. corporate investment. At the heart of the federation's relationship with the CIA was the commitment to anticommunism and farcical class collaborationism that dug its roots in the labor bureaucracy during WWI.

Anticommunism was weaponized by the conservative labor leadership domestically during WWI with the goal of neutralizing militants and radicals in unions and forging a rapport between the federation, employers, and the state. In the 1930s and during WWII, the labor bureaucracy joined big business and the U.S. government in prioritizing international affairs.

The Soviet Union served as a convenient boogeyman for the U.S. ruling class, and provided justification for imperialist policies and interference in foreign lands. Some figures in labor and business even advocated supporting Hitler and the Nazis against the USSR, including National Civic Federation (NCF) president Ralph Easley. The NCF emerged shortly after the Spanish-American War with the purpose of fostering collaboration between labor bureaucrats, employers, and the government. Founded on the asinine notion that workers and bosses have shared interests, the NCF sought to settle labor disputes and develop a peace accord between business and labor, as class struggle at home impeded preparations for imperialist endeavors abroad. The flimsiness of the NCF's assumption regarding common interests between labor and business was shown quite clearly in the violent struggles that occurred in the years following its creation.

In the 1930s, the decrepit NCF's primary spokesman was AFL vice-president and close Gompers collaborator Matthew Woll. A lifelong Republican and opponent of the New Deal, Woll served as the AFL's international affairs chairman and consistently headed the AFL's convention resolution committee. Woll helped develop a 'Pan-American' strategy for spreading business unionism to Latin America. Woll's 'Pan-American' scheme was designed to assist the U.S. government's imperialist ventures in the Caribbean and Central and South America. When the CIO was founded in the mid-1930s, Woll became one of the new federation's most vicious adversaries. Despite the antagonism between Woll and the CIO's founder, John L. Lewis, the two men would both find themselves serving on a committee beside Herbert Hoover shortly before the U.S. became involved in WWII. The committee's objective was to encourage Adolf Hitler to invade and dominate the USSR (Morris 1967:49).

Through his associate David Dubinsky, the right-wing president of the International Ladies' Garment Workers' Union (ILGWU), Woll was introduced to Jay Lovestone, who would come to play an integral role in crafting the AFL's foreign affairs policies. In the 1920s, Lovestone served as the general secretary for the Communist Party of the United States of America (CPUSA), before he was expelled for his support of Bukharin and the Right Opposition in the Soviet Union. After his expulsion, Lovestone founded the American Communist Party (Opposition), nicknamed 'Lovestoneites', but by the 1930s, Lovestone had become vehemently anticommunist. With Lovestone, Woll and Dubinsky formed the American Labor Conference on International Affairs (ALCIA).

One of the ALCIA's primary objectives was to disrupt the rise of the CIO. Through its organization of millions of unskilled or semiskilled workers, the CIO shifted the foundation of U.S. labor from craft unionism to industrial unionism. The ALCIA recognized the threat the CIO's industrial unionism posed to its imperialist agenda, and was particularly troubled by the CIO's renouncement of racism and commitment to anti-fascism. As villainous as Lewis appeared to ALCIA and the AFL leadership, it was the rank-and-file unionists and their radical leaders in the CIO affiliates who really stood to imperil the labor bureaucracy. Lewis and other anticommunist CIO leaders did not share the progressive vision of the rank and file, and were not comfortable with the federation's connection to left politics. Lewis' primary concern, which he shared with other CIO union leaders, was obtaining contracts and representation rights, not building a new society through class struggle (Lynd 2015:58–59).

Eventually, the philosophical rift between the rank and file and his administration would prove too much for Lewis. As the CIO became increasingly associated with Roosevelt and the New Deal, Lewis, who advocated for negotiating an agreement with Hitler, was forced into retirement as president of the federation in 1940. His successor, Philip Murray, supported FDR and the New Deal, and during his presidency, the CIO joined Soviet and British trade unions in sponsoring the World Federation of Trade Unions (WFTU). The AFL, with encouragement from the State Department, responded to the CIO's newly won prominence with red-baiting and fomenting factionalism.

With funding from ILGWU and eventually the CIA (through its front organization the J.M. Kaplan Fund), ALCIA published anticommunist and anti-Soviet literature and distributed it to unions. In 1943, when it became clear that the Nazis were going to be defeated in the USSR, the ALCIA held a conference at the Commodore Hotel in New York. The special conference featured a speech delivered by Raphael Abramovitch, an anti-Soviet exile, who hoped (and predicted correctly) that a cold war against the USSR would follow the end of WWII. At an AFL convention in 1944, a resolution drafted by Lovestone was passed and the federation established the Free Trade Union Committee (FTUC), a nominally independent entity that would control AFL foreign policy through the 1940s and 1950s. Lovestone served as executive director of the FTUC, and in 1963, he became the international affairs director for the AFL-CIO. The FTUC provided financial support to anticommunist political and labor organizations, while much of its own funding was provided by the CIA (McKenzie 2022:4).

By the late 1940s, the CIO's internal struggles and political factionalism, in addition to the AFL's extreme red-baiting campaigns and the 1947 Taft-Hartley Act, ruptured the federation's unity. In 1948, the CIO convention in Portland, Oregon, was largely committed to adapting the federation's policies to suit the narrative of the Cold War, ensuring division in the CIO's ranks. At a convention a year later in Cleveland, Ohio, the CIO expelled at least 10 unions for refusing to support the Cold War. The anticommunist purges, which reduced the federation's membership by 1.7

million, severely damaged the CIO's prestige and organizing drives (Parenti 2001:43). As the CIO adopted the practices of the AFL, it began to look increasingly like a federation of old, conservative, business unions, complete with domineering bureaucracy and hysterical anticommunism. Expelled unions were raided, black workers left in droves, and intensified anticommunist policies effectively immobilized the labor movement. It would not be long before Woll and his associates were collaborating with CIO leaders, all enthusiastically throwing their clout behind the Cold War.

In 1949, the AFL, joined by other international anticommunist federations, formed the International Confederation of Free Trade Unions (ICFTU). Former CIA agent Philip Agee divulged in his 1975 memoir *Inside the Company: CIA Diary* that ICFTU was "set up and controlled by the CIA to oppose the World Federation of Trade Unions (WFTU)" (Agee 1975:540). In March 1951, George Meany, at the time secretary-treasurer of the AFL, boasted in a pamphlet published by the federation titled *The Last Five Years* about the AFL's "world network in the fight against communism" (Morris 1967:59). Though the AFL (and U.S. intelligence) essentially directed the ICFTU, Meany underscored the international operations exclusive to the AFL, and bragged about the activities of the Lovestone-directed FTUC. Meany praised the AFL's anticommunist literature, printed in various languages and distributed internationally, and noted the federation's representatives (including CIA asset Irving Brown) in Europe, Japan, India, and Latin America.

Meany was not the only one putting pen to paper for the anticommunist cause. William Green, Gompers' successor to the AFL presidency, penned his own anticommunist propaganda in editorials for *The Federationist*, the monthly magazine of the AFL and later the AFL-CIO. In one of his editorials published in 1950, Green warned of the communist threat to Christian society, and the same issue of *The Federationist* included a salute from Green to the Free China Labor League (FCLL), a CIA operation based in Taiwan. A year later, Meany confirmed in a speech delivered in Chicago that the AFL was linked to the FCLL. In a 1951 editorial, Green praised the Supreme Court's decision to uphold the Smith Act, and supported the imprisonment of top leaders of CPUSA.

Matthew Woll's editorials for the International Free Trade Union News gained significant international attention. His bellicose anticommunism was popular among 'Hitlerite' West Germans, who yearned for a real war against communism and perceived Woll's writings as calls to action. In

March 1953, the New York *Daily News* reported that, "The American Federation of Labor is sponsoring a spy organization in Berlin". The report continued, "The AFL transmits approximately $10,000 a month to the U.S. Central Intelligence Agency, which in turn, passes the money to the group called Kampfgruppe (combat group)" (Morris 1967:67). The Kampfgruppe gegen Unmenschlichkeit (Combat Group against Inhumanity) was an anticommunist terrorist organization based in West Germany, and many of its members were formerly associated with the Nazi Party. The Kampfgruppe engaged in sabotage, arson, poisoning, kidnapping, murder, and bombing, among other reprehensible activities (adding soap to powdered milk that was to be given to children in East German schools, for example) with financial support from the CIA (Blum 2003:61).

Following the merger of the AFL and CIO, U.S. labor would find itself increasingly involved in CIA operations around the world. The AFL-CIO's collaboration with U.S. intelligence and its involvement in coups and paramilitary projects caused U.S. labor to become alienated from international labor movements and trade unions. As the AFL-CIO assisted corporations in making the world safe for capitalism, it dug its own grave at home. The decimation of left-wing labor and political movements abroad opened up the world to globalization and capitalist expansion. Corporations closed up their factories in the United States and moved them elsewhere, where they could find cheaper labor to exploit. In addition to globalization, crushing left-wing political parties and movements has allowed right-wing authoritarianism, ethno-nationalism, and pseudo-populism to rise almost unchallenged on a global scale. Without the impediment of Communist or other left-wing parties and labor movements standing in the way, rebranded fascism has taken advantage of the chaos of capitalism and its crises, and today holds worldwide influence and political power.

Neoliberalism has proven unable to halt the rise of the right. This is primarily because, like the right and its fascist trends, neoliberal 'centrists' do not challenge the legitimacy of capitalism. Thus, the U.S. labor movement has not only served the purposes of the ruling class and imperialist state through direct participation in its operations, but also through its seemingly unassailable connection to the neoliberal Democratic Party.

The Graveyard of Social Movements

The Democratic Party is an organization with an observable history of co-opting, absorbing, manipulating, and moderating progressive social movements, the labor movement chief among them. The political consequences of this are worth analyzing. The Democratic Party "has often been called 'the graveyard of social movements,' and more often than not the social struggles in the United States end their useful lives digging their own graves" under the party's influence (Eagleburger and Rusk 2017:1). A ruling class political institution, the Democratic Party, oftentimes by merely pointing out the grotesqueness of the Republican Party, attracts and absorbs progressive social movement activists hoping that collaboration with the political establishment will further their causes.

The institutionalized social movements end up functioning as appendages of the Democratic Party without seeing anything done for them in return. In contrast, social movements associated with the Republican Party embrace institutionalization because conservative and reactionary movements are able to experience institutionalization without sacrificing militancy or political integrity. As the movements associated with the Republican Party are unabashedly conservative, capitalist, and even reactionary, they do not pose a threat to the power structure, and are therefore given license to be as extreme as they would like. Left-wing movements, on the other hand, "become more restrained, more concerned with keeping their leaders happy, less confrontational, and less powerful" when they associate with the Democratic Party (Eagleburger and Rusk 2017:2).

In the past, the Republican and Democratic parties were confronted by challenges from independent political and labor organizations, including the Socialist Party, the Industrial Workers of the World and other militant unions, and eventually the Communist Party. The two dominant political parties still maintained the capitalist power structure, but it was more difficult to convince the working class that alternatives did not exist. It was a coalition of left-wing parties, unions, and groups espousing radical alternative politics that forced Roosevelt to introduce the New Deal, which, despite being far from perfect, did meaningfully impact the lives of workers. The working-class parties, unions, and organizations did not collaborate with the Democratic Party to bring about such concessions—on the contrary, the progress came about as a result of workers refusing to be controlled by the Democrats.

The communists organized councils of unemployed workers that demanded jobs while engaging in direct action and protest (Foner 2022:27). Militant unions led strikes in multiple U.S. cities, including remarkable sit-down strikes in auto plants. In the Jim Crow South, communists organized racially integrated unions in steel mills and other manufacturing institutions. The working-class groups did not negotiate with elite institutions or follow the prescribed methods of the Democratic Party, and this autonomy allowed them to remain radical, militant, and uncompromised.

The successful strikes and the growing support for alternative parties and political organizations opened the door for the most powerful working-class organization ever to emerge in the United States: The Congress of Industrial Organizations. The creation of the CIO was fueled by rank-and-file militancy and strikes, many of which were illegal and all of them disturbing to capitalists and their political institutions. The labor bureaucrats who broke away from the AFL to form the CIO merely harnessed the energy of the working-class radicalism which erupted in the 1930s in the form of strikes and clandestine worker committees on the shop floor (Davis 2018:60). However, when the time came to decide the course of the new federation, it was the cautious union leaders who were to choose between organizing workers and lashing out against the power structure with all of the risks involved, or accepting contracts which would allow them to take a more comfortable position that did not require incessant struggle. The CIO leadership, considering the potential encroachment of other opportunistic and boss-friendly union leaders, chose the latter.

The contradiction of the contract is that it simultaneously records gains by workers while acknowledging employers' control of industry (Glaberman 1952:24). While contracts serve workers in taking at least a degree of power from bosses, they also allow union leaders to become comfortable and apathetic. When union officials become severed from the rank-and-file, and are not held accountable by a militant union or revolutionary politics, self-interest and comfort have the tendency to become their primary motivators. Rather than pursue the interests of workers through militant struggle, comfortable union leaders attend conferences with the masters of industry, shake hands with politicians, and assist in the maintenance of the power structure.

Association with the Democratic Party helped union bureaucrats redirect worker militancy into orderly political campaigns which bolstered the Democratic Party but weakened the autonomy and radicalism of the U.S. labor movement. After WWII, the CIO's leaders collaborated with the Democratic Party (and the U.S. government as a whole) in the purging of communists and other radicals from their unions, and then complied with the Taft-Hartley Act's prohibition of radicals from union ranks. This further served to moderate the labor movement by stripping unions of their most effective and militant organizers.

This moderation and institutionalization of the labor movement aided the power structure in multiple ways, including the mythmaking regarding peaceful protest and nonviolent action. In truth, historical social movement action and protest, which did involve nonviolent demonstrations, also involved participants engaging in armed conflict with police, reactionary terrorist organizations, and even the U.S. military. The violent, disruptive, and militant histories of labor and other social movements are downplayed because such history is inconsistent with the power structure's façade of openness and tolerance.

The labor movement is hardly the only example of a social movement being absorbed, institutionalized, and defanged by the Democratic Party. The Civil Rights movement stands as a particularly tragic example, as the movement that had sprouted as a call for human decency, equality, and solidarity would eventually be called to uphold the Democratic Party's abhorrent policies, including support for the Vietnam War, hostility toward the antiwar movement, and participation in CIA operations. Organizations within the Civil Rights movement that remained outside of the control of the Democratic Party, such as the Black Panther Party, were met with violent state repression.

Social movements that collaborate with the Democratic Party assist ruling class institutions in maintaining a mask of legitimacy, and redirect activists and participants from radical grassroots efforts to institutionalized outlets which pose no threat to the power structure. The void that has been created and maintained as a result of strong left-wing alternatives to the Democratic Party being dismantled or disoriented has led to social movements substituting Democratic Party electoral campaigns for actual grassroots organizing, which helps the Democratic Party, but hinders challenges to the ruling class. The few concessions given by the Democratic Party to social movements are preemptive safeguards which serve the purpose of warding off the emergence of an opposition movement—it is a process much like loosening a valve to release steam. Thus, rather than giving the working class a voice in the political arena, the Democratic Party stifles labor and other grassroots movements while adopting their radical vocabularies—using words like 'justice', 'equality', 'progress', 'activism', and so on—in order to maintain a vestige of legitimacy.

References

Agee, Philip. 1975. *Inside the Company: CIA Diary*. American ed. New York, NY: Stonehill.

Blum, William. 2003. *Killing Hope: US Military and CIA Interventions since World War II*. London, England: Zed Books.

Cochran, Bert. 1977. *Labor and Communism: The Conflict that Shaped Labor Unions*. Princeton, NJ: Princeton University Press.

Davis, Mike. 2007. *In Praise of Barbarians: Essays Against Empire*. Chicago, IL: Haymarket Books.

———. 2018. *Prisoners of the American Dream: Politics and Economy in the History of the U.S. Working Class*. London, England: Verso Books.

De Leon, Daniel. 1913. 1913: Industrial Unionism. *Marxists.org*. https://www.marxists.org/archive/deleon/works/1913/130120.htm.

Dubofsky, Melvyn. 1969. *We Shall Be All: A History of the Industrial Workers of the World*. Chicago, IL: Quadrangle Books.

Eagleburger, Hart, and Jack Rusk. 2017. Deliver Us to the Lesser Evil: How Social Movements Bury Themselves in the Democratic Party. *Left Voice*. http://www.leftvoice.org/deliver-us-to-the-lesser-evil-how-social-movements-bury-themselves-in-the-democratic-party.

Foner, Philip. 2022. *The History of the Labor Movement in the United States, Vol. 11 the History of the Labor Movement in the United States, Vol. 11: The Depression*. New York, NY: International.

Glaberman, Martin. 1952. *Punching Out*. Edmonton, Alberta: Thought Crime.

Haskins, James. 1976. *The Long Struggle: The Story of American Labor*. Louisville, KY: Westminster John Knox Press.

Industrial Workers of the World. 1905. Preamble, Constitution, & General Bylaws of the Industrial Workers of the World. *Iww.org*. https://www.iww.org/resources/iww-constitution-en.pdf.

Kimeldorf, Howard. 1999. *Battling for American Labor: Wobblies, Craft Workers, and the Making of the Union Movement*. Berkeley, CA: University of California Press.

Kolin, Andrew. 2019. Repression, Resistance, and Development of the Labor Movement in the United States. In *The Palgrave Handbook of Social Movements,*

Revolution, and Social Transformation, ed. Berch Berberoglu. New York, NY: Palgrave Macmillan.
Lens, Sidney. 1961. *The Crisis of American Labor*. Beaminster, England: Barnes.
Lynd, Staughton. 2015. *Solidarity Unionism: Rebuilding the Labor Movement from Below*. 2nd ed. Oakland, CA: PM Press.
McKenzie, Rob. 2022. *El Golpe: US Labor, the CIA, and the Coup at Ford in Mexico*. London, England: Pluto Press.
Montgomery, David. 1987. *The Fall of the House of Labor: The Workplace, the State, and American Labor Activism, 1865-1925*. Cambridge, England: Cambridge University Press.
Morris, George. 1967. *CIA and American Labor: The Subversion of the AFL-CIO's Foreign Policy*. New York, NY: International Publishers.
Murolo, Priscilla, and A.B. Chitty. 2018. *From the Folks Who Brought You the Weekend: A Short, Illustrated History of Labor in the United States*. New York, NY: New Press.
Parenti, Michael. 2001. *Blackshirts and Reds: Rational Fascism and the Overthrow of Communism*. San Francisco, CA: City Lights Books.
Savage, Marion Dutton. 1922. *Industrial Unionism in America*. New York, NY: The Roland Press Company.
Stark, Louis. 1935. Fist Fight puts A.F. of L. in Uproar; Lewis and Hutcheson, Labor Leaders, Trade Punches on Convention Floor. Climax to Bitter Row, Constitution Amended to Bar Reds from State and Central Labor Groups. *The New York Times*, October 1935. P. 22
Stepan-Norris, Judith, and Maurice Zeitlin. 2002. *Left out: Reds and America's Industrial Unions*. Cambridge, England: Cambridge University Press.
United Electrical, Radio and Machine Workers of America (UE). n.d. *Member-Run Unionism: The Democratic Alternative That Works*. Pittsburgh, PA.
Werstein, Irving. 1969. *Pie in the Sky: An American Struggle: The Wobblies and Their Times*. New York, NY: Dell Publishing.
Yates, Michael. 2009. *Why Unions Matter*. New York, NY: Monthly Review Press.

CHAPTER 4

The U.S. Labor Movement Since 1955

Since the merging of the AFL and CIO in 1955, mainstream labor unions have principally operated as political lobbying organizations. C. Wright Mills (who, it should be noted, called himself a Wobbly) writes in his examination of U.S. labor *The New Men of Power* that the bureaucracies of business and mainstream labor have been amalgamated for the purpose of 'stabilization'—that is, for the preservation of the capitalist power structure (Mills 1948:223). Gone are the days of sit-down strikes, sabotage, solidarity boycotts, of worker sentries watching for scabs outside the factory. The relationship between big business and 'big labor' has been one not of conflict, but overall, one of cooperation. In this arrangement, the politically moderate or conservative union bureaucrats act as a barrier between the bosses and the rank-and-file workers. This ensures that the workers are given at minimum an illusion of representation on the job, and the bosses (and their profits) are not significantly impacted by union activity.

In order for this relationship between union bureaucrats and employers to function properly, rank-and-file radicals, 'unauthorized' militant leaders who might call for a wildcat strike or other direct action, must be eliminated. In the past, unions did not have such a relationship with the bosses—the class distinctions and power dynamics were apparent, as was, in the words of the IWW, the "irrepressible conflict between the capitalist class and the working class". However, in the era of 'stability,' the safe,

A. Barrington, *The U.S. Labor Movement in the 20th and Early 21st Century*, Social Movements and Transformation,
https://doi.org/10.1007/978-3-031-30077-6_4

moderate AFL-CIO works alongside business and the state, guaranteeing a workforce that will not, and arguably cannot (so long as it adheres to the 'rules') slip back into the militancy and radicalism which characterized earlier periods of the U.S. labor movement.

The AFL-CIO is the weakest link in this arrangement between business, labor, and the state. As Mills warned a little over 70 years ago, the connection of business, labor, and the government has resulted in the state adopting the interests of business while dismantling the strength and purpose of organized labor. This feat is accomplished in part by the evangelizing of the conservatives preaching the gospel of cooperation (class collaboration), insisting the impossible: that the interests of the worker and the capitalist can be reconciled.

Today, over 60 years since the merging of the AFL and CIO, unions in the United States are starved, if not of money, then at least of power. The function of some of the larger unions within the AFL-CIO, including its three largest affiliates: the American Federation of Teachers (AFT), United Food and Commercial Workers (UFCW), and the American Federation of State, County, and Municipal Employees (AFSCME), is predominantly to act as instruments of the Democratic Party. As UE points out in its pamphlet mentioned above, labor became entrenched in the machinery of the Democratic Party during the (FD) Roosevelt administration, and it has remained largely connected to the Democrats (the exceptions being police unions and the building trades, which tend to be more conservative and connected to the GOP) ever since.

When a political campaign for a Democratic candidate emerges, the AFL-CIO is one of the primary organizations funneling money to the campaign and getting feet in the street. Regardless of how much funding and volunteer work the labor federation provides, however, the Democratic Party is reluctant, nearly to the same extent as the Republicans, to provide any structural assistance to workers or labor unions. In many cases, rank-and-file workers pay their union dues like they would pay into some kind of insurance program, and they are only contacted by their local union or the AFL-CIO when it is campaign season and a Democratic candidate needs people to knock doors and call voters.

This pathetic devotion to mainstream electoral politics, rather than devotion to organizing the unorganized and building worker power, is not unnoticed by the average worker. However, confronted with the overwhelming problems and contradictions inherent to the power structure, the worker is immobilized—they know something must be done, that something must change, and yet they do not see a meaningful, practical way to engage in struggle. This is because the weaponry once used by workers to confront the power structure is covered in cobwebs. The militant, radical unionism of the past which workers used to build solidarity and class-conscious challenges to the ruling class has been locked away. The workers have been left with a woeful labor federation beholden to the cause of stability and bogus cooperation with employers, and sutured to the capitalist Democratic Party.

Labor and the Democrats: A Parasitic Relationship

Following the New Deal, the close organizational ties between labor and the Democratic Party were firmly established, and by the 1960s, organized labor took its place as the Democratic Party's most influential ally in national elections (Francia 2010:293). However, despite the labor movement's role as essentially the Democratic Party's campaign and election branch, unions have received little more than lip service for their efforts. An analysis from the Center for Responsive Politics covering the years 1989 to 2009 revealed that of the top 20 organizations providing financial support to politicians and political parties, 12 were labor PACs (political action committees). Unlike the corporate and business firms that financially support both Republican and Democratic candidates, labor PACs support the Democratic Party overwhelmingly. As campaign finance reforms have deregulated funding to 501(c) and 527 organizations, alternatives to PACs have become more prominent in elections. Many of these 501(c) and 527 organizations are directly tied to organized labor (Francia 2010:295).

The Campaign Finance Institute reported that the American Federation of State, County, and Municipal Employees (AFSCME) spent $30.7 million through its 527 in 2008, and the 527 of the Service Employees International Union (SEIU) spent $27.4 million, the combination of which topped all other 527 organizations. However, when the Center for Responsive Politics categorized individual donors based on employment and occupational information, the data show that the campaign finance system is dominated by corporate donors. In 2008, the funds given by corporate donors to the Democratic Party amounted to 15 times that provided by labor, which might explain why labor's demands and political concerns never seem to get addressed. It should be noted, though, that political contributions from unions and ideological groups are often classified as business contributions by the CRP.

The most valuable resource provided by the labor movement, however, is not financial, but human. The AFL-CIO reported that during the 2008 election process, union "volunteers knocked on 10 million doors, made 70 million phone calls, distributed 27 million worksite fliers, and sent 57 million union mail pieces" (Francia 2010:297). The outreach tactics undertaken by the rank and file of the AFL-CIO paid off for the Democratic Party, as exit poll surveys of union members showed that in battleground states, 68 to 69% of union voters supported the Democrats. Despite all of the money and campaign assistance provided by the AFL-CIO, the labor federation's relationship with the Democratic Party has been one-sided.

The Democratic Party has certainly reaped the benefits of the AFL-CIO's support, but labor's priorities have been largely disregarded by the Democrats, even when the Democratic Party is in a political position to implement legislation that would benefit the workers who tirelessly campaigned for the party's candidates. There have even been instances in which Democrats have directly opposed the goals of labor. One such occasion was when Senator Joseph Lieberman (a Democrat until 2006 and then an Independent who caucused with the Democrats) threatened to join the Republicans in a filibuster if a provision for a public option was included in the Affordable Care Act. Lieberman's stance effectively killed public healthcare, a longtime goal of organized labor. The Democratic Party, even after securing filibuster-proof majorities, refuses to allow any major legislative victories for unions and the working class in general.

Labor's dependence on the Democratic Party has rendered it incapable of both fighting for and achieving political victories that would benefit and empower workers. Because the labor movement allowed itself to become moderate, institutionalized, and dependent on a political party owned and operated by the ruling class, it has limited its options. The future of the U.S. labor movement is thus dependent on a change in course. The AFL-CIO's partnership with the Democratic Party has resulted not in victories for the working class, but victories for the corporate donors and their pet politicians who make their careers getting elected and preserving the power structure.

The AFL-CIO and the CIA

Even before WWII officially came to a close, the United States was already preparing itself for conflict with the Soviet Union. After the war, the U.S. government, and especially its military and intelligence sectors, was concerned about the influence of Communist parties in the postwar world, which had gained significant support among the masses for their commitment to antifascism, and for the partisan resistance militias they had organized in fascist-occupied territories during the war.

The left-wing guerilla troops in Greece, who had refused to disarm and accept British rule after fighting the Nazis, gave Truman the pretext for launching the Cold War. Though the U.S. accused Stalin of wanting to invade Western Europe, there is no real evidence that this was the case. Stalin told the Greek Communists to lay down their arms and accept the authority of the British, and the Greeks chose to ignore his instructions (Bevins 2021:16). Similarly, Stalin advised the Italian and French Communists to disarm, and unlike the Greeks, they complied. The civil war in Greece gave the right-wing Greek government, with backing from the U.S., the opportunity to try a new chemical weapon that had just been cooked up in a Harvard lab: napalm. The Royal Hellenic Air Force dropped the incendiary chemical on the left-wing guerillas who had fought Hitler during the war, and secured a victory for the Kingdom of Greece in 1949. The Italian and French Communists, who had agreed to disarm after the war, remained popular in their countries and looked to elections as a means to obtain power. The CIA, fearful that Communist parties would win parliamentary victories, decided it was necessary to intervene.

In a top-secret CIA report dated September 15, 1951 titled "Analysis of the power of the Communist Parties of France and Italy and of measures to counter them", Allen Dulles, then deputy director of the CIA, describes a meeting that took place on July 9, 1951 involving the CIA, Department of State, Department of Defense, and ECA (Economic Cooperation Administration, a former government agency established for carrying out the Marshall Plan in 1948). The purpose of the meeting, according to Dulles, was "to consider the implications for the defense of Western Europe, of the continuing power of the Communist parties in France and Italy, as evidenced by their popular vote in the 1951 Italian municipal elections and the French elections for the Chamber of Deputies" (Dulles 1951:1). Dulles states that the results of the elections were "disappointing", especially considering the "electoral mechanisms had been manipulated so as greatly to reduce Communist representation in the French Chamber and in Italian municipalities" (Dulles 1951:1).

Despite the meddling of U.S. intelligence in the elections, the Communist parties of France and Italy still garnered a significant number of votes and were popular in their respective countries. As much as anti-communist idealogues bellowed about their commitment to democracy, they were certainly willing to interfere in democratic elections where they found communists winning them. Likely sensing no irony in his writing, Dulles goes on to describe how the participants in the July meeting agreed they had to develop "new techniques" in order "to deprive the French and Italian Communists of their power", as the Communists posed "a continuing threat to democratic government" (Dulles 1951:2).

In addition to the respectability the Communist parties of France and Italy acquired through their antifascist resistance movements during the war, Dulles noted that the "single most important element of the strength of these two Communist parties" was their influence in their countries' labor movements (Dulles 1951:6). Dulles writes that "in France the communists absolutely control the CGT which is the dominant trade union organization, while in Italy they likewise dominate the powerful CGIL" (Dulles 1951:6). In the United States, the ruling class feared the entrance of labor into the political arena, and so through the state and private entities it crushed politically motivated unionism and purged 'reds' and militant unions from the AFL and CIO. After this was largely accomplished, it looked to other nations where the U.S. hoped to gain influence, and, seeing the same threat, sought to do the same abroad.

The General Confederation of Labour (Confédération Générale du Travail) (CGT) in France was heavily associated with the French Communist Party, which it supported until the 1990s, when the federation took a moderate turn. In Italy, the Italian General Confederation of Labour (Confederazione Generale Italiana del Lavoro) (CGIL) was connected to the Italian Communist Party, and today, is still associated with its heir, the Democratic Party.

In order to crush the French and Italian Communist parties, Dulles recommended the use of "measures to break the strength of the Communist labor unions", a task which would require the "continuing aid of American labor" (Dulles 1951:9). Through the FTUC and its leading position in the ICFTU, the AFL (and to a lesser extent the CIO) had proven U.S. labor's value as an asset to intelligence operations and combating militant unionism internationally. After the AFL and CIO combined, U.S. labor's connection to the CIA and U.S. intelligence and paramilitary operations abroad deepened, and in 1962 the AFL-CIO established the American Institute for Free Labor Development (AIFLD), the instrument with which the federation and the CIA would disrupt and subdue the world's left-wing labor movements.

AIFLD

The architect of the merger of the AFL and CIO in 1955 was a lawyer from Chicago named Arthur Goldberg. In 1948, Goldberg was appointed to the CIO's general council, and helped orchestrate the purges of 'reds' from the federation. Goldberg would go on to become Secretary of Labor, then an associate justice of the Supreme Court, and in 1965, United States Ambassador to the United Nations. Thus, Goldberg's work, particularly his involvement in the purges of the late 1940s, paid off. The AFL-CIO, since its inception in the Cold War United States, has been devoted to upholding the values of the ruling class and spreading the gospel of capitalism around the world.

AIFLD was developed largely under the direction of Jay Lovestone, and its purpose was to provide training and anticommunist 'education' to Latin American unionists who, upon returning to their respective countries, would combat left-wing elements in the labor movement and keep their nations safe for foreign investment. AIFLD's leadership consisted of representatives from labor, the U.S. government, and corporations, including Jay Lovestone, George Meany, J. Peter Grace, Brent Friele, Juan Trippe, Charles Brinkerhoff, Robert C. Hill, and William M. Hickey (Morris 1967:92). Grace was president of W.R. Grace & Co., director of the National City Bank of New York and Stone & Webster, and had investment interests in Latin America as a member of the Colombian Chamber of Commerce and president of Brazilian Technical, Inc. Trippe was president of Pan-American World Airways; Brinkerhoff was president of Anaconda Copper; Hill represented Merck & Co., and Hickey represented the United Corporation. The corporate presence in AIFLD might have been enough to dispel any notion that the Institute served any interests of working people, but it operated under the banner of U.S. labor and would directly impact working-class populations and unions in a number of countries.

Jay Lovestone and his ilk were invaluable to the U.S. government and labor bureaucrats who collaborated with the state in intelligence operations. Ex-leftists who could provide information regarding how left-wing organizations functioned and, more importantly, how they could be neutralized were in high demand. David Dubinsky hired Lovestone to help denigrate and isolate left-wing rank-and-file unionists in the ILGWU, and Lovestone's rise as a person of influence in the AFL, and later the AFL-CIO, shows that Dubinsky was not the only right-wing labor leader who recognized the value of Lovestone's services. During George Meany's tenure as president of the AFL and then the AFL-CIO, Lovestone served as his closest advisor on foreign affairs. Under Lovestone's direction, the FTUC participated in clandestine operations, assisted the CIA in collecting intelligence on labor unions and activists overseas, and siphoned CIA funds to anticommunist organizations that were friendly to U.S. business interests (Murolo and Chitty 2018:209).

Lovestone began reporting to James Angleton, chief of counterintelligence for the CIA, in 1954. Lovestone and Angleton, who became friendly on a personal level, communicated almost daily for 20 years (McKenzie 2022:28). Like Lovestone, Angleton was an anticommunist cold warrior, and viewed labor unions as critical to the fight against communism. Angleton oversaw some of the CIA's most infamous surveillance efforts on U.S. soil, including Operation CHAOS, which targeted the anti-war movement, left-wing activists and organizations, civil rights leaders, and feminists, among others. In Lovestone, Angleton found a link to U.S. labor and labor activities abroad, and after Lovestone was put in charge of the AFL-CIO's international affairs in 1963, Angleton was kept abreast of any new information or rumors regarding the labor movement. Lovestone and other sordid characters would come to play a major role in the development and execution of the AFL-CIO's foreign policy programs during the Cold War.

Serafino Romualdi, an Italian exile who fled to the United States in the 1920s, joined the ILGWU's Editorial and Publicity Departments in 1933. Before getting involved in organized labor, Romualdi served as counsel on labor matters to Nelson Rockefeller's Coordinating Committee on Latin American Affairs. In 1944, Romualdi was hired by the Office of Strategic Services (OSS), the predecessor of the CIA, to study the impacts of U.S. foreign policy in South America. He was assigned by the AFL in 1945 to establish contacts in Latin American trade unions, and his work was instrumental in developing the ICFTU Inter American Regional Organization of Workers (Organización Regional Interamericana de Trabajadores) (ORIT). After the 1955 merger, Romualdi was named

Inter-American Representative and Executive Secretary of the AFL-CIO's Inter-American Affairs Committee. In 1962, he was made the executive director of AIFLD. Philip Agee describes Romualdi in *Inside the Company: CIA Diary* as "AFL representative for Latin America and principal CIA agent for labour operations in Latin America" (Agee 1975:544).

When Guyana (at the time British Guiana) elected its first native-born prime minister, Dr. Cheddi Jagan, in 1953, Winston Churchill suspended the constitution and had Jagan thrown in jail. After his release, Jagan went on to win re-election in 1957 and again in 1961, much to the dismay of the UK and U.S. governments. The Kennedy administration shared Churchill's concerns regarding Jagan's popularity and his progressive politics, and thus found it necessary to disrupt his government through the incitement of race riots and strikes (organized by CIA operatives under the guise of the U.S. labor movement) in 1962 and 1963 (McKenzie 2022:12). Fully aware of the imperialist influences behind the attacks on his government, Jagan asserted that the CIA and AIFLD were responsible for the tumult, and identified Serafino Romualdi as one of the leading figures involved. Romualdi was also actively involved in CIA operations in Guatemala, Brazil, and Chile, among other places.

Another influential figure in U.S. labor's foreign policy was Irving Brown. Before the 1955 merger, Brown supported the AFL's anticommunist foreign policy through his work with the FTUC and ICFTU. Brown had been a follower of Jay Lovestone back when Lovestone headed the American Communist Party (Opposition), and like Lovestone, Brown had strong ties to the CIA. Brown directed the FTUC's European operations during the 1950s, providing funding and support to right-wing unions in France, Italy, and elsewhere. In a top-secret Current Intelligence Bulletin dated November 7, 1952, the CIA reported that "The American Embassy in Paris warns that the growing antagonisms between French non-Communist labor leaders and American labor representatives in Europe might create a serious incident in French-American relations" (CIA 1952:7). The bulletin further reported, "AF of L representative Irving Brown has also aroused resentment by his 'outspoken recommendations' on French policy questions" (CIA 1952:7). In other words, there was a feeling even among conservative unionists in France (and probably elsewhere) that the Americans were overstepping boundaries, and Brown's 'outspoken recommendations' likely revealed motives beyond assisting Europe's postwar labor movements.

The CIA's Foreign Broadcast Information Service archive contains an article published April 18, 1962 in the Russian newspaper *Trud*, which prior to the collapse of the USSR had been the paper of the All-Union Central Council of Trade Unions. The article, titled "Espionage Record of U.S. Agent Exposed", covers the work of "The Agent Known Under the Alias of 'The Bronzed'", who was identified by a member of an "underground fascist organization" with the alias 'Marek' as Irving Brown. According to Marek, Brown ('the Bronzed') was introduced to him by two 'syndicalists' who worked as instructors at an "espionage center" near Munich. Marek informed his colleagues, writing that the espionage center "was in fact guided by our friend 'the Bronzed' from the trade unions, and finally this is nothing else but the American intelligence service, subordinated to one and the same center" (FBIS 1962:2). The article goes on to describe Brown's efforts in France and Belgium, where he urged (and bribed) the CGT's leaders to purge left-wing workers from their unions, and then in Greece and Nigeria, where he engaged in similar activities.

In the 1980s, Brown was made an international affairs director of the AFL-CIO, and he used his position's influence to support the apartheid regime in South Africa and the right-wing Contras in Nicaragua. In 1981, Brown, who had already been exposed as a CIA operative, joined the right-wing AFL-CIO president Lane Kirkland on a visit to Poland in support of the anticommunist Solidarność (Solidarity) movement. Speaking out against the Communists of Eastern Europe, leader of the Solidarity movement, Lech Wałęsa, would declare in 1990 '"a gang of Jews had gotten hold of the trough and is bent on destroying us"' (Parenti 2001:71). Such were the friends of U.S. labor bureaucrats.

The primary goal of U.S. intelligence, in terms of labor movements overseas, was to break the influence of leftists, progressives, and specifically communists in unions and labor federations in order to make the targeted countries safer for corporate investment and exploitation. The labor bureaucrats and intelligence assets who participated through FTUC, ICFTU, and AIFLD had plenty of experience doing the same type of work in labor unions in the United States, which purged, blacklisted, vilified, and isolated left-wing and progressive unionists and labor leaders, and made the U.S. labor movement less of a threat to capital at home. After militancy and radicalism were thoroughly snuffed out in U.S. unions, the AFL and CIO, with guidance from intelligence assets like Lovestone, Romualdi, and Brown, were able to assist the U.S. government and its dominant intelligence apparatus, the CIA, to do the same to unions elsewhere.

Guatemala

During the CIA's first paramilitary effort, the 1954 overthrow of President Árbenz in Guatemala, the U.S. labor bureaucracy threw its weight behind the coup and parroted the U.S. government's anticommunist sentiments. Árbenz was widely popular in Guatemala among the working class and peasantry, and his government implemented land reforms and promoted union organizing in powerful firms such as the United Fruit Company. Árbenz instituted a campaign to combat illiteracy and introduced programs to increase democratic participation in the Guatemalan government, and his Agrarian Reform Law (Decreto 900) redistributed land to the peasantry, much to the chagrin of wealthy landlords and foreign business firms. While Árbenz was not a communist, his reforms were enough to frighten Washington, and with the backing of the Eisenhower administration, the CIA began working to overthrow him. The AFL (and to a lesser extent the CIO), taking cues from Serafino Romualdi, emulated the U.S. government's attitude toward Árbenz, and supported intervention in Guatemala (Morris 1967:81).

Four months before CIA-backed troops in Honduras invaded Guatemala in June 1954, George Meany wrote a letter to Árbenz (the contents of which were publicly distributed for propaganda purposes) expressing U.S. labor's anxiety about the 'communistic' character of his government. Meany urged Árbenz to purge Guatemalan unions of communists, to cease his criticism of the U.S. government, and to stop supporting youth and peace organizations which Meany asserted were communist front groups. In the March 1954 issue of *The Federationist*, Meany criticized opponents of intervention in Guatemala, including other Latin American governments, and praised the U.S. government's announcement regarding its plans to disrupt Árbenz.

After the coup, a right-wing dictatorship was established by Colonel Carlos Castillo Armas. Castillo Armas decimated the Guatemalan labor movement, seized land from peasants and returned it to landlords and corporations, and initiated a violent anticommunist campaign with the establishment of the National Committee for Defense against Communism, which led to the interrogation and imprisonment of thousands of Guatemalans, many of whom were executed, or 'disappeared' (Immerman 1982:199). The legal recognition of over 500 Guatemalan labor unions was canceled with Castillo Armas' political reforms, and any unions seeking registration under his regime had to be approved by the National Committee for Defense against Communism.

None of this prevented Serafino Romualdi from writing glowingly of the coup and praising Castillo Armas in the September 1954 issue of *The Federationist*. Romualdi boastfully recalled the role that he played alongside representatives of the CIO and the pro-Batista Cuban Federation of Labor in helping the 'liberated' Guatemalan workers find their place under the new regime (Morris 1967:82). To Washington and the CIA, the operation in Guatemala was a success. United Fruit and other firms had an ally in the pro-business Castillo Armas, and the U.S. government could rest easy knowing that the sinister Árbenz was no longer around to offer the rest of Latin America the threat of a good example.

Brazil

After becoming president of Brazil in 1961, João Goulart, a member of the Brazilian Labour Party (PTB), enacted the kinds of political and economic reforms known to make Washington nervous. He extended voting rights, expropriated and redistributed land, reduced illiteracy, and introduced an income tax on the wealthy and multinational corporations. Though Goulart initially sought to establish a cordial relationship with the Kennedy administration, it did not take long for Washington's opinion of the Brazilian leader to sour. Kennedy and his cabinet viewed Goulart's domestic and foreign policies as hostile to U.S. interests, and were particularly troubled by Goulart's refusal to aid U.S. attempts to destroy the revolutionary government in Cuba (Domingos 2018:544). The conditions were ripe for another coup.

AIFLD centers in Brazil were set up in 1962, and in January 1963 the first batch of Brazilian students reported to Front Royal, Virginia, for training (McKenzie 2022:20). The training sessions at Front Royal included courses on U.S. labor history and anticommunist strategies. Upon returning to Brazil, the AIFLD students actively participated in clandestine operations which culminated in the overthrow of Goulart in April 1964. Romualdi was at the very least aware of the CIA's plans for the coup, and the AFL-CIO made no attempts to hide their involvement. William C. Doherty, Jr., executive director at AIFLD's Washington, DC, headquarters, boasted of the AIFLD students' participation in the coup against Goulart in interviews and AFL-CIO broadcasts (Morris 1967:94). The Brazilian Communist Party called for a general strike at the outset of the coup, and the unionists trained by AIFLD assisted the military by splitting the labor movement and keeping communications systems running, allowing the anti-Goulart troops to coordinate their operations.

Following the coup, a right-wing military dictatorship was established with the installation of Gen. Humberto de Alencar Castelo Branco as president. Castelo Branco, who in his younger days trained at Fort Leavenworth in Kansas, purged the government and trade unions of left-wing and center-left leaders, and violently suppressed dissent under a fanatically anticommunist regime. With its strategic position in Latin America, Brazil became one of the U.S.'s most significant Cold War allies, and would not hold a democratic election again for over two decades (Bevins 2021:111).

Chile

The role of the U.S. government in the overthrow of Salvador Allende in Chile has received considerable and deserved attention. However, the AFL-CIO's contributions to the coup warrant closer study. Allende himself said in his final speech to the Chilean working class that "professional unions" were behind the insurrection, and specifically the unions whose leaders were trained by AIFLD (Hirsch 1977:9). One of AIFLD's first students in Chile, Manuel Rodriguez, declared in a 1974 speech (during an event which had Gen. Augusto Pinochet as the other main speaker) that the September 11, 1973 coup which overthrew the democratically elected Allende government could not have been accomplished without the actions of the 'professional unionists'.

As in the other nations that served as hosts to CIA/AIFLD operations, the labor movement in Chile was strongly tied to left-wing politics, and the Central Unitaria de Trabajadores de Chile (CUT), Chile's dominant labor federation, was targeted by U.S. cold warriors even before Popular Unity took power in 1970. In 1962, Serafino Romualdi, then AIFLD Executive Director, expressed his opinion that the only way to crush the '"Communist CUT"' was to break it apart (McKenzie 2022:42). AIFLD identified several sectors of Chilean labor which it believed would be sympathetic to its anticommunist crusade, including the *gremios*—guilds of white-collar and government workers, shopkeepers, and small business owners in trucking and other industries. After the coup, Pinochet praised the gremios for their role in the toppling of Allende's Popular Unity government. In addition to the gremios, AIFLD targeted the maritime and copper unions. The goal was to build a bloc within the CUT that would have enough power to shift the federation's politics to the right, and eventually split the CUT along ideological lines (a tactic which the AFL-CIO had nearly perfected by that time).

AIFLD served U.S. intelligence by gathering information on Chilean unions and workers, mapping their political leanings, and providing training and funding to those with anticommunist (and anti-Allende) proclivities. Shortly after Allende was elected, Nixon ordered Kissinger to "make the economy scream", but by that time AIFLD had already been fomenting the social and economic tension that would allow the coup to take place. Though it failed to inflict enough damage to break apart the CUT, including through the establishment of short-lived rival federations, AIFLD was able to instill its influence in a few major unions and build the groundwork for economic turmoil.

AIFLD also acted as a conduit for covert U.S. government funding of International Trade Secretariats (ITSs), nominally independent organizations which assisted in collecting intelligence on Latin American workers and unions and deciding which should be put on the CIA payroll. Over $4 million was pumped into Chile by the CIA to fund the gremios and support their campaigns against Allende (Hirsch 1977:22). In 1971, AIFLD began funneling CIA money to the Chilean maritime union, Confederación Marítima de Chile (COMACH), the leaders of which were supportive of efforts to undermine the Allende government, and likely directly involved in the coup.

Salvador Allende had been scrutinized by the U.S. government even before his 1970 election. Allende was a lifelong socialist, and worked as a physician before getting involved in politics. Elected to the Chamber of Deputies and then Minister of Health in the late 1930s, Allende was one of the 76 members of the Chilean Congress who signed a telegram sent to Hitler condemning Kristallnacht and the Nazis' violent persecution of the Jewish people. Allende had several unsuccessful presidential campaigns before his successful bid in 1970, including in 1964, when he lost to Eduardo Frei. According to declassified State Department reports, the CIA began providing covert funding to Frei and the Christian Democratic Party in 1962 at the suggestion of the U.S. Ambassador to Chile and Richard Goodwin, an advisor to John F. Kennedy (National Security Archive 2004). In total, the CIA spent $2.6 million directly financing Frei's campaign, and spent an additional $3 million on propaganda against Allende and the Popular Action Front (FRAP) between 1962 and 1964. The Kennedy and Johnson administrations were pleased with the results of this investment.

Leading up to and during the 1970 Chilean presidential election, the CIA used a similar strategy as they had in the 1960s, but this time their efforts would prove less effective. According to the Church Committee's report, "Covert Action in Chile: 1963-73", it was decided that, rather than support any particular candidate, the U.S. government would fund 'spoiling' operations against Allende and Popular Unity in order to influence the outcome of the election (Church Committee 1975:19). The CIA spent between $800,000 to $1 million on propaganda and covert action projects, including funding right-wing "civic action" groups and a "scare campaign" that equated Allende with violence and Stalinism (Church Committee 1975:20–21). Washington had hoped to accomplish two goals through their covert operations: (1) disrupt the communists and other leftists in their efforts to build a coalition which could win them the presidency, and (2) strengthen right-wing and anticommunist politicians and political parties to defeat Popular Unity in the 1970 election.

This time, the CIA's attempts to undermine democracy failed. In part, this was due to their inability to sway the political opinions of Chilean workers to the right. In assessments of their operations in Chile between 1965 and 1969, the CIA found that their labor and 'community development' projects were "rather unsuccessful in countering the growth of strong leftist sentiment and organization among workers, peasants and slum dwellers" (Church Committee 1975:19). The efforts of the CIA and AIFLD to sabotage the CUT were unproductive, as they were unable "to find a nucleus of legitimate Chilean labor leaders to compete effectively with the communist-dominated" labor federation (Church Committee 1975:19). Even after Allende was elected by a plurality, the CIA continued its activities in a desperate endeavor to prevent him from taking office. When propaganda projects again failed, it was determined that economic pressures were necessary.

Washington's "economic offensive" against Allende, according to the Church Committee, "was intended to demonstrate the foreign economic reaction to Allende's accession to power, as well as to preview the future consequences of his regime" (Church Committee 1975:25). However, even this was ineffective against Allende and his Popular Unity program taking power, and so Nixon "instructed the CIA to play a direct role in organizing a military coup d'état in Chile" (Church Committee 1975:25). The U.S. government had the backing of massive corporations, including ITT, which owned the telephone companies in Chile, as well as Anaconda,

Kennecott, and W.R. Grace, the heads of which were influential members of AIFLD.

Though the CIA and AIFLD were unable to dismantle the CUT, the funding and resources they provided their friends in trade associations in key sectors of Chilean industry certainly worked wonders in plunging the economy into chaos during Allende's presidency. In addition to anticommunist trade associations and their leaders, the CIA financed violent reactionary political organizations linked to the gremios. CIA-backed right-wing paramilitary groups such as Patria y Libertad (Fatherland and Liberty) aided the strikes by the 'professional unions', effectively coordinating their efforts to interrupt the economy. During the truckers' strike in October 1972, Patria y Libertad spread steel tacks "on highways in order to help bring the country's transportation system to a halt" (Church Committee 1975:31). Without the CIA's money, the strikes, which persisted up until the coup on September 11, 1973, could not have lasted, and surely not solely on union funds. When Allende referred to 'professional unions' in his final words, he was primarily referring to the Chilean Confederation of Professionals, or CUPROCH. CUPROCH was not a union, but rather an association of mine supervisors, and the organization was crucial to the shutdown of copper mines after Allende pushed for nationalization. AIFLD members Kennecott and Anaconda were particularly impacted by Allende's copper mine nationalization plan (Hirsch 1977:27).

After the coup, AIFLD's allies were rewarded for their loyalty and assistance in bringing down Allende and Popular Unity. AIFLD provided COMACH with gifts, including a new radio system, and leaders of the CIA-backed unions and associations, including CUPROCH, were moved into top labor positions after the CUT was outlawed under the Pinochet regime. Pinochet's Junta outlawed over a thousand unions in the Santiago area alone, and replaced the unionists and labor leaders they murdered with figures sympathetic to the new reactionary government. CUT member Luis Figueroa, after escaping Chile following the coup, noted that it was with the AFL-CIO's funding and support that Pinochet's Junta sought to reform Chilean unions into meek, pro-government organizations.

AIFLD and its friends in Chile were active even after the Junta prohibited all other union activities. AIFLD's leaders, like William C. Doherty, saw no contradictions in their participation in the operations of Pinochet's fascist terror state. In fact, Doherty believed U.S. labor had introduced democracy to Chilean unionism, stating in July 1974 that AIFLD would bring Chilean labor "a democratic-dominated movement for the first time in many years" (Hirsch 1977:34). During Allende's time as president, the number of Chileans attending trainings in AIFLD's Front Royal program drastically increased. AIFLD's education program for Chilean workers included courses with titles such as "Why are We Against Communism?", "Communist Trade Union Trickery Exposed", and "What Unions Can Do to Promote Democracy in Latin America" (Hirsch 1977:35). Between the day of the coup and May 1974, nearly 40 Chilean students graduated AIFLD's Front Royal program. As far as AIFLD was concerned, Pinochet was a true champion of democracy, and U.S. labor had done its part to bring him to power.

AIFLD's intelligence gathering operations, which included the distribution of questionnaires and the creation of reports on the political orientations of Chilean unions and their leaders, helped the Junta identify problematic workers, activists, and organizations. AIFLD gathered information regarding the political positions of thousands of Chilean unionists and worked with the larger U.S. intelligence apparatus in service to the Pinochet regime, which used lists compiled by the CIA and AIFLD to target, torture, and murder an estimated 40,000 people.

In 1975, the Junta set up its own labor schools, following the AIFLD model, and staffed them with graduates of AIFLD's 'Little Anti-Red Schoolhouse' in Front Royal, Virginia. The AFL-CIO's ties to the Junta were something of an open secret—in the summer of 1975 alone, George Meany sent Pinochet nine telegrams, though he had communicated with Pinochet throughout the 1970s (McKenzie 2022:53). Even after Pinochet suppressed unionism and abolished collective bargaining; even after workers, labor leaders, and activists were arrested and thrown into concentration camps; even after the mass graves, firing squads, and helicopters dropping tortured people into the ocean, the AFL-CIO felt comfortable about having a close relationship with the Junta.

This is not to say, however, that the rank-and-file members of the AFL-CIO's unions approved of what the leadership of the federation did in Chile or elsewhere in Latin America. There had already been some dissent against the AFL-CIO's foreign policy from the UAW and other affiliates before the 1973 coup in Chile. The egregiousness and documented brutality of the Pinochet regime ignited furious protest from a number of unions and leaders, including Fred Hirsch, member of Plumbers and Steamfitters Local 393, whose 1977 book *The CIA and the Labour*

Movement detailed the AFL-CIO's complicity in the overthrow of Allende and in the fascist savagery of the Pinochet regime. Other leaders from unions including the Amalgamated Meat Cutters and Butcher Workmen of North America, United Packinghouse Workers, International Association of Machinists and Aerospace Workers, and the International Longshore and Warehouse Union, spoke out against the Junta and the AFL-CIO's involvement in the Pinochet regime's operations.

During the 1980s, there would be a wider revolt within the U.S. labor movement against the AFL-CIO's foreign policy, but the neoliberal experiment in Pinochet's Chile, led by the 'Chicago Boys', a group of Chilean disciples of Milton Friedman, had already set the stage for global privatization and substantial damage to international labor, including in the United States. Friedman himself visited Chile during Pinochet's reign and gave his approval to what was happening there. After Ronald Reagan became president, the neoliberal program became dogma for both the Republican and Democratic parties. By 1983, the effects of this turn toward neoliberalism were painfully noticeable to workers in the United States. With plant closures, automation, and wage deceleration, the gains won by organized labor over the past 40 years crumbled (Davis 2018:106).

The AFL-CIO's participation in the U.S. government's anticommunist project would come back to the federation like a vindictive boomerang. As it turns out, making the world safe for capitalism meant making the world safe for corporate expansionism, and the bosses running transnational corporations saw (and see) little reason to invest in the United States when they could (and can) exploit more desperate workforces elsewhere. Crushing left-wing militant unions and social movements opened the world to the spread of neoliberal globalization, and in this way, U.S. labor dug its own grave. The AFL-CIO's collaboration with U.S. intelligence did not end with the horrors of Chile.

El Salvador

El Salvador is a nation all too familiar with brutal repression, military dictatorships, and economic control by wealthy elites. In the late twentieth century, El Salvador's economy was dependent on exportable agricultural products, and impoverished rural peasants made up over half of its population. A vast majority of the land was owned by a few wealthy families and plantation owners. There were occasional eruptions of discontent and protest against the established order, but they tended to be short-lived and easily crushed. Between 1960 and 1970, the number of landless peasants significantly increased, as they were forced from their land by large producers of sugar, cotton, and coffee. The vast stretches of land designated for export crops meant lower food production for the people of El Salvador, and the result was malnutrition, starvation, and an accelerated infant mortality rate.

Though unions were illegal, peasants began forming cooperatives in the early 1960s. Facing intense opposition from the ruling class and its violent protector, the military, the peasants advocated for land redistribution and improved conditions for agricultural workers. In 1966, AIFLD, with the blessing of the government of El Salvador, began investing in infrastructure projects, developing training programs for agricultural workers, and building relationships with the peasants and their cooperatives (McKenzie 2022:59). The Salvadoran ruling class and military government supported AIFLD's efforts, which they viewed as an alternative to the militant, grassroots organizing being led by left-wing peasant leaders. In 1968, AIFLD created the Salvadoran Communal Union (UCS), which, despite being a union and therefore technically illegal, was backed by the government.

In 1972, Colonel Arturo Molina was dubiously elected president over the Christian Democratic leader José Napoleón Duarte, whose coalition of center-left and left-wing parties drew the ire of the right-wing National Party of Conciliation (PCN) and its military backers. Following the election Duarte was arrested and forced into exile. In 1973, the new government sought to impede the peasant and cooperative movement, which it perceived as a communist plot, and Molina ordered AIFLD to leave the country, although the UCS was allowed to survive. However, even after 'leaving' El Salvador, AIFLD continued communication with its contacts there, sent Salvadorans to its training seminars, and kept U.S. government funding flowing into the UCS. Molina's government oversaw death squad terrorism against peasants and activists, and assassinations of priests. At home in the United States, the AFL-CIO remained steadfast in its vitriolic anticommunism, and supported the Carter administration's policies. During the Reagan years, the federation's leaders wholeheartedly endorsed his administration's odious agenda in El Salvador.

Molina's successor, General Carlos Romero, was ousted by 'reformist' military officers in a bloodless coup in 1979. The new government initially supported land reform, which it figured would appease the peasant movement, and called for an end to state corruption. AIFLD returned to El

Salvador and picked up where it left off working with UCS, which had an annual budget of $2 million almost entirely supplied by the Institute. It would not be long before right-wing military officers seized control of the government, and any hopes of reform were crushed. Violent repression remained the state's primary method of controlling the population, and by January 1980, nearly all members of government not tied to the military had resigned in disgust. Later that year, José Napoleón Duarte, who returned to El Salvador from his exile, was installed as president of the junta. Left-wing political parties and activists recognized that change could not be brought about peacefully. Guerilla troops united to form the Farabundo Martí National Liberation Front (FMLN), and opposition groups with various political ideologies organized the Democratic Revolutionary Front (FDR).

Left-wing groups and labor organizations were driven underground, and dissident protests were met with violent reactions from the government, including snipers firing into crowds, crop-duster planes dropping DDT on demonstrators, bombings, kidnappings, rapes, torture, and disappearances. Following the brutal repression of a general strike in March 1980, with 54 people murdered in the capital alone, Archbishop of San Salvador Óscar Romero urged the Carter administration to stop supporting the death squads and right-wing government with military aid. Shortly thereafter, Romero was assassinated by a death squad led by fanatical anti-communist and School of the Americas trainee Major Roberto D'Aubuisson (Bevins 2021:224). At Romero's funeral, a bomb was thrown into a crowd of mourners, followed by rifle and machine gun fire. At least 40 people were killed and hundreds were injured (Blum 2003:355). Duarte blamed the left for the violence.

In the summer of 1980, AIFLD branched out from its peasant operations and helped finance the creation of a Christian Democrat labor organization called Popular Democratic Unity (UPD). The primary focus for UPD, which became the largest labor federation in El Salvador in 1982, was support for Christian Democratic candidates and Duarte, whose junta presidency the AFL-CIO still supported. Though AIFLD had been welcomed as an accessory to other reactionary governments in Latin America, the Institute's relationship with the right-wing military regime in El Salvador was more complicated. In January 1981, two American AIFLD employees, Michael Hammer and Mark Pearlman, were murdered, along with Salvadoran labor leader José Rodolfo Viera, by soldiers while dining at the Sheraton Hotel in San Salvador. This incident, and the Salvadoran government's reluctance to prosecute the killers, brought political problems for Reagan, and caused tensions to emerge in the AFL-CIO, which continued to back the Reagan administration's policies in El Salvador even after the murders.

Later that year, in December 1981, Salvadoran troops used U.S.-made assault rifles to massacre more than 900 men, women, and children in the village of El Mozote (Bevins 2021:224). The U.S.-backed terror regime adopted a 'scorched earth' policy, which translated into mass executions and accelerated violence against not only perceived political enemies, but also the elderly, children, and other vulnerable and helpless citizens. Reagan appointed Elliot Abrams to serve as assistant secretary of state for human rights and humanitarian affairs, and his primary job was to make excuses for the administration's endorsement of terrorism and savagery in El Salvador. Abrams called reports of the massacre in El Mozote communist propaganda, and Washington kept up its support of the right-wing military government for years, actively preventing any negotiation between the regime and the guerilla rebels. From 1980 to the early 1990s, the U.S. gave billions of dollars in military aid to the Salvadoran government, and because of how the aid was categorized ('development' aid), the total cost for the military hardware is unknown (Blum 2003:357).

While the leadership of the AFL-CIO never wavered in their support of U.S. government foreign policy, a number of unions and their leaders within the federation (as well as a few unaffiliated unions) spoke out against Washington's operations and expressed their solidarity with the working class and peasantry of El Salvador. The International Longshore and Warehouse Union (ILWU), the International Association of Machinists (IAM), the United Auto Workers (UAW), and the United Electrical, Radio and Machine Workers of America (UE) openly criticized the AFL-CIO for its complicity in the brutal repression in El Salvador, and the locals of various other unions, including United Steel Workers (USW), Service Employees International Union (SEIU), the American Federation of State, County, and Municipal Employees (AFSCME), and American Federation of Teachers (AFT), adopted resolutions opposing U.S.-sponsored terror against Salvadoran peasants and workers. Some unions even engaged in direct action.

The *Guardian* reported on May 6, 1981 "The ILWU has displayed the most dramatic solidarity to date with the people of El Salvador", after the longshore union "initiated a boycott of all U.S. military equipment bound for the Duarte regime" (Schaal 1981). The AFL-CIO responded to the growing dissent in its ranks with intimidation tactics, and Lane Kirkland, president of the federation, flew William Doherty to union and labor council meetings across the country to disrupt any progressive rumblings. The *Guardian* article goes on to describe the 'peasant cooperative' established by AIFLD that fervently supported the junta and "played a major role in carrying out the repressive land reform". In the United States and abroad, the AFL-CIO lobbied for the right-wing military government in El Salvador, even though the regime "outlawed municipal worker unions, militarized all industry, prohibited strikes and bombed most union halls".

Despite the AFL-CIO's attempt to squash dissent, unions and rank-and-file workers who disagreed with the federation leadership's position on El Salvador did not roll over. The National Labor Committee in Support of Democracy and Human Rights in El Salvador (NLC) was formed in September 1981 by leaders in the Amalgamated Clothing and Textile Workers Union (ACTWU), UAW, and IAM, and within a few years they brought leaders of 23 other national unions into their ranks (McKenzie 2022:68). The NLC teamed up with non-labor organizations, sponsored speaking tours for Salvadoran labor leaders, lobbied Congress, and, among other work in solidarity with the working class of Central America, fought against U.S. military aid going to the Contras in Nicaragua. The conservative leadership of the AFL-CIO would reward the NLC's efforts with red-baiting.

At the 1983 AFL-CIO convention, the NLC was successful in proposing and passing a resolution which curbed the AFL-CIO's unconditional support of the junta. In El Salvador, the AIFLD-funded UPD also changed its policies regarding Duarte and the Christian Democrats during the 1984 presidential election. UPD decided it would no longer support Duarte without demands being met, including wage increases, human rights improvements, labor participation in government, and negotiations with the FMLN/FDR. When the Christian Democrats agreed to most of the UPD's demands, the federation put its weight behind Duarte and helped win him the election. Reagan and his administration considered Duarte's victory a tremendous success. The NLC did not share Reagan's enthusiasm, and viewed Duarte and the Christian Democrats as a front for U.S. interests in El Salvador.

The UPD's ardor for Duarte was short-lived. Duarte's government failed to make good on the promises of his campaign, and feeling the pressure of a revitalized left-wing labor movement challenging its dominance as a federation, the UPD began openly criticizing Duarte. This intensely displeased AIFLD, which responded by trying to force UPD unions into a different, more easily controlled federation, the Confederation of Democratic Workers (CTD). UPD unions that rebelled lost AIFLD funding. Open conflicts emerged between unions and federations, and UPD leaders denounced AIFLD's corruption and use of blackmail, destabilization, and intimidation tactics against unions that stepped out of line. From El Salvador, the AFL-CIO would turn its attention to Nicaragua.

In 1984, the AFL-CIO supported Reagan's request for another $70 million in military aid to El Salvador. The federation's reversal of its 1983 resolution fueled the strife between the AFL-CIO's leadership and the NLC, which by 1985 contained a majority of the federation's membership. At the October 1985 AFL-CIO convention, the NLC unions denounced the Reagan administration's policies in Central America, including its support of the right-wing Contras, while the federation's foreign policy staffers focused their energy on bashing the Sandinistas. While the result was a compromise resolution, with no explicit language opposing the Contras but broad anti-war sentiment expressed, the 1985 convention was historic in that it was the first time foreign policy had been debated on the floor of an AFL-CIO convention in the federation's existence.

Mexico

By the 1980s, the Institutional Revolutionary Party (PRI) enjoyed nearly five decades as the ruling force in the Mexican government (albeit with several changes to the party's name and political persuasion). In the late 1940s, the party moved to the right from its center-left position, and during the 1988 presidential election, it would fully embrace a neoliberal perspective. The PRI selected conservative Carlos Salinas de Gortari as its candidate. Cuauhtémoc Cárdenas, son of former PRI president of Mexico Lázaro Cárdenas, left the PRI to challenge Salinas as the candidate for the Authentic Party of the Mexican Revolution (PARM).

The election was befouled by fraud at the hands of the PRI, which resorted to altering vote tallies, among other tactics, in order to prevent Cárdenas from defeating Salinas. The PRI already had significant advantages as an institution in Mexico, and so the rigging of the 1988 election served the purpose of bolstering the regime's symbolic strength and intimidating opposition parties (Cantú 2019:720). The fraud in the 1988 election differed from previous examples of tampering in Mexican elections, however, in that the ruling party was confident that it would defeat the opposition, and only at the eleventh hour resorted to fraud after realizing just how unpopular its candidate was.

The Confederación de Trabajadores de México (CTM), the largest labor federation in Mexico, was effectively an arm of the PRI while the party was in power. The CTM's history parallels that of the CIO in at least two ways: (1) the federation, founded in the 1930s, began as a militant force, welcomed radicals into its ranks, and won substantial victories for workers, but later ousted leftists and progressive nationalists in order to invite government support, and (2) it formed an alliance with a center-right political party, the PRI, just as the CIO did with the Democratic Party in the United States (Schuhrke 2022). The CIA and the AFL-CIO subverted militant left-wing unionism in Mexico during the Cold War, and the CTM would prove to be one of the AFL-CIO's crucial allies in its crusade against communism and radical unionism. The site of perhaps the most blatant and violent episode of yanqui interference in the Mexican labor movement was a Ford plant in Cuautitlán in January 1990.

A December 1983 secret CIA report titled "Mexico: Labor-Government Relations" characterized the CTM as "almost wholly co-opted by the ruling party", but noted "signs of militancy" in Mexico's labor movement resulting from economic hardships and austerity (CIA 1983:iii). The report also spelled out the concerns of the U.S. government plainly: "The continued loyalty of organized labor … is essential for the maintenance of IMF-mandated austerity and for short-term political stability" (CIA 1983:iii). According to the CIA, pro-government unions maintained their control by expelling "recalcitrant workers", preventing "Dissident victories", and using violence (called 'physical persuasion' in the report) when necessary (CIA 1983:1). Focusing specifically on the internal structure of the CTM, the CIA described the federation as "hierarchically ordered and relatively noncompetitive", with elections serving only a ceremonial purpose and leadership "based largely on personal loyalty" (CIA 1983:16). The CTM's structure paralleled that of the PRI, and according to the CIA, the federation implemented requirements for elected leaders which ensured anyone the government opposed never gained an influential position.

Despite the observable discontent and spirit of rebellion in Mexican labor at the time, the CIA did not believe that this alone would be enough to endanger U.S. corporate interests. If the Mexican government could maintain its positive relationship with the CTM, and prevent economic catastrophe from exacerbating tensions between the ruling party and the working class, disruption of the established order could be avoided. Unfortunately for the PRI, a 1985 earthquake in Mexico City would unravel any remaining faith the working people of Mexico had in the government.

On September 19, 1985, a magnitude 8.1 earthquake struck Mexico City, followed two days later by a sizeable aftershock. The National Seismological Service estimates that the earthquake killed at least 40,000 people (Servicio Sismológico Nacional n.d.). Roughly, 200,000 people were left without homes, condemned to live as refugees in shelters for months. A considerable number of buildings were demolished, signaling the PRI government's inadequate enforcement of building codes, and in a callous divulgence of its priorities, the government sent the army to protect factories rather than assist in aid and rescue operations (Kirkwood 2000:203). Instead of removing the corpses of workers from the rubble, the military assisted factory owners in salvaging their machinery. The PRI government was accused of brutal repression and torture, which it repeatedly denied, long before 1985, but such claims were validated when the police headquarters in Mexico City was severely damaged by the earthquake. With much of the building demolished, the torture chambers within were exposed.

The PRI government's slipshod response to the earthquake spurred citizens to take matters into their own hands. Workers, students, grassroots organizers, and left-wing groups developed coordinated efforts to provide clothing, food, shelter, medical supplies, and rescue services to people impacted by the devastating event. Opposition parties grew in popularity, nourished by the shortcomings of the PRI and the people's resentment toward the government. Still, even as the 1988 presidential election approached, the PRI felt little need to fear the opposition. It was not until the July 6 election, as the results were coming in, that the ruling party discovered its victory was not as secure as its leaders had thought. Their response was to shut down the computers tallying the votes, and when they turned the computers back on, the PRI candidate, Salinas, was shown as the winner. Salinas's PRI government would go on to introduce numerous neoliberal reforms and assist in bringing NAFTA to fruition.

In 1983, the Reagan administration proposed the creation of the National Endowment for Democracy (NED) to serve as an instrument for funneling government funds to AIFLD and other CIA operations. After Congress passed the National Endowment for Democracy Act, Washington had a stand-in for the CIA which it would use to destabilize governments abroad that it perceived as threatening to U.S. financial and political interests. The United States Agency for International Development (USAID) and Congress provided funding for NED, which then gave the money to the Free Trade Union Institute (FTUI), which in turn distributed it to AIFLD and other organizations. In 1985, a NED/AIFLD grant was proposed to subsidize the PRI and strengthen the ties between the CTM and AFL-CIO. The program, for reasons not entirely known, was scrapped, but by 1986, AIFLD had already set up its base in the new CTM headquarters in Mexico City (McKenzie 2022:117). The unrest that followed the 1988 election deeply concerned the U.S. government and the major auto manufacturers who saw in Mexico a reservoir of cheap and exploitable labor.

In April 1988, the AFL-CIO and CTM held a joint meeting to discuss the 'twin plant' ("Maquiladora") system, which meant parts were exported from the U.S. to Mexico, assembled in a plant, and then sent back to the United States. The AFL-CIO, and in particular the UAW, had by then established a close relationship with the leaders of the CTM through AIFLD, and consequently the CIA had a foothold in Mexican labor. The CTM did not represent all union autoworkers in Mexico, but its Ford affiliate was its largest and considered its best organized, which made its leadership the obvious choice to represent the CTM in meetings with the AFL-CIO's industrial group, the Automotive/Transportation Committee.

Flying about the U.S. in private jets, CTM leaders were hosted by the AFL-CIO for meetings in Washington and San Diego to discuss the Committee's operations in Mexican auto factories. Around the same time, the CTM union at Ford was preparing for a national election. The CTM leadership collaborating with the AFL-CIO faced opposition from reformers who sought to regain what the workers had lost in the 1987 CTM contract with Ford. Workers at the Cuautitlán Ford factory elected a new local Executive Committee with a reformist agenda in 1988, and because the Cuautitlán plant had the largest number of union members, it seemed likely that the Cuautitlán candidates would win the 1989 CTM Ford national election. Worried that a militant rank-and-file movement within the factories would disrupt their arrangement, Ford management and the CTM old guard conspired to suppress dissidents.

Ford introduced a profit-sharing bonus in the run-up to the election, and hoped that the untaxed windfall would shift the balance to favor the CTM establishment. This would not turn out to be the case, as the reformist candidates continued to gain momentum, and so with the support of the CTM, Ford fired four of the six members of the Cuautitlán Executive Committee. The terminations of the four committee members brought fear and uncertainty to the workers at the plant, but they also spurred the formation of the Ford Workers Democratic Movement (FWDM). The fired committee members set up shop outside the Cuautitlán factory and continued organizing the rank-and-file autoworkers and leading the local union throughout 1989.

In December 1989, with agreement from CTM leadership, Ford began withholding the taxes which it did not collect from the profit-sharing payments, resulting in workers receiving miniscule paychecks, and some workers receiving no payment at all (some were even told they owed Ford money). In response, workers walked off the job, demanded restored pay and bonuses, and formed a commission independent of the CTM to negotiate with Ford. When Ford refused to recognize the legitimacy of the commission, the workers called on the CTM to meet with the Executive Committee. After recognizing that the workers would not back down, the CTM agreed to a meeting.

The meetings with the CTM would bear no fruit for the dissident workers. Just before the holiday shutdown of the plants from Christmas through New Year's Day, hired thugs targeted one of the dissident leaders, Jaime Flores Durán, forced him to dig a grave (implied to be his own), and interrogated him about being a Marxist or communist (McKenzie 2022:129). Such intimidation tactics were commonly used by the CTM against workers who threatened the federation's hegemony, as were violence and kidnapping. Flores Durán was visited by plant security the next day at his work station, and the guards took him back to the site of his grave near a scrap heap. If not for a work stoppage organized by Flores Durán's coworker, Gabriel Abogado, who noticed him missing from the factory, Flores Durán may not have escaped and returned to the assembly area to inform the workers of what had happened to him.

On January 5, 1990, two days after work resumed at the Cuautitlán factory, a gang of about 30 thugs, including hired goons of the CTM, Ford, and Mexican mobsters, with the protection of the police, attacked and kidnapped workers handing out leaflets. The kidnapped workers were later released after their coworkers organized a sit-down strike and barricaded themselves inside the plant. It is not entirely clear who formed the group that attacked the workers, but it is apparent that the CTM and Ford were likely involved. Over the weekend, unfamiliar people with Ford uniforms and ID badges were entering the factory, and the workers, suspecting that the strangers would be there when they returned to work on Monday, prepared themselves for conflict.

When Monday morning arrived, 300 gangsters armed with clubs, pistols, and machine guns and wearing Ford uniforms and ID badges greeted the workers at the Cuautitlán plant. Leaders of the January 5 work stoppage found the locks on their lockers changed, and the gangsters, many of whom were drunk or intoxicated by other substances, harassed and intimidated workers on the assembly lines. The workers took up tools and defended themselves against the thugs, who responded by opening fire inside the factory, killing one worker and wounding eight others. Upon hearing of the outbreak of violence from local leaders, the press, wives of factory workers, and others surrounded the plant. Though Ford security guards had locked the gate, the furious wives and family members of the workers tore down the fence and opened a passage for ambulances and news reporters to the factory.

There is no 'smoking gun' that suggests Ford and the CTM were solely culpable for what happened at the Cuautitlán factory in January 1990. Many of the factors involved, including how quickly the 300-man gang was organized, the fact that they were equipped with expensive machine guns, and that they carried out their attack against unarmed workers with no apparent fear of retaliation, point to at least some connection with higher levels of authority in Mexico and the United States. The U.S. government certainly had an incentive to crush militant unionism in Mexico, as the North American Free Trade Agreement (NAFTA) was being developed and big business needed an investment-friendly climate in Mexico in order to implement their neoliberal agenda. While the workers at the Cuautitlán plant fought back with a strike following the January 1990 attack, it was not enough to prevent Salinas and the PRI from bringing Mexico into NAFTA.

Corporate Globalization: U.S. Labor's Reward for Cold War Loyalty

At this point, it is necessary to further clarify again that co-optation does not fully explain the decline of the U.S. labor movement, although it certainly played (and continues to play) a role in the AFL-CIO's policies and operations. One cannot suggest without ignoring much of the events described above that the sorry state of the U.S. labor movement is due solely to infiltration and co-optation by representatives of the ruling class, although the facts suggest that something of this sort happened at various points in the movement's history. The point is that infiltration, co-optation, and institutionalization would not have been possible without conservative labor leaders who embraced class collaborationism—figures like Gompers, Green, Meany, and Kirkland—men in high places who thought the ruling class and the working class shared common interests. For this reason, it would be incorrect to describe the catalyst of the labor movement's transformation as 'co-optation', for how can a movement with the germs of conservatism and reaction already operating within it be co-opted by conservative and reactionary forces?

If not for the presence of influential willing participants in the ruling class's socioeconomic program, the labor movement would not have followed the path chronicled in this book. The labor movement's marriage to the Democratic Party since the New Deal broadened the base of the Democratic Party, but has delivered very little to workers or their unions (Davis 2018:102–103). The class collaborationism of the labor bureaucracy, and the constraints placed on labor due to its connection to a bourgeois political party, reproduce and reinforce the astonishing absence of class consciousness in and the depoliticization of the U.S. working class.

It can be argued that there have always existed multiple labor movements, and this is true beyond the United States. Historically, one finds on the one hand the labor movement of revolution, of the Wobblies, of the socialists and communists, of the anarchists and syndicalists, the labor movement that decried capitalism and condemned bigotry while embracing working-class internationalism, and on the other hand, the labor movement of the craft unions, the labor movement of purges, of segregation, of beating the war drum when the state demanded it, of collaboration with the CIA to bring down militant unionism in Latin America and around the world. It is far more accurate, therefore, to advance a perspective of the U.S. labor movement which acknowledges these various tendencies, and through concrete analysis one finds that the labor movement was the site of a battle between competing ideologies, and the victor happened to be, perhaps unsurprisingly, the side supported (financially and otherwise) by the ruling class.

The movement was not so much co-opted by the ruling class as it was vivisected, splintered, and reshaped. The Wobblies, who, while marginalized, still organize and agitate in workplaces across the United States and elsewhere today, were not co-opted, but they were violently crushed, raided, and nearly eradicated through the collaborative efforts of the state, employers, and business unions. If the IWW and other maligned militant unions, including the UE and ILWU, still exist and operate independently, one cannot say the labor movement has been entirely co-opted and institutionalized. Similarly, on the other side of the coin, one cannot say the AFL-CIO has been co-opted, since this assertion ignores that the federation collaborated with the ruling class since its earliest days, as did the AFL and CIO prior to their combination.

If only the labor leaders at the helm of the AFL, CIO, and then AFL-CIO during the Cold War years had listened to the Wobblies who told workers "The working class and the employing class have nothing in common", they might have been more careful about collaborating with institutions that viewed organized labor as a nuisance. When the AFL and CIO endorsed the Red Scare purges, and when the AFL-CIO colluded with the CIA through AIFLD, they were aiding in the dismantling of radical, militant unionism and left-wing political movements, the barriers that stood between the workers of the world and neoliberal hegemony. Once these barriers were effectively removed, multinational corporations were able to move about the globe threatening labor and diminishing living standards without fear of challenge or reprisal.

In its review of the impact of NAFTA on U.S. labor, the Economic Policy Institute (EPI) notes that the trade agreement resulted in the loss of 700,000 jobs, lower wages, and the acceleration of upward redistribution of wealth (Faux 2013). NAFTA gave employers in the United States, Canada, and Mexico the power to move their factories to regions with cheaper labor and either less effective or no unions. In the U.S., employers used NAFTA to break union drives and coerce workers to accept lower wages and less benefits by threatening to move their jobs if they did not comply with the bosses' orders. In Mexico, according to the EPI, several million workers were dislocated by NAFTA, and the trade agreement destructively impacted the agricultural and small business sectors. Thus, NAFTA was a primary cause of the significant increase in undocumented workers immigrating to the United States in search of opportunities in the U.S. labor market. This had the effects of (1) suppressing wages by prompting workers in the U.S. to compete with undocumented immigrant workers, and (2) fostering resentment and xenophobia in U.S. workers who blamed the undocumented workers themselves rather than the ruling classes of the U.S. and Mexico for thrusting both the U.S. and Mexican working classes into increasingly precarious circumstances.

It is worth noting that such resentment and xenophobia did not arise after the implementation of the Canada-United States Free Trade Agreement (CUFTA) in 1989. U.S. workers did not fear that Canadian workers were going to come after their jobs. One might suggest this implies a racial (or racist) component in the tendency of workers in the U.S. to fear undocumented Mexican labor but not competition from Canadians, and this cannot be easily dismissed. In fact, U.S. workers contributed to the purpose of the agreement in that they provided cheaper labor than their Canadian counterparts and the experiences of Canadian workers after the implementation of the CUFTA might have served as a warning to workers in the United States. From the implementation of CUFTA in 1989 to 1991, roughly 435,000 manufacturing jobs left Canada as employers relocated to lower wage regions in the U.S. and Mexico (Moody 1995:104–5).

Free-trade agreements are not imposed upon other nations by the ruling class of another. They are collaborative, conscious efforts by international elites to establish an arrangement which suits their interests. One must keep in mind that, while the United States retained much of the power in NAFTA and the CUFTA before it, U.S. business did not force Mexico and Canada into these agreements. The ruling elites of Canada and Mexico were just as enthusiastic about the neoliberal agenda as their counterparts in the United States, and they practiced similar relocation tactics to undermine workers and their unions. In Mexico, businesses moved their operations from central to northern Mexico, where the border region contained less of a threat from unions and allowed the companies to escape regulations pertaining to the health and safety of workers (Roman and Velasco Arregui 2017). In the developed nations, industrial production dropped by roughly 20% between 1980 and 2008, as corporations, liberated by the neoliberal paradigm, moved production to underdeveloped countries with more easily exploitable labor (Tigar 2016).

The path to neoliberal hegemony was paved by U.S. interference in the politics and economies of other nations, and the participation of the AFL, the CIO, and the AFL-CIO was crucial in the quelling of left-wing and nationalist movements that stood in the way of the global domination of transnational corporations. With the implementation of NAFTA, the U.S. labor bureaucracy was bestowed with the reward for their assistance. Job loss and insecurity, weakened unions, lower wages, and a diminished standard of living in the United States and elsewhere are not glitches in the neoliberal scheme: they are necessary components. Recently, the responses to the crises introduced to the world by neoliberalism have been just as, if not more, concerning as the disastrous impacts of the system itself. With the international left rendered, with few exceptions, disorganized, disjointed, and meek, the prominent critiques of neoliberalism have emerged from increasingly authoritarian right-wing sources. This phenomenon will be explored in more depth in the next chapter.

Before delving further into the crisis of neoliberalism and the alarming growth of reactionary ideologies on a global scale, it would be unfair not to include examples of vibrant labor activism that surfaced after the 1955 merger of the AFL and CIO, including recent developments which have offered promising signs of revitalization in the labor movement.

Worker Militancy After 1955

Despite the U.S. labor bureaucracy's non-confrontational, class-collaborationist approach to unionism, there have been numerous eruptions of rank-and-file militancy after the merger of the AFL and CIO which require recognition and study. Some of these events mentioned below, including the Memphis Sanitation Workers Strike of 1968 and the formation of the Dodge Revolutionary Union Movement (DRUM), were responses not only to the abuses experienced by workers at the hands of their employers, but to the racism which pervades capitalism and capitalist relations of production.

Wildcat strikes, including those led by postal workers in 1970 and the 2018–19 teacher strikes, showed rank-and-file commitment to solidarity and direct action and the willingness to take risks from which the labor bureaucracy consistently shies away. ILWU and UE continue to show a progressive alternative to the boss-friendly unionism of the AFL-CIO, and the emergence of independent and worker-led unions, including the Amazon Labor Union (ALU) and Starbucks Workers United (SWU), indicates a turning away from class collaborationism and toward militant, rank-and-file organizing strategies largely unseen since the 1930s.

The material conditions in which the U.S. working class and labor movement struggle today, particularly after the *Janus v. AFSCME* case and the COVID-19 pandemic (which produced the 'Great Resignation' and to some extent 'Striketober'), have transformed, and the uptick in labor activism and union organization indicates that the attitudes of workers regarding the rules of engagement with the capitalist class have undergone a transformation as well. Whether this change in perspective will produce a new labor movement is yet to be seen, but regardless, it is necessary to examine instances from the past and in these times during which the rank and file have taken matters into their own hands.

The Memphis Sanitation Workers Strike of 1968

Workers faced substantial risk during the Memphis Sanitation Workers strike of 1968, a famous wildcat that was notable for its participants being predominantly black as well as for the support given to the strikers by Dr. Martin Luther King, Jr. shortly before his assassination. The strike in Memphis began following the deaths of sanitation workers Echol Cole and Robert Walker, who were crushed by a malfunctioning truck. The deaths occurred at a time when workers had been voicing their concerns about low pay, poor safety standards, no sick leave, and the overt racism they experienced on the job.

Dr. King went to Memphis to support the workers after they called a strike—illegally—and said to the workers "“You are reminding not only Memphis, but you are reminding the nation that it is a crime for people to live in this rich nation and receive starvation wages”" (Weber 2018:3) This statement was made only weeks before Dr. King was assassinated. Henry Loeb III, the mayor of Memphis, viewed the union and the strike as illegitimate, and declared that public employees could not engage in actions against their employer. Photographs of armed soldiers and police confronting the striking workers show the belligerent environment in which the sanitation workers carried out their strike. With the approval of Loeb, the police attacked the workers and crowds of supporters. Sixteen-year-old Larry Payne was killed by a police officer who accused him of looting. Payne was actually waiting for Dr. King to arrive so that he could hear the Civil Rights leader speak.

The striking workers remained unshaken even after 4000 National Guard troops were called in and Loeb declared martial law. The strike continued, with the workers becoming both somber and more militant after the assassination of Dr. Martin Luther King, Jr. Coretta Scott King returned to Memphis only four days after her husband's assassination to support AFSCME Local 1733, and the widow of Dr. King marching alongside the striking workers brought their movement strength and kept the participants fiercely committed to their cause. Shortly after, the union won recognition and the city agreed to raise the sanitation workers' wages.

DRUM and the League of Revolutionary Black Workers

The year 1968 also saw the rise of the Dodge Revolutionary Union Movement (DRUM). Formed by black members of the United Auto Workers at Chrysler's Dodge plant in Hamtramck, Michigan, DRUM emerged in the aftermath of the rebellions against police brutality and miserable housing conditions that shook Detroit the previous summer. While "more than 60 percent" of the workforce in the plant was composed of black workers, "the leadership of United Auto Workers Local 3, plant management, and lower-level supervision was all white" (Weber 2018:5).

Though the UAW had given support to the civil rights movement in the 1950s and 1960s, it was slow to offer leadership roles to black workers, which led DRUM to confront not only Chrysler but the UAW as well. DRUM's July 1968 wildcat strike erupted in response "to a 40 percent increase in assembly line speed and tensions exacerbated by management and union intransigence" (Weber 2018:5). Nearly 4000 members participated in the strike, which prevented the production of roughly 3000 cars over the course of almost three days. The DRUM wildcat strike encouraged workers elsewhere around Detroit to take similar action. There was the Ford Revolutionary Union Movement at Ford's River Rouge Plant, for example, as well as the Eldon Ridge Revolutionary Union Movement.

While the revolutionary workers did not quickly achieve many of their goals, the strikes did create meaningful change, with the respective incipient movements coalescing to form the League of Revolutionary Black Workers in the Detroit-area. According to the League's constitution, the organization was built to fight for change '"wherever there are Black Workers"', be it in the United States or '"the mines of Bolivia, the rubber plantations of Indonesia, the oil fields of Biafra, or the Chrysler plant in South Africa"' (Weber 2018:6). Thus, the militant actions of the revolutionary black workers in the Michigan auto plants swelled into a new radical internationalism, and although disagreements in tactics, focus, and organizing led to the dissolution of the League, the examples of DRUM and the militant worker organizations it inspired remain relevant and encouraging to workers and unions seeking to challenge the power structure.

Postal Workers' Strike of 1970

The Postal Workers' Strike of 1970 serves as another example of militant worker action that is worth studying. After Congress gave itself a 41% wage increase but voted for only a 4% increase for postal workers, infuriated postal workers shocked Nixon, their union, and the nation by walking off the job. The postal workers labored under abysmal conditions, were unable to negotiate wages, and often had to work second jobs to survive. Having had their fill of abuse, postal workers, much to the dismay of the union leadership, decided to engage in a wildcat strike in March 1970.

Over 210,000 workers, from letter carriers to office clerks, participated in the wildcat strike. Richard Nixon, deeply troubled by this militant worker activity, appeared on national television and threatened to have the military deliver mail if the workers refused to go back to work. However, rather than frighten the striking workers, Nixon spurred more postal workers to join their striking comrades, and as a result, workers at nearly 700 more locations across the nation walked off the job. The workers crippled the mail system, and their strike even affected the stock market, with predictions of a complete shutdown occurring if the strike went on long enough.

By mid-March, Nixon appeared on television again to inform the country and the striking workers that the military would begin delivering the mail. In the same television appearance, Nixon declared a national emergency with Proclamation 3972. Nixon sent in the National Guard to carry out basic mail operations in 17 New York post offices while simultaneously negotiating with the wildcat strikers (Murolo and Chitty 2018:236). After the strike ended eight days later, not a single postal worker lost a job, and shortly thereafter, the National Postal Reorganization Act became law, providing collective bargaining rights to the four unions representing postal workers.

The Postal Workers' Strike of 1970 in particular shows the power of militant collective action. The Nixon Administration was hostile toward unions, and the striking workers faced not only fines but also incarceration for their actions. By lashing out as a united force, the workers were able to challenge the power structure and bring about meaningful changes that had seemed impossible earlier. It was not with institutional aid or by conforming to elite rules of engagement that the goals of the striking workers became reality—it was through militant, disruptive, and risky tactics, traits that characterize the wildcat strike and distinguish it from other forms of worker action.

ILWU and UE: Continuing the Legacy of Progressive Labor

By the time it held its 1949 convention, the CIO had already been ignoring or encouraging raiding of 'red unions' and actively purging its federation of progressives and leftists, all considered to be 'communist' whether they belonged to the Communist Party or not. Albert Fitzgerald, president of the United Electrical, Radio and Machine Workers of America (UE), the 'Red Fortress', explained to reporters covering the convention that he hoped the CIO would stop encouraging and financing the raiding of UE (Stepan-Norris and Zeitlin 2002:268). UE was among a faction of progressive unions in the CIO that took racial equality and women's rights seriously, and its policies, in contrast to the more class-collaborationist unions at the time, were markedly pro-labor and implemented with the well-being of the membership in mind. Whatever criticisms and accusations the CIO's leadership lobbed at UE, they could not charge the union with neglecting its members.

When Harry Bridges, president of the ILWU, came to the defense of UE at the 1949 CIO convention, he noted that no charges had been made against UE involving the economic workings of the union, or any involving neglect or exploitation of its membership. Bridges pointed out that the charges against UE were political, and brought against the union because UE did not support the Marshall Plan or the North Atlantic Treaty, two initiatives the ILWU disapproved of as well. When Bridges asked if his own union's disagreements with the politics of the CIO would lead to ILWU's expulsion, an ensemble of delegates bellowed '"Yes!"' (Stepan-Norris and Zeitlin 2002:271).

Remarkably, ILWU and UE did not meet the fate suffered by numerous other 'red unions', which after being purged from the CIO were isolated and raided until they eventually shriveled up and disappeared. ILWU and UE have been able to maintain their unions and continue supporting their members while preserving the spirit of progressive unionism through consistent engagement in worker-led social justice campaigns and activism. Neither the ILWU nor the 'Red Fortress' sacrificed their commitments to the labor movement as a mechanism for organizing and mobilizing the working class toward a more just and egalitarian future. The fact that both have retained this militant perspective while continuing to conduct their meaningful work outside of the AFL-CIO is arguably as remarkable as their survival of the Red Scare.

For years, the ILWU has disrupted port operations along the U.S. and Canadian west coast in solidarity with numerous progressive movements and causes, including a 2008 May Day work stoppage in protest against the Iraq War, a 2014 picket against Israeli cargo shipments in support of the people of Palestine, work stoppages in 2020 in memorial of George Floyd and in solidarity with the nationwide protests which erupted in the wake of his murder, and most recently the union's refusal to handle Russian cargo in protest of the invasion of Ukraine. The ILWU's unwavering support for social justice and activism inside and outside of the workplace shows that labor's place at the forefront of civil rights and progressive movements has not been completely forgotten.

Similarly, UE has remained a vigilant presence on U.S. labor's left since its 1949 departure from the CIO. UE's commitment to worker-led organization is summed up by its slogan, 'the members run this union'. UE was way ahead of other U.S. unions in the fight against racism, and by the mid-1950s, practically all of UE's contracts had anti-discrimination clauses included in them. In the 1960s, UE led a successful strike campaign against General Electric (GE), and its membership grew through the 1970s. In the 1980s, UE began to experience a decline in membership as a result of plant closings and capital flight, which continued into the 1990s.

Recognizing the threat that NAFTA posed to the working class not only in the United States but also in Mexico, UE formed an alliance with the left-wing Mexican labor federation Frente Auténtico del Trabajo (FAT—Authentic Labor Front) in 1992. Early on the frontline in the struggle against globalization and the IMF, UE formed alliances with progressive international groups outside the labor movement as well. UE's important alliance-building has continued into the present. After the COVID-19 pandemic laid bare the callousness of employers and exacerbated the indignities suffered by workers across the United States, UE teamed up with the Democratic Socialists of America (DSA) to form the Emergency Workplace Organizing Committee (EWOC). EWOC provides resources, training, and other forms of support to workers seeking to organize their workplaces, and is a bright example of what left-labor alliances can do to rebuild the labor movement.

Labor After Janus Versus AFSCME

The purpose of the 2018 *Janus v. AFSCME* case, which ended in a victory for corporate funders of union-busting legislation, was to further diminish the power and resources still held by unions (Richman 2018:1). The plaintiff of the case, Mark Janus, claimed that his freedom of speech was violated by the 'fair share' fee associated with working in a unionized workplace.

A fair share fee is a percentage of money paid by nonunion workers that goes to a union in order to help pay for the benefits of having a unionized workplace (representation, protection, sustained wage increases, etc.). Fair share fees, also called 'agency fees', are compensation for the costs, both pecuniary and operational, of representing and providing services to all workers in a bargaining unit. Because the American Federation of State, County, and Municipal Employees (AFSCME) has open ties to the Democratic Party, Janus claimed that he was paying for political speech with which he did not agree.

While it was pointed out by AFSCME's attorney that their political fund is completely voluntary and one must agree to pay into it, and that it is illegal for unions to use dues money for political purposes, the Supreme Court still sided with Mark Janus, making it illegal for public sector unions to collect fair share fees. Thus, *Janus v. AFSCME* essentially made 'right-to-work' the law of the land. AFSCME's attorney also noted, interestingly, that employers often secure agency fees for unions in return for no-strike clauses in contracts, and that the disappearance of such clauses could lead to increased worker militancy—and more headaches for employers.

The 2018–19 Teacher Strikes and the Return of the Wildcat

In the aftermath of the *Janus v. AFSCME* case, to the chagrin of institutional anti-union forces and elites, a renewed enthusiasm for industrial union tactics, worker militancy, and coordinated disruption has emerged. Workers have taken the task of confronting capital upon themselves, collectively rejecting the restrictions placed upon them by bosses, the state, and business unionism. This was clearly the case in the 2018–19 wave of teacher strikes. Notably, many of the strikes took the form of a wildcat strike, a tactic most commonly associated with syndicalist and industrial unions defined by workers striking without the approval of employers, the state, or union bosses. The wildcat strike is likely named after the black cat symbol of the Industrial Workers of the World, the 'sabocat' or 'sabo-tabby' ('sabo' being short for 'sabotage,' another form of militant worker action), depicted fiercely with arched back, fangs bared—an omen of bad luck for the boss. The power of the wildcat is in its radicalism, militancy, and refusal of compromise.

The noticeable resurgence of militant worker tactics arguably began with an unexpected February 2018 teacher wildcat strike in West Virginia. The West Virginia wildcat was followed by similar strikes across the country, from 'conservative' states like Arizona and Oklahoma to 'liberal' California and Colorado. The teachers leading the wave of strikes put class-centered demands and critiques of racism at the forefront, contrasting them with the U.S. teacher strikes of the 1970s, which had the unfortunate consequence of exacerbating tensions between teachers and the communities they served (French 2019). The striking teachers were unafraid of emphasizing class struggle in their wildcat demonstrations and demands, calling for higher taxes for the rich and corporations to better fund public education. The teacher strikes, therefore, had an undeniable aura of class-based worker militancy unseen in the institutionalized U.S. labor movement for decades.

The demands made by the striking teachers are significant, as their orientation is openly class-based: an end to the closures of public schools and the expansion of charter schools, more support staff, and a lower student-to-teacher ratio. The demands listed here are not simply teacher-centered (higher pay, etc.)—they are founded on the concepts of community interest, shared experiences, and common strength and vulnerability. Because of the community-oriented approach to their strikes, teachers garnered widespread support from the public. The teachers presented demands not only for their own benefit, but also for the benefit of their communities, and established working-class solidarity by attacking the ruling class that is hoarding its wealth and dismantling public education.

The community- and class-based disposition of the teacher strikes forged unity between the striking teachers, students, and parents, thus making the strikes more than just a battle between the teachers and their employers. The teachers in West Virginia demanded higher taxes on their state's natural gas industry while teachers in Arizona successfully defeated a proposal that would have increased funding for education by cutting Medicaid and other social programs. The Arizona teachers, like their counterparts in West Virginia, insisted that education should be funded through higher taxes on the rich. In Los Angeles, striking teachers made it abundantly clear that the heart of their struggle was protecting their students and their communities against privatization.

The striking teachers in Oakland declared that their fight was in opposition to racism and assaults on public education by the wealthy, and they won substantial victories by uniting teachers, students, parents, and others members of their community against the forces of privatization, including a compromised schoolboard. By conducting themselves as a militant, unified front within the frame of the greater struggle between classes, Oakland teachers achieved reduced class sizes, decreased caseloads for support staff, and higher wages. Perhaps most significantly, however, they secured the word of the Board of Education president for a five-month school closure stoppage and a resolution bringing an end to the expansion of charter schools in the Oakland Unified School District.

The strike that ignited the brushfire of militant worker activism, the West Virginia wildcat, deserves considerable attention, especially from social movement activists hoping to understand the dynamic between the power structure and movements seeking to challenge it. The wildcat strike began as a teacher walkout in opposition to low pay and the rising cost of health insurance. By mid-February 2018, a settlement seemed to have been reached, with Governor Jim Justice promising teachers a 5% pay raise (Richman 2018:2). While union leadership accepted the deal, the rank-and-file were not satisfied, and refused to go back to work. Every public school in West Virginia remained closed during the strike, which went on for nine days, and came to an end only after the West Virginia legislature agreed to a 5% pay increase for all state workers and the formation of a committee to address the workers' concerns regarding healthcare. The West Virginia teacher wildcat strike starkly resembled militant worker activity prior to the National Labor Relations Act (NLRA).

Wildcat strikes are effective in part because of their spontaneity. This is not to say that they do not require planning, coordination, and discipline—no coordinated worker action is ever truly 'spontaneous'. However, a short work stoppage, walkout, or slowdown can take place without the bureaucratic process of obtaining official union approval, and it might be ignited simply by a rude comment from a manager, or a change in workplace policy that does not suit the workers. While collective bargaining contracts contain 'no-strike' clauses, preventing workers from striking throughout the duration of the contract, workers organized and militant enough to wildcat strike take action whenever it appears necessary to do so (Glaberman 1952:13). More often than not, union bureaucrats are just as eager to prevent wildcat strikes as employers are.

Wildcats can also involve acts of sabotage (the name deriving, after all, from the ferocious 'sabocat'). While the heyday of the wildcat strike might rest in the pages of history before the passage of the National Labor Relations Act, there have been notable occasions when the black cat has been stirred from its slumber after the implementation of the NLRA. For example, workers in the Lordstown, Ohio, General Motors factory in 1972 threw loose screws into a gas tank, hoping for the line to get shut down and for a brief interruption of their toil. While the leadership of the UAW bargained for higher wages, the factory workers at Lordstown wanted to work at a slower pace. The Lordstown workers organized a 22-day wildcat strike demanding management settle grievances, rehire laid-off workers, and reduce the pace of work.

The striking teachers in West Virginia schools were faced with peculiar circumstances, having no formal collective bargaining or contracts, only a degree of union recognition, contentious tenure and grievance procedures, and pay and benefits across the state dependent on legislative lobbying. Such an environment does not seem in the least to be friendly to labor organizing, nor conducive to union militancy. However, the teachers in West Virginia, among the lowest paid in the United States, showed courage rather than fear when they decided to walk off the job in February 2018. The conditions in which the wildcat strike in West Virginia emerged, both in the schools and in the general political atmosphere, make the strike remarkable. The teachers went up against not only a school system but also a state apparatus that could have imprisoned them for the action they took. Small wonder, then, that their victorious action inspired the wave of strikes by teachers across the nation who followed West Virginia's example.

Since the implementations of the National Labor Relations Act, Taft-Hartley Act, and Labor Management Disclosure and Reporting Act, the illegality of such action has reinforced the wildcat's power rather than diminish it. After the National Labor Relations Act was signed into law in 1935, workers lost control of striking, as such action was made illegal during the duration of a contract with management (Weber 2018:1). Taft-Hartley and the Labor Management Disclosure and Reporting Act went further in their abatement of worker power, with Taft-Hartley requiring workers to submit notices to management prior to a strike and the Labor Management Disclosure and Reporting Act criminalizing solidarity strikes (when a union supports the strike of another union).

Union members have been unable to carry out any effective militant actions with the blessing of the law for quite some time, and this has led to a resurgence in illegal worker actions—such as the wildcat strike—as workers have come to realize that playing by the rules of the ruling class is no way to bring about change. When workers engage in wildcat strikes, they disregard the state's legal restrictions, with all of the risks involved, and do not concern themselves with the opinions of union bureaucrats. As it so happens, this highly illegal tactic is also highly effective.

The West Virginia teacher strike, which involved roughly 20,000 teachers and thousands of other workers in the public school system shutting down schools across all of the state's 55 counties, reintroduced militancy and tenacity to the U.S. labor movement and inspired workers across the country to take similar action (Karp and Sanchez 2018:7). The teacher strikes that followed West Virginia in states such as Colorado, North Carolina, Oklahoma, Arizona, and Kentucky represented struggle beyond the classroom. The strikes embodied a battle waged by workers and their communities against privatization and austerity, two prominent features of the capitalist power structure. Most of the strike actions took place in 'right-to-work' states, which have stricter laws regulating unions, and right-wing legislators who welcome severe cuts to public school funding and diminished compensation for teachers.

In the case of the teachers in Arizona, the governor, Doug Ducey, joined by a Republican Legislature, attempted to extinguish the strike by offering pay increases and minor restoration of public school funding. At the time, Ducey was scheming with the Koch brothers, trying to figure out how to privatize the Arizona public school system entirely. However, while the movement was sometimes referred to as a series of "red state revolts", there were strikes in the 'purple' state of Colorado and the 'blue' state of California as well. Regardless of political leadership, the states embrace similar economic policies, and decreases in funding to public education and other social services afflict the nation as a whole.

The hardships faced by educators across the country are symptoms of a broader economic assault on the working class. Diminished pay for teachers signals the impact of the gutting of funding to public schools. Underfunded public schools have been a consistent feature of the U.S. education system, and in many states, this problem is accelerating. The underfunded schools served as incubators for teacher wildcat strikes, which emerged in a wider climate of economic assaults on already vulnerable communities. Thus, the teacher wildcat strikes are unique, for they cannot simply be branded as contained struggles by workers fighting only for better conditions on the job. The teacher strikes serve as an example of a wide, inclusive working-class social movement that recognized the strike, and more specifically the wildcat strike, as the most effective method of lashing out against the power structure. The cutting of teacher pensions and health benefits and slashing of public education budgets are part of a more general attack on public social programs and services which has resulted from a 'bipartisan' devotion to austerity and privatization.

The strikes were, then, not only disruptive actions in response to low wages and large class sizes, but militant reactions to policies enacted for the benefit of the ruling class. Viewed in this context, the wave of teacher wildcat strikes appears to be an indication of a greater rumbling of working-class consciousness, organization, and militancy. The collaboration between reactionary elite institutions and establishment politicians is more than a suspicion, and this has become more apparent to working-class Americans as time has rolled forward.

During the 2018–19 teacher wildcat strikes, the right-wing State Policy Network, funded by the Koch brothers and the Walton Family Foundation, published a list of talking points to assist legislators in disparaging the teachers and their strikes. However, it was (and is) not just conservative elite groups and right-wing politicians urging privatization and austerity. President Obama's Secretary of Education, Arne Duncan, embraced austerity and privatization as means to increase 'innovation' in public schools. Bipartisan support has been enthusiastically given to the project of dismantling public schools, decreasing teacher compensation, and privatizing education. According to the Education Law Center (ELC), the states ranked lowest for teacher pay include several controlled by Democrats.

Despite the attempts by corporate elites and their pet politicians to nudge public policy in an anti-teacher and anti-union direction, teachers and strike actions are overwhelmingly supported by the public, and this is another ingredient in the power of the wildcat teacher movement. A poll conducted by Associated Press-NORC showed that 78% of the U.S. population considers teacher pay too low, and a majority supports the use of strikes (AP-NORC 2018). The public, therefore, must be ignoring the corporate media, which consistently pump out stories blaming teachers for the hardships experienced by public schools while failing to mention the market zealots crusading for privatization and the austerity policies dismembering public education.

The Amazon Labor Union

Some of the most exciting and successful union organizing campaigns in recent years have been conducted not by professional organizers or the AFL-CIO, but by rank-and-file workers who have built independent unions in industries dominated by powerful and well-known corporations. Much of what professional organizers have been taught are essential components to successful organizing drives has been thrown out the window by these rank-and-file workers, who have taken it upon themselves to figure out how best to build solidarity and consciousness among their fellow workers and collectively challenge their employers.

Workers have become more audacious, and more willing to challenge their bosses and pursue unionization to fight for common interests. In part, this is due to the precariousness and lousy working conditions of jobs in the service and warehouse/factory sectors. The workers toiling in such industries tend to move from one job to the next relatively often anyway, and so the threat of being fired has lost its vicious prestige. This willingness to take risks on the job is one aspect of the recent worker-led organizing campaigns. Another, which is arguably more important, is that the workers leading these drives have mostly or completely ignored the 'traditional wisdom' of labor organizing.

The organizational success of the Amazon Labor Union (ALU) should be a loud and clear signal to the disciples of labor's 'traditional wisdom' that the rules of engagement have changed. For example, in a union organizing drive, a professional union organizer would be met with either incredulity or laughter from the union's executive board if they proposed filing for a union vote with authorization cards signed by only 30% of the workforce. Yet, this is precisely what the ALU organizers did, and the victorious result speaks for itself.

The organizing efforts at Amazon's JFK8 warehouse in Staten Island began as a worker-led protest against Amazon's lackadaisical policies at the height of the COVID-19 pandemic. After the lead organizer at JFK8, Chris Smalls, was illegally fired for his activities at the warehouse, Smalls and his fellow workers were undeterred. Smalls, who is now president of ALU, posted up at a bus stop near the warehouse with a team of rank-and-file organizers and maintained a constant presence there to talk to workers as they started and ended their shifts. After a December 2021 Amazon-NLRB settlement which required Amazon cease its union-busting practices, ALU organizers were able to talk to their coworkers inside the warehouse as well as continue their efforts outside (Brooks 2022).

ALU's first petition for a union election, filed in October 2021, was rejected by the NLRB because the organizers had not collected the legally required number of signatures (30% of the workforce). ALU filed again in December, and this time the NLRB approved it, and set the election date for March 2022. The 'traditional wisdom' of labor organizing tells one that they should expect at least 10% of workers who sign authorization cards to rescind their support during the election process, and so organizers are encouraged to collect signatures from 70–80% of the workforce before filing for a union election. Fortunately, the workers leading the union drive at JFK8 did not heed this advice, and filed for an election after collecting the minimum required number of authorization cards.

Following the NLRB's announcement of the union election, Smalls and two other rank-and-file organizers were arrested while delivering food to workers in the JFK8 parking lot. Amazon had called the police in an attempt to prevent ALU representatives from garnering more support from the workforce, but it completely backfired. Videos of the arrest circulated among workers at the warehouse. In the context of the 2020 civil rights uprisings which erupted across the country, the footage of Smalls and his comrades being taken away by police for simply providing food for their fellow workers stimulated righteous anger in the JFK8 workforce. According to Smalls, this event was a turning point in the ALU's battle with Amazon (Brooks 2022).

The ALU's unprecedented union election victory, a little over a month after the arrests, was achieved through both tried-and-true labor organizing methods (face-to-face conversations with workers, identifying and developing leaders, disrupting anti-union efforts by the company, etc.) and the eschewal of labor organizing orthodoxy. The ALU leaders were not professional organizers, but rank-and-file workers, and they did not rely on the support of an already established union or labor federation. ALU was built from the ground up by the workers themselves, who harnessed the momentum that surfaced in events such as the protests against Amazon's COVID-19 policies, Smalls' termination, and the arrests of ALU representatives after the NLRB's election announcement. Using momentum and moving quickly was advantageous for the ALU organizers, and had they relied on the slower, more careful structure-based approach preached by adherents of labor's 'traditional wisdom', they very well might have lost their union election. Sustaining momentum and worker enthusiasm while seizing opportunities for growth is essential to successful organizing campaigns, and ALU's victory at the JFK8 warehouse is a testament to the fact that it is not professional organizers and paid union staff or executive board bureaucracies that will determine the fate of the labor movement, but the workers themselves.

Starbucks Workers United

At the time of writing, a year has passed since the first organizing committee meeting of Starbucks Workers United (SWU). Starbucks Workers United has since won union elections at 225 locations across the United States and brought over 6000 Starbucks workers into the labor movement (Pitkin 2022). Dozens of Starbucks stores are currently waiting for union elections and new petitions are being filed to the NLRB by Starbucks workers each week. With a third of the organized Starbucks stores going on strike and hundreds of locations still in the process of organizing, the company has responded with store closings and targeted firings of organizers and union leaders. The company has even filed a suit against the NLRB, which it claims is colluding with Starbucks Workers United.

Despite Starbucks' nefarious union-busting efforts, workers across the country continue to organize their shops. Recently, Starbucks Workers United introduced the 'No Contract, No Coffee' pledge, which invites community members and sympathetic organizations to connect with and support Starbucks workers and get involved in their union drives. Community support for the rank-and-file Starbucks union organizers has adopted numerous forms, including 'sip-ins', during which union supporters pack a store and, while drinking coffee, disrupt management's union-busting actions or boost morale before an election vote. Community members have also joined Starbucks workers on their picket lines, and helped shut down Starbucks stores by clogging drive-through lines and preventing managers and scabs from entering the stores to serve coffee.

The success of Starbucks Workers United is extraordinary for a number of reasons. First, like their counterparts in the Amazon Labor Union, the rank-and-file workers are leading the Starbucks national organizing drive (although there has been assistance from Workers United, the SWU's parent union). Second, the union's success indicates an attitudinal change among unorganized service industry workers. There is an assumption that such 'low-level' jobs are not worth the trouble and resources to organize, and that workers who are dissatisfied with their jobs should simply quit and find work elsewhere. The workers behind Starbucks Workers United appear to have rejected this perspective, opting rather to organize their workplaces and fight for dignity and respect where they are. The Starbucks workers are quite right to rebuff the 'find a better job' line of thought, as it only keeps workers desperately chasing a 'kinder, gentler boss' instead of building class consciousness and solidarity and forming unions, which are effective regardless of the boss's character. Lastly, the stunning speed with which Starbucks Workers United has organized stores across the United States is in itself remarkable. Over 200 shops and 6000 workers in a single year—one would be hard pressed to find anything comparable in the U.S. labor movement in recent memory.

The Great Resignation and Striketober

The successful union campaigns by ALU and Starbucks Workers United are part of a larger resurgence in labor activity in the United States. While one must carefully avert the temptation to compare what happened in 2021 as anything close what happened in the 1930s or 1940s, the combination of the 'Great Resignation'—a term used to describe the ongoing trend of millions of workers quitting their jobs *en masse*—and the walkouts and strikes of October 2021 (known as 'Striketober') did offer workers an encouraging glimpse of their shared power and how it can be put to use. Some mainstream media commentators even compared the Great Resignation to a general strike (Lichtenstein 2021).

The frustration, anxiety, sickness, and death introduced by the COVID-19 pandemic brought about an economic reshuffling, and the post-pandemic 'labor shortage' gave workers leverage. Workers were instilled with the confidence that their bosses needed them, but they did not need their bosses. Though the Great Resignation may not constitute an organized labor mass action, its impact has been significant, and the comparisons to a 'quiet' general strike may not be unwarranted. After all, the millions of workers who quit their jobs were, through abandoning their employers, protesting the unsatisfactory conditions they encountered at work. Many workers who had been laid off during the pandemic refused to return after their bosses called them back to their jobs. Because the U.S. working class is largely unorganized, workers rely on individual actions, like quitting, when they are dissatisfied with their employment. The Great Resignation, which peaked in 2021 but continues as an ongoing trend, is an aggregate of individual actions taken by workers. However, there was considerable organized labor activity that complemented the Great Resignation, particularly during what is known as Striketober.

In 2021, workers in multiple sectors, including manufacturing, health care, entertainment, fast food, and higher education, organized and launched strikes and work stoppages, the bulk of which occurred in October and November. According to a February 2022 Labor Action Tracker report compiled by Cornell University's School of Industrial and Labor Relations, there were 265 work stoppages in 2021, involving an estimated 140,000 workers (Kallas et al. 2022).

In August 2021, Nabisco workers represented by the Bakery, Confectionery, Tobacco Workers and Grain Millers' International Union (BCTGM) went on strike, first in Portland, Oregon, and then across the United States, demanding better wages, an improved healthcare plan, and protection against the outsourcing of jobs to Mexico. The first strike of 'Striketober' was the October 1, 2021 strike initiated by hundreds of nurses represented by Communications Workers of America (CWA) at Mercy Hospital in Buffalo, New York. On October 4, 1400 Kellogg's workers represented by BCTGM went on strike, followed by a strike involving approximately 10,000 John Deere workers represented by United Auto Workers (UAW) on October 14, and a walkout/strike led by graduate student workers (also represented by UAW) at Columbia University. A surprising finding from the February 2022 Labor Action Tracker report is that 32.8% of 2021 strikes were by nonunion workers, which suggests that workers are organizing and engaging in direct action even without the formal recognition of a labor union.

As exciting as the labor actions were in 2021, the level of strike activity during Striketober was lower than in 2018 and 2019, and did not get anywhere close to the numbers recorded in the decades prior to the Reagan years (Henwood 2022). However, though Striketober may have fallen short of a 'strike wave', the fact remains that over 100,000 workers across the United States engaged in strike actions, and in addition to the Great Recession, this uptick in worker action did result in some concessions from employers. Many employers began offering increased benefits, including healthcare and college scholarships. According to the Atlanta Fed's Wage Growth Tracker, in December 2021, wages increased by 4.5% (Atlanta Fed 2022).

Reckoning with the Past and Organizing in the Present

Rebuilding the U.S. labor movement and regaining the courage, idealism, and militancy that characterized its most vital and exciting periods means acknowledging labor's mistakes and rectifying its transgressions. This requires more than a 'what went wrong?' analysis, although recognizing consistent patterns and elements that have produced certain results is undoubtedly a necessary part of solving the contradictions of labor. More necessary, though, is developing coherent and tangible strategies for rebuilding the labor movement in such a way that it is capable of engaging in successful struggles faced by the working class *today*.

It is easy for one to fall into the trap of trying to solve today's contradictions with yesterday's solutions, or, to put it another way, of trying to fight today's battles with yesterday's weapons. There are methods and tactics that remain useful for workers, and it is appropriate for organizers and unions to continue implementing them when they can be effectively put to use. However, such methods and tactics, ranging from communication strategies for organizing workers to work stoppages or wildcat strikes, must be continually scrutinized and sharpened, lest they become outdated or blunted.

The conditions have changed, but the obstacles impeding the organization of the workers into a revolutionary class remain the same: limited opportunities for political participation, the concentration of wealth and ownership of property, tremendous inequality of income, exhaustion and alienation, and so on. Inspiration can be found when speculating about what yesterday's radicals would do if confronted by today's conditions (and contradictions), but speculation is not the task of the architects of a new labor movement. The task of the workers and organizers who will build a revived militant, visionary labor movement is to analyze the current situation and seize opportunities to build class consciousness and solidarity. This does not mean putting undue faith in spontaneity (nothing is spontaneous), nor does it mean the leaders of the movement must be opportunistic. Organizing in the present means firmly grasping the revolutionary purpose of the labor movement and working toward tangible goals with the available tools.

The globalized neoliberal market system has made working-class internationalism more imperative than ever. Building a new labor movement in the United States requires establishing organizational ties with progressive and militant unions and labor federations abroad, as workers in every land are impacted by neoliberal globalization, and degradation and exploitation are unique to no nation (Davis 2018:326–327). This process will necessarily entail reckoning with the fact that U.S. labor's dominant institution, the AFL-CIO, has a long and brutal history of conspiring with capital and the state to break progressive political movements and radical labor unions around the world. Understandably, progressive labor unions and federations abroad have little reason to trust the AFL-CIO, even with AIFLD being discontinued. This is another reason why the new U.S. labor movement must be independent of the AFL-CIO—it must be unblemished by the labor bureaucracy's past (and present) nefarious practices.

The builders of the new labor movement must study what has been done to militant labor movements abroad, and unabashedly proclaim and denounce U.S. labor's role in the toppling of progressive governments, crushing of militant unions, and opening of the world for neoliberal globalization. Similarly, the leaders of the new labor movement must be unafraid to impart clear connections and comparisons between what was done to unions in other nations by the CIA and AFL-CIO and what happened in the United States during the Red Scare(s): the purges, anticommunist hysteria, interrogations, and violence that squelched the progressive wing of U.S. labor.

Connections must also be drawn between the crushing of left-wing governments and radical labor movements and the rise of the right in its current form. Had progressive political movements and parties, and militant labor federations and unions not been extinguished, the right would not have been able to opportunistically seize the 'anti-globalization' socio-political space. Legitimacy in this area, among others, is with the left, and the left remains the only political force capable of truly challenging the global neoliberal paradigm. The major question before the architects of the new labor movement is: what is 'the left'? These same workers and organizers will have to decide that through their efforts.

In any case, the inability of the AFL-CIO to lead the charge toward a revitalized labor movement is clear. Its leadership is too connected politically and economically to the ruling class. Over the years, it has become an institution which hinders rather than serves the interests of the working class. To be sure, militant, progressive workers should still join and organize within AFL-CIO unions, as abandoning the workers who are members of the federation to whatever bourgeois or conservative elements exist within their unions does little (and is in fact harmful) for the cause of revolutionary unionism (Lenin's 1920 pamphlet *"Left-Wing" Communism: an Infantile Disorder* includes a scathing critique of the 'left communist' tendency to promote disengagement in non-revolutionary trade unions which should be read and reread by today's labor organizers). However, the fact remains that the new labor movement will need to exist independently of the AFL-CIO, and the development of an alternative, left-wing labor federation will be necessary in order to challenge the AFL-CIO's hegemonic position in U.S. labor. This struggle will be indispensable in the larger fight against neoliberalism and capitalist hegemony.

The task ahead of the workers and organizers who will develop the new labor movement involves several components (these are not the only components, to be sure, but they are, I argue, the most glaring): understanding labor's essential place in a progressive mass political movement, reckoning with U.S. labor's past, rejecting class collaborationism, and building an internationalist, working-class program to challenge the right's pseudo-populism and ethno-nationalism. New labor's architects must also accomplish that which has been either put off or rejected by cautious labor leaders for decades: the creation of a Labor Party.

The void created in the sociopolitical arena by the expulsion of an organized, coherent left and radical labor unions has opened space for the right, which has taken advantage of the absence of a legitimate challenge in a time when the status quo appears to offer nothing to the masses. The left and progressive labor have the only true answers to the problems faced by the international working class. Without a coherent, disciplined left, the pseudo-populist right has been able to bulldoze its way into power. If they are to be understood and overcome, the dynamics and implications of the rise of the right must be closely examined.

References

Agee, Philip. 1975. *Inside the Company: CIA Diary*. American ed. New York, NY: Stonehill.

AP-NORC. 2018. American Attitudes toward Teacher Pay and Protests. *AP-NORC*. https://apnorc.org/projects/american-attitudes-toward-teacher-pay-and-protests/.

Bevins, Vincent. 2021. *The Jakarta Method: Washington's Anticommunist Crusade and the Mass Murder Program that Shaped Our World*. New York, NY: PublicAffairs.

Blum, William. 2003. *Killing Hope: US Military and CIA Interventions since World War II.* London, England: Zed Books.

Brooks, Chris. 2022. How Amazon and Starbucks Workers Are Upending the Organizing Rules. *In These Times.* https://inthesetimes.com/article/amazon-starbucks-workers-organizing-unions-momentum-movement-moment.

Cantú, Francisco. 2019. The Fingerprints of Fraud: Evidence from Mexico's 1988 Presidential Election. *The American Political Science Review* 113 (3): 710–726. https://doi.org/10.1017/s0003055419000285.

Church Committee (U.S. Senate Select Committee to Study Governmental Operations with Respect to Intelligence Activities). 1975. *Covert Action in Chile 1963-73.* Washington, D.C.: U.S. Government Printing Office.

Davis, Mike. 2018. *Prisoners of the American Dream: Politics and Economy in the History of the U.S. Working Class.* London, England: Verso Books.

Directorate of Intelligence. 1983. Mexico: Labor-Government Relations. *Freedom of Information Act Electronic Reading Room.* https://www.cia.gov/reading-room/docs/CIA-RDP84S00897R000100040007-7.pdf.

Domingos, Charles Sidarta Machado. 2018. Ligações Perigosas: A Deterioração Das Relações Entre Os Governos de João Goulart e John Kennedy No Ano de 1962. *Tempo (Rio de Janeiro, Brazil)* 24 (3): 525–545. https://doi.org/10.1590/tem-1980-542x2018v240306.

Dulles, Allen W. 1951. Analysis of the Power of the Communist Parties of France and Italy and of Measures to Counter Them. *Freedom of Information Act Electronic Reading Room.* https://www.cia.gov/readingroom/docs/CIA-RDP80R01731R003200020013-5.pdf.

Faux, Jeff. 2013. NAFTA's Impact on U.S. Workers. *Economic Policy Institute.* https://www.epi.org/blog/naftas-impact-workers/.

Federal Reserve Bank of Atlanta. 2022. Wage Growth Tracker. *Federal Reserve Bank of Atlanta.* https://www.atlantafed.org/chcs/wage-growth-tracker.

Foreign Broadcast Information Service (FBIS). 1962. Espionage Record of U.S. Agent Exposed. *Freedom of Information Act Electronic Reading Room.* https://www.cia.gov/readingroom/docs/CIA-RDP75-00149R000100500026-1.pdf.

Francia, Peter L. 2010. Assessing the Labor-Democratic Party Alliance: A One-Sided Relationship? *Polity* 42 (3): 293–303. https://doi.org/10.1057/pol.2010.7.

French, Nick. 2019. A Different Kind of Teachers' Strike Wave. *Jacobinmag.com.* http://jacobinmag.com/2019/03/a-different-kind-of-teachers-strike-wave.

Glaberman, Martin. 1952. *Punching Out.* Edmonton, Alberta: Thought Crime.

Henwood, Doug. 2022. No Strike Wave in 2021. *LBO News from Doug Henwood.* https://lbo-news.com/2022/01/17/no-strike-wave-in-2021/.

Hirsch, Fred. 1977. In *The CIA and the Labour Movement*, ed. R. Fletcher. Nottingham, England: Spokesman Books.

Immerman, Richard H. 1982. *The CIA in Guatemala: The Foreign Policy of Intervention*. 1st ed. Austin, TX: University of Texas Press.

Kallas, Johnnie, Leonardo Grageda, and Eli Friedman. 2022. Labor Action Tracker. *The ILR School*. https://www.ilr.cornell.edu/worker-institute/blog/reports-and-publications/labor-action-tracker-annual-report-2021.

Karp, Stan, and Adam Sanchez. 2018. The 2018 Wave of Teacher Strikes. *Rethinking Schools*. http://www.rethinkingschools.org/articles/the-2018-wave-of-teacher-strikes.

Kirkwood, Burton. 2000. *The History of Mexico*. Westport, CT: Greenwood Press.

Lenin, Vladimir. 1920. 'Left-Wing' Communism: An Infantile Disorder. *Marxists.org*. https://www.marxists.org/archive/lenin/works/1920/lwc/ch06.htm.

Lichtenstein, Nelson. 2021. Are We Witnessing a 'General Strike' in Our Own Time? *Washington Post*. https://www.washingtonpost.com/outlook/2021/11/18/are-we-witnessing-general-strike-our-own-time/.

McKenzie, Rob. 2022. *El Golpe: US Labor, the CIA, and the Coup at Ford in Mexico*. London, England: Pluto Press.

Mills, C. Wright. 1948. *The New Men of Power: America's Labor Leaders*. London, England: Harcourt, Brace & Co.

Moody, Kim. 1995. NAFTA and the Corporate Redesign of North America. *Latin American Perspectives* 22 (1): 95–116. https://doi.org/10.1177/0094582x9502200107.

Morris, George. 1967. *CIA and American Labor: The Subversion of the AFL-CIO's Foreign Policy*. New York, NY: International Publishers.

Murolo, Priscilla, and A.B. Chitty. 2018. *From the Folks Who Brought You the Weekend: A Short, Illustrated History of Labor in the United States*. New York, NY: New Press.

National Security Archive. 2004. Chile 1964: CIA Covert Support in Frei Election Detailed. *Gwu.edu*. https://nsarchive2.gwu.edu/news/20040925/index.htm.

Office of Current Intelligence, CIA. 1952. Current Intelligence Bulletin. *Freedom of Information Act Electronic Reading Room*. https://www.cia.gov/reading-room/docs/CIA-RDP79T00975A000900240001-5.pdf.

Parenti, Michael. 2001. *Blackshirts and Reds: Rational Fascism and the Overthrow of Communism*. San Francisco, CA: City Lights Books.

Pitkin, Daisy. 2022. Interview: Starbucks Workers Are in the Fight of Their Lives for a Contract. *Labor Notes*. https://labornotes.org/blogs/2022/08/interview-starbucks-workers-are-fight-their-lives-contract.

Richman, Shaun. 2018. The West Virginia Teachers' Strike Has Activists Asking: Should We Revive the Wildcat? *In These Times*. http://inthesetimes.com/working/entry/20987/west_virginia_teachers_strike_wildcat_janus.

Roman, Richard, and Edur Velasco Arregui. 2017. The NAFTA Consensus. *Jacobin.com*. https://jacobin.com/2017/08/nafta-trans-pacific-partnership-trump-free-trade.

Schaal, Dennis. 1981. Unions Blunt U.S. Salvador Policy. *Freedom of Information Act Electronic Reading Room*. https://www.cia.gov/readingroom/docs/CIA-RDP90-00806R000100070005-8.pdf.

Schuhrke, Jeff. 2022. Trader Joe's Workers Have Won Their First Unions in America. *Jacobin.com*. https://jacobin.com/2022/08/trader-joes-union-minneapolis-ma-interview.

Servicio Sismológico Nacional. n.d. El Sismo de 1985: En Cifras. *Internet Archive*. https://web.archive.org/web/20080610175800/http://www.ssn.unam.mx/website/jsp/Carteles/sismo85.jsp.

Stepan-Norris, Judith, and Maurice Zeitlin. 2002. *Left out: Reds and America's Industrial Unions*. Cambridge, England: Cambridge University Press.

Tigar, Michael E. 2016. Job Loss, the Clintons, NAFTA, and a New Progressive Labor Rights Agenda. *MR Online*. https://mronline.org/2016/11/17/tigar171116-html/.

Weber, Brandon. 2018. When Workers Say 'No!': A Whirlwind Tour of Wildcat Strikes. *Progressive.org*. http://progressive.org/dispatches/when-workers-say-no180831/.

CHAPTER 5

Filling the Void: The Reactionary Response to Neoliberalism and Its Crises

The crises caused or exacerbated by neoliberalism, including mass job insecurity, diminished standards of living, lower wages, military conflicts, and towering income inequality, have brought into the sociopolitical space an alarming reaction from the right on an international scale. While working-class organizations (including labor movements) and the left naturally oppose neoliberalism and its global 'race to the bottom' strategy, the rapid rise of right-wing critiques of neoliberalism is worth examining, as it is indicative of a massive ideological and political shift with global implications.

Global capital has used the crises and contradictions that have ripened since the dawn of neoliberalism to advance reactionary sociopolitical and economic agendas (Berberoglu 2021a:4). In addition, numerous social and political developments have emerged alongside the campaigns of reactionary world leaders which appear to have been borne by distrust in established institutions and the void created by the obliteration (or near obliteration) of the left and independent, internationalist labor movements. These developments include: (1) the rise of pseudo-populism; (2) the promotion of ethno-nationalism; and (3) emboldened authoritarianism/neofascism.

Pseudo-populism has been a useful tool for the right in that it establishes an 'us against them' binary, heightens the sense of being threatened in the masses of supporters, and allows political and economic 'insiders' to

A. Barrington, *The U.S. Labor Movement in the 20th and Early 21st Century*, Social Movements and Transformation,
https://doi.org/10.1007/978-3-031-30077-6_5

cast themselves as 'outsiders'. The instability and uncertainty fostered by neoliberalism (and capitalism in general) instill a yearning in particular sectors of the populace (notably the petty bourgeoisie) for a 'strong man' figure, a leader who might bring the nation back to a nebulous bygone era of 'prosperity' and 'comfort'. This desire for glory-via-submission is a dominant feature of past fascist movements and is indeed critical to today's reactionary resurgence. Finally, ethno-nationalism serves the dual purpose of cultivating an identity for a particular group and inventing the sinister 'other'. For ethno-nationalists in the United States and Europe, the sinister other mostly takes the form of immigrants or refugees, but the label can be applied to any person or group who does not fit the reactionary ideal of 'Western culture'. The common origin of all of these components of reaction is economic crisis.

The reactionary response to neoliberal globalization, including the elements listed above, presents an antithetical perspective to that of the left/labor, at least in the sense that it opposes the internationalism and working-class solidarity which mark left-wing and progressive labor movements. It should be noted, however, that the right's nationalist, ethnocentric rhetoric has enjoyed some appeal in segments of the working class (Davis 2018:184–185). The nativist ideals held by some of today's conservative unions (a vast majority of which represent law enforcement) and workers evoke the infamous anti-Asian sentiment harbored by U.S. labor in the late nineteenth and early twentieth centuries, which was fueled by similar displacement-based anxiety and racism (Montgomery 1987:85–86).

Without an accessible or widely publicized left-wing response to globalization, many workers have joined in the exuberant circus of reaction. In fact, a tactic used by reactionary leaders, Trump chief among them, has been to lump the left in with the neoliberals (recall how he chastised the 'radical leftist' Democrats in his numerous bombastic speeches). In response, the neoliberal establishment has tried to cram the right and left beneath the same irrational 'populist' umbrella, equating social democrat Bernie Sanders with the reactionary Donald Trump (Reed 2021).

In any case, the political establishment certainly prefers the right to the left. This has been evident since long before the dawn of the neoliberal era, shown clearly in the preference of the U.S. and other capitalist states for right-wing autocrats over any government even remotely on the left. When the AFL and the CIO purged U.S. unions of radicals and militants, and when the AFL-CIO aided the CIA's international anticommunist programs, trampling independent progressive labor movements and propping up right-wing tin-pot dictatorships, the labor federations were doing their part in making the world safe for capitalism, and consequently for neoliberal globalization. The neoliberal paradigm's destabilization of governments, economies, and social relations has resulted in the rise of right-wing demagoguery on an international scale. With no coordinated militant left to stand in its way, reactionary forces may very well drag organized human life over the precipice.

Pseudo-Populism: Exploiting Discontent

The primary reasons the so-called 'populism' of current reactionary movements is a fraud are (1) the movements are organized and funded by members of the ruling class, and (2) the application of the term 'populism' serves the purpose of equating the right with the left. The legitimate ingredient in the pseudo-populist movements is the discontent of the working class and some sectors of the middle class. Neoliberalism, as with capitalism in general, introduced social and economic anxiety and insecurity to working people, and this anxiety is exploited by members of the ruling class who seek to prevent challenges to the capitalist power structure. Neoliberalism is still the guiding force behind global capitalism today, even in the midst of crises, and any attempt to disassociate the capitalist system from neoliberal globalization is confused at best and nefarious at worst (and the attempts by the elites behind the reactionary movements are of the latter category). The confusion of working- and middle-class participants in right-wing 'populist' movements is to the advantage of the ruling class puppet masters pulling the strings.

The members of the ruling class leading the reactionary 'anti-globalization' movements have little interest in dismantling neoliberalism. Rather, they are interested in preserving capitalism, and know that mass discontent can lead to socioeconomic transformations which have the potential to challenge their interests. Thus, they exploit this discontent, and shift the direction of mass rage and mistrust away from capitalists and toward sinister 'Others', such as immigrants, unions, minority groups, and other nations. The capitalist class has long weaponized the fomentation of antagonism and resentment in workers against other workers along racial, ethnic, and national lines to diminish working-class solidarity (Yates 2009:142–143). To preserve neoliberal hegemony, the capitalist class incites prejudice, chauvinism, and distrust in public institutions in order to keep the blame for capitalism's crises directed elsewhere.

This approach was especially apparent in past eras of reactionary 'populism', those of the first and second Red Scares. The public was fed anxiety through incessant streams of ruling class propaganda portraying immigrants and leftists as agents of destruction and doom, and even labor organizations, including the AFL and the CIO, participated in the witch hunts, kangaroo courts, and purges which crushed militant challenges to the capitalist paradigm. As I hope to have shown through the analyses in this book, this would be to the detriment of workers in the United States and abroad, but to the benefit of the global ruling classes.

If the current trends of reaction are 'populist', then those of the periods of anticommunist hysteria surrounding WWI and WWII certainly were as well. The point of the Red Scares was to encourage working- and middle-class Americans to view the enemies of the ruling class as their own. Groups including the American Legion (which notably murdered members of the IWW in the Centralia Massacre of 1919) and the Ku Klux Klan embodied supposed 'right-wing populism' which, in fact, can be more accurately described as the ruled doing the dirty work of the rulers (Dubofsky 1969:455). There is nothing really populist about reactionary movements, as their sole purpose is to preserve the power and control of the ruling class. However, 'populist' is a favorable description for reactionary movements as far as the institutions (mainstream media, etc.) which seek to preserve the power structure are concerned, as it allows them to equate the right-wing with the left-wing, placing both beneath the populist umbrella, and thus all critiques of the status quo can be dismissed as irrational and incomprehensible. It must be said, however, that ruling class institutions, even those purporting their liberalism, favor the right's supposed brand of 'populism' over that of the left.

While individual participants in right-wing 'populist' movements may feel they are engaged in a battle against the neoliberal socioeconomic arrangement, the contradictions inherent to reactionary 'populism' result in such movements being little more than cheerleaders for ruling class domination, and thus more or less for the preservation of the status quo. They do not like the way things are, yet they champion the very structural conditions which displease them (decrying the 'elite' while embracing favors for the wealthy, etc.).

Therefore, there is no right-wing populism, as the populist label suggests more than mere dissatisfaction with the present socioeconomic structure. While it is true enough that reactionaries are dissatisfied with current social and political trends, populism also suggests bottom-up demands for *something else* politically and economically—redistribution of wealth, more assistance for the lower classes, improved public housing, and so on. For example, in the late nineteenth century, the People's Party, also known as the Populist Party, which was connected to organized labor and had socialist leanings, was detested by capitalists, conservative labor bureaucrats, and wealthy farmers because it sought to challenge the power structure and empower industrial and agricultural workers (Davis 2018:36–37).

The demands of right-wing movements, even those described as 'populist', can be boiled down to the insistence on a socioeconomic arrangement even more favorable to the ruling class (less taxes for the rich, less regulation of businesses, etc.). There is nothing populist about demanding more of the same but to an accelerated degree. The contradictions of reactionary 'populism' will be explored further later, but the main point here is that a reactionary movement, which by definition has no interest in challenging the capitalist power structure but rather seeks to embolden it, cannot be populist, especially since right-wing 'populism' is guided by members of the elite.

While remaining committed to the capitalist model, reactionary movements can, however, bring about political and social changes through efforts to destroy solidarities across groups and identities, inflame chauvinism and ultra-nationalism, and dismantle democratic institutions, but this is not populism. This is something else—it is fascism. Historically, ruling classes have typically held a favorable view of fascism, particularly when confronted with labor, communist, and left-wing populist movements. In distinguishing between phony right-wing 'populism' and the legitimate populism of the left, it is helpful to examine recent examples of how ruling class institutions perceive and approach divergent 'populist' movements.

Even a cursory glance at the differences between two exemplars of right and left 'populism', the Tea Party movement and the Occupy movement, is enough to dispel the myth of 'right-wing populism'. The Tea Party was arguably ignited by inflammatory comments made by CNBC commentator Rick Santelli on the floor of the Chicago Mercantile Exchange in February 2009. Santelli's tirade and call for a Tea Party insurrection was in response to the Obama administration's Homeowners Affordability and Stability Plan. By 2010, the Republican Party had a Tea Party Caucus, and the movement was receiving substantial funding from the Koch brothers through their foundation Americans for Prosperity. Reactionary mainstream politicians including Sarah Palin, Michelle Bachman, Ron and

Rand Paul, and Ted Cruz, among numerous others, all were either directly involved in the Tea Party movement or at the very least gave it their enthusiastic support. Controversies surrounding the Tea Party movement include its threats of violence directed toward public figures and politicians, vandalism, and other forms of thuggery and intimidation. Yet, one finds the movement was not targeted, monitored, or disrupted by law enforcement, which is quite unlike the treatment exacted by institutions of the ruling class against the Occupy movement.

The Occupy movement began as a call for mass protest in 2011 by the Canadian publication *Adbusters* (Gandesha 2018:49). In response to corporate influence in politics, instability brought by neoliberalism, and surging wealth inequality, *Adbusters* proposed an occupation of Wall Street, which materialized in September 2011. Occupy Wall Street, despite criticisms of disorganization (some of which are legitimate), was able to operate its own library, media, and encampments, as well as coordinate decisions through a democratic assembly.

Unlike the Tea Party movement, Occupy did not have a specific program or agenda beyond protesting corporate greed and wealth inequality, and it did not have the support of mainstream elites, although influential authors, musicians, and academics made appearances at some of Occupy's demonstrations. Occupy became a nationwide movement, with cities across the country developing their own versions of what was being done by protestors in New York City. The movement's decline was due in part to its lack of progressive strategy, leadership, and coherent plans or projects for continuation. Another factor that distinguishes the actually populist Occupy movement from the pseudo-populist Tea Party movement is the law enforcement response to Occupy.

Heavily redacted FBI documents show that the Occupy movement was under surveillance as early as a month prior to the beginning of the protests. According to the Partnership for Civil Justice Fund, the FBI met with the New York Stock Exchange in August 2011 to discuss the upcoming protests, and the FBI notified businesses in the area that they could be targeted by the movement (PCJF n.d.). The documents also revealed collaboration between the FBI, Department of Homeland Security, and corporations in response to the Occupy movement, a particularly clear display of the state's role in protecting big business and the interests of the ruling class.

Labor's role in the Occupy movement is also noted in the documents, as the Naval Criminal Investigative Services (NCIS) reported on port actions by Occupy in coordination with organized labor to the Domestic Security Alliance Council (DSAC). FBI and law enforcement agencies around the United States, including those based in Virginia, Florida, Indiana, Wisconsin, Mississippi, Tennessee, and Colorado, harmonized their surveillance programs to blunt the Occupy movement, which they viewed as criminal and potentially a source of domestic terrorism.

The law enforcement approach directed at Occupy contrasts starkly from its perception and handling of the Tea Party movement. The reason for this contrast is simple: Occupy, whatever its shortcomings, sought to challenge the power structure. The Tea Party movement did not. The contrast in how the ruling class and its guardians in law enforcement respond to right-wing versus left-wing movements was made even more explicit during the inauguration and then departure of Donald Trump.

During Trump's inauguration in 2017, there was an enormous police presence in Washington, DC, with more than three thousand officers from various agencies joined by five thousand members of the National Guard, some surrounding the area in armored vehicles (Beckett 2022). The police and National Guard were prepared to suppress any protests or civil disobedience that might erupt in response to the inauguration of Trump, considered odious then and now by a significant percentage of U.S. citizens (after all, he lost the popular vote in 2016 by three million). Nothing of the sort happened which might have justified such an excessive police and military presence.

Compare this with the law enforcement response to the events which unfolded on January 6, 2021, when a mob of fanatical Trump supporters, urged by their leader, smashed their way into the Capitol building armed with guns and zip ties, with which they could capture and detain members of Congress. The mob even erected gallows outside the Capitol—whether they would have really used it if given the opportunity is anyone's unfortunate guess. The Capitol Police "After-Action Report" for the "January 6, 2021 Event", dated June 4, 2021, includes a section on intelligence which states the law enforcement assessment of the planned demonstration on January 6 "did not express the severity of the threat or the fact that USCP actually had knowledge of a plan in place. The statement that protesters may be armed was included, but it was never expressed with the urgency that they planned to overtake the Capitol and target Members of Congress" (USCP 2021:19).

According to a March 7, 2022 assessment from the U.S. Government Accountability Office, many Capitol Police officers "felt discouraged or hesitant to use force because of a fear of disciplinary actions" (GAO 2022:47). Regardless of whether the cause of the inadequate law enforcement response on January 6, 2021 was confusion, lack of preparation, or malfeasance, or a mixture of all of these potential factors, it is clear from the police and military presence at Trump's 2017 inauguration that vigorous and coordinated law enforcement operations can be developed and deployed when the powers that be feel it is necessary. For whatever reason, such actions were not deemed necessary when an armed right-wing mob attacked the Capitol, ransacked Congressional offices, and came within a few feet of Vice President Mike Pence, who the mob clearly intended to apprehend and, as suggested by the gallows and the chants of 'hang Mike Pence', execute.

In consideration of the elements and incidents described above, there is little reason to regard the trends of mob violence, incoherent restlessness, and elite-sponsored mobilization on the right 'populist'. There is, however, every reason to view these trends as signs of an emergent fascism that extends well beyond the United States, as witnessed in the UK (Brexit), Hungary under Viktor Orbán, Poland under Andrej Duda, Turkey under Recep Tayyip Erdogan, India under Narendra Modi, the Philippines under Rodrigo Duterte and now under Bongbong Marcos, Brazil under Jair Bolsonaro, and in various political parties in France (Rassemblement National), Germany (Alternative für Deutschland), Italy (Fratelli d'Italia), and elsewhere. While there are some political differences in right-wing parties abroad, the common feature is that they exploit the insecurity, instability, and diminished living standards experienced by workers and the middle class caused by neoliberalism, and direct the legitimate frustration of the masses away from capitalism and toward sinister 'others'—immigrants, refugees, academics, LGBTQIA+ citizens, minorities, unions, secularists, and so on.

The reason these political movements cannot be described as populist is that such 'populism' is itself a contradiction (Bonanno 2021:20). The political and economic 'insiders' behind these movements fraudulently declare themselves 'outsiders'; the right-wing leaders claim to care deeply about the working class but promote further tax cuts and 'incentives' for the wealthy and the stigmatization of labor unions; they condemn neoliberalism and globalization, but call for more deregulation; they denounce 'elites' while advocating for the elimination of welfare programs and public assistance. Thus, the right-wing 'populist' movements, supposedly new currents in international political scenes, are actually more of the same from conservative and reactionary forces which find success in the exploitation and misdirection of popular anxiety and discontent. This has been the right's game for quite some time.

In the United States, the fairly obvious reason that 'Trumpism' cannot be the 'populist' insurgency within the Republican Party that mainstream media commentators are wont to paint it as is that the Trumpite agenda bears practically no difference to that which the GOP has advanced at least since the Reagan years. Arguably, Trump's bombastic churlishness and buffoonery distinguish him from other Republican leaders who at least try to appear as though they accept the political rules of engagement, but what has Trump said or done that separates him from the rest of the party? He cut taxes for the rich and giant corporations, demonized immigrants, embraced the military-industrial complex, dismantled efforts to combat climate change, and exhibited the all-too-common misogyny and chauvinism one should come to expect from the right. Trump's boorishness does nothing to distinguish him from the rest of the GOP, and the Republican Party has not become 'the party of Trump'—it has harbored the same beliefs and goals since long before his presidency. As this is the case, it is time to see the GOP for what it is, with or without Trump: a proto-fascist party. There is nothing 'populist' about it.

The second component to the right's strategy is the advocacy of ethno-nationalism, which combats internationalist solidarity with chauvinism, racial/ethnic fearmongering, and the weaponization of national identity.

Ethno-Nationalism: Identity Politics of the Right

A charismatic 'strongman' leader is not enough for the masses to consent to right-wing programs. There must be a level of insecurity, uncertainty, and perceived degradation of the 'national character' in order for the right to appeal to the populace. The right has long used identity politics as a means of obtaining support, and this practice is not unique to the United States or other 'Western' nations. In Modi's India, for example, Muslims, secularists, and civil rights leaders, among others, are decried as enemies of the Indian nation and its traditions and targeted by Hindutva ethno-nationalists (Kumbamu 2021:171–172).

Right-wing identity politics has enjoyed a long, sordid history in the United States. When Richard Nixon adopted the 'Southern Strategy' in his pursuit of the presidency, he was fully aware that he was capitalizing on the prejudice and racial anxiety of lower- and middle-class white Americans who were hostile towards integration and the Civil Rights movement (Spector 2021:76). The right in the U.S. long ago adopted racial/ethnic fearmongering and xenophobia as part of its political program, and continues to make use of racism and ethno-nationalism in the present.

Reagan's racist attacks on 'welfare queens' and George H.W. Bush's infamous 'Willy Horton' campaign ad are further examples of how racism and right-wing identity politics are used to garner votes. Bigotry directed towards Muslims and Arabs, including widespread stereotyping and violent attacks on American Muslims and Arabs, was accelerated by unfounded stories of how Muslim and Arab Americans 'cheered' after the September 11, 2001 attacks. While the popularized anti-Muslim and anti-Arab prejudices following 9/11 are part of the legacy of the George W. Bush administration, Trump breathed new life into such sentiments when he revived the debunked 'cheering Muslims' story in 2015 during his presidential campaign (Phelps 2015). Trump's 'Build the Wall' slogan and his racist fearmongering directed at the peoples of Mexico and Central America made ethno-nationalism a centerpiece of his 2016 presidential campaign, and much of it carried over into his 2020 campaign as well.

Hungarian Prime Minister Viktor Orbán has received praise from the U.S. right for his ethno-nationalism and proposals for 'illiberal democracy'. Speaking at the August 2022 Conservative Political Action Conference (CPAC) in Dallas, Orbán announced, "the globalists can all go to hell, I have come to Texas!" During his speech, Orbán touted his tough stances on immigration and 'gender ideology', as well as his contempt for liberals and 'leftist media' (Smith 2022). Orbán warned the audience at CPAC that 'western civilization' is under attack by progressives and leftists, who seek to dilute the ethnic purity of 'Christian' nations and destroy the traditional family. The 'clash of civilizations' narrative is a common ingredient in ethno-nationalist doctrine, and like other conspiracy theories, it reinforces the anxiety and sense of victimhood which arise in times of crisis.

The Hungarian prime minister's recent CPAC speech was certainly not unique, nor was it unprecedented. Opposition to immigration, references to 'globalists', and fearmongering about the collapse of Christian values have long been hallmarks of his political persona. In a February 2018 speech delivered at the annual general meeting of the Association of Cities with County Rights in Veszprém, Orbán declared, "We must state that we do not want to be diverse and do not want to be mixed: we do not want our own colour, traditions and national culture to be mixed with those of others" (Orbán 2018).

Orbán has put his political philosophy of 'illiberal democracy' into practice by seizing control of the judiciary, eroding checks and balances, and maintaining power through election fraud (Marcetic 2022). Orbán and his far-right Fidesz party have also facilitated a massive transfer of wealth to the rich at the expense of Hungary's working class. According to a 2018 report by Germany's Friedrich Ebert Foundation (Friedrich-Ebert-Stiftung), Orbán's restructuring of the Hungarian welfare system has resulted in "a profound shift in the direction of redistribution towards the better-off" (Szikra 2018:3).

One may find it surprising, therefore, that much of the support for Orbán's government is based in the working class and materially deprived underclass. A July 2020 report by the Budapest-based 21 Research Center is enlightening on this matter. According to the report, titled "The Fidesz Party's Secret to Success: Investigating Economic Voting in Hungary," Orbán has been able to win the support of Hungarians belonging to the 'underclass' through scapegoating immigrants, the homeless, George Soros, and, paradoxically, the poor (Róna et al. 2020:35).

This is the open secret of ethno-nationalism: by nurturing a sense of national identity in the masses which undermines class consciousness, right-wing leaders like Orbán and Trump (and their political parties) are able to pursue agendas which offer tremendous gifts to the ruling class while appearing as 'populists' and agents of the common citizen. Thus, ethno-nationalism, like pseudo-populism, is a useful tool for reactionary zealots, as it allows them to direct popular discontent away from the ruling class and the power structure. Ethno-nationalism serves the purpose of undermining internationalist class consciousness and solidarity, keeping the global working class in a perpetual state of alienation and disoriented competition.

Authoritarianism/Fascism

Reactionary pseudo-populism is based in real socioeconomic anxiety, but it offers no way forward for its proponents to fundamentally change anything about the current mechanics of the power structure. In fact, it only stimulates greater support for the conditions which produced the socioeconomic anxiety and instability in the first place. This is not accidental. Despite the fact that some workers might get swept up in the nationalist euphoria effused by reactionary pseudo-populism and come to believe in its authoritarian solutions, the class character of right-wing authoritarianism prevents workers *as a class* from identifying with the reactionary movement (Paxton 2005:103). Indeed, historically the working class (and its representative organizations—socialist/communist parties, labor unions, etc.) has been the predominant target of right-wing authoritarian movements, as well as the primary source of opposition to the forces of reaction. Right-wing authoritarianism's promise of restoring 'law and order' is specifically directed at the petit bourgeoisie (the self-employed middle class), a class confronted with loss of prestige and diminished status—a class which fears its eventual transition into the proletariat.

Authoritarianism is not a potential undesirable consequence of reactionary and/or right-wing belief systems: it is the objective of such belief systems. In order to better understand the 'logic' of authoritarianism and its appeal to particular segments of the population, we must briefly examine two of history's most consequential reactionary, authoritarian regimes: Fascist Italy and Nazi Germany.

While there has been much important scholarly debate on the problem of what is and is not fascism, in this chapter I use the terms 'authoritarianism' and 'fascism' more or less interchangeably. My interchangeable use of the terms should not imply any carelessness regarding minor or substantial differences between reactionary movements or regimes that have emerged in various places and at various times. In efforts to determine the exact nature of fascism, it was posited by fascists themselves that there is not one 'fascism' but numerous 'fascisms' (Bosworth 2006:171). Regardless of the differences between 'fascisms' of one kind or another, they share, among other things, a commitment to authoritarianism, and so I find it, if not useful, at least not harmful, to call right-wing authoritarianism fascism and *vice versa*. I agree with Palmiro Togliatti, who warned that one must not assume that fascism adopts the same forms anywhere or anytime it appears (Togliatti 1976 [1935]:2). Still, while I argue that one must be careful about the application of the term 'fascist', authoritarian right-wing movements offer little reason for one to distinguish their professed ideals from fascism as an ideology.

Authoritarianism (or fascism) serves a specific purpose in the capitalist framework: it arrives in times of crises and instability to protect the power structure from systemic disintegration and/or revolutionary upheaval (Berberoglu 2021b:278–279). In his 1935 lectures at the Lenin School in Moscow, Togliatti remarked that the most complete definition of fascism is "the open terrorist dictatorship of the most reactionary, most chauvinistic, most imperialist elements of finance capital" (Togliatti 1976 [1935]:1). This definition, first delivered at the 13th meeting of the Enlarged Executive of the Communist International, might be simplistic, and it certainly is not the only definition given to fascism (by the Communists or anyone else). However, the direct connection to capitalism identified in the definition is crucial, for it is impossible to understand fascism without understanding its relationship with the capitalist power structure.

In his lecture, Togliatti identifies what he viewed as a major shortcoming in earlier left-wing attempts to discern the causes and purposes of fascism: the lack of an effort to connect "the dictatorship of the bourgeoisie and the movement of the petty-bourgeois masses" (Togliatti 1976 [1935]:2). There had been disagreement on the left regarding what kind of movement fascism was, with some comrades suggesting it merely signaled a petty-bourgeois revolt against the bourgeoisie. Such descriptions ignored two explicit features of the fascist program: (1) the fascists' collaboration with the 'big' bourgeoisie, and (2) the fascists' animosity toward the working class and working-class organizations (labor unions, communist/socialist parties, etc.).

Another definition of fascism, perhaps more enlightening than Togliatti's, is provided by Daniel Guerin in *Fascism and Big Business*: "a strong state intended to artificially prolong an economic system based on profit and the private ownership of the means of production" (Guerin 1973:381). Fascist movements are financed by the capitalist class to both crush the working class/working-class institutions and to protect the capitalist power structure from systemic disturbances. The fascist state functions first and foremost as a servant of capitalists—it crushes unions, paralyzes proletarian resistance, slashes wages, squelches class struggle, and delivers total control of production to capitalists (Guerin 1973:239). Under fascism, capitalists are given more representation in the state, and through their positions on government labor and economic committees, collaborate with the fascists to systemically stifle working-class organizations and disrupt proletarian solidarity.

Fascism's anti-worker (and anticommunist) and pro-capitalist character made it appealing to the ruling classes of both Italy and Germany even prior to the establishment of fascist states in these nations. Before Mussolini seized power in Italy, paramilitary squadrons of Fascists routinely terrorized workers and peasants, and violently disrupted the success of the left. In November 1920, *squadristi* (Blackshirts, the paramilitary wing of the

National Fascist Party) protested the victory of the Socialists in the local elections in Bologna by attacking leftists in the streets, tearing down red flags, and eventually occupying town hall to prevent the installation of a new Socialist mayor (Bosworth 2006:134).

The Fascists formed alliances with landlords and factory owners who feared working-class radicalism, left-wing labor unions, and the influence of the socialists and communists. The Blackshirts were employed by the capitalists and landowners as strike breakers and disciplinarians for workers and peasants. Throughout 1920–21, the Fascists subdued communist-led strikes, raided union offices, and attacked, and sometimes murdered, left-wing activists, labor organizers, workers, and peasants, all with the backing of the capitalist class. The violent repression of the left and labor accelerated after Mussolini took power following the March on Rome in 1922. By 1925, independent labor unions were dissolved under the Fascist government, and in 1926, strikes were explicitly prohibited under the 'Rocco law' (Bosworth 2006:226).

In Germany, the Nazis enjoyed the active support or passive consent of both the petit bourgeoisie and ruling class elites. They went a step further than the Italian Fascists in their attacks on left-wing parties and the labor movement. The Nazis not only violently attacked workers and destroyed working-class institutions, but also sought to prevent working-class solidarity through eliminating the 'social' aspect of labor. The Nazi State Executive, in collaboration with the capitalists, implemented systemic efforts to undermine worker solidarity and class consciousness, fragmenting the working class and imposing rivalry as an institutional feature of the workplace (Mason 1995:250).

The Nazi-capitalist scheme had a devastating impact on the German working class, both in terms of union and political representation and working-class solidarity. Under the Nazi regime, workers were politically and socially isolated. Repression and terror at the hands of the *Sturmabteilung* (SA, the Nazi Party's paramilitary wing), including the ransacking of union offices and the torturing and killing of leftists and labor officials, cleared a path for the *Arbeitsordnungsgesetz* (AOG, Law on the Organization of National Labor) to institute a program intended to atomize the working class and give employers complete control over production (Mason 1995:250).

Analyses of fascism which include descriptions of the movement as anti-bourgeois or somehow dangerous to capitalists (analyses which, more often than not, it seems, derive from bad faith attempts to equate fascism and communism) ignore the intrinsic connection between fascist movements and the ruling classes of the respective nations in which fascism emerges. Far from being a movement which threatens the capitalist socioeconomic establishment, fascism offers the power structure protection from working-class radicalism and the left. Establishment conservatives in government, ruling class elites, and the anxious petty bourgeoisie (the self-employed, small-time merchants, etc.) all discovered in fascism a guardian from the class-conscious proletariat and impending working-class revolution (or, in the case of the petty bourgeoisie, from proletarianization).

Fascism forged its coalitions with conservative government officials, capitalists, and reactionary elements in the masses primarily through (1) allowing the political right to obtain parliamentary majorities without making concessions to the political left, and (2) fascism's ability to pull sections of the working class away from Marxism (Paxton 2005:103). Fascism's hostility toward the left and its promotion of nationalism as an antidote for working-class Marxism (which had limited success in practice) gained fascists the support of parliamentary conservatives as well as the capitalist ruling class. These characteristics of fascism which appeal to conservatives, capitalists, and the petty bourgeoisie make all the more sense when one considers the fact that fascism emerges in times of economic crisis—especially when the left and working-class radicalism gain momentum and demands for alternative socioeconomic arrangements (e.g., socialism and communism) become more popular.

Two particular conditions, it seems, must be met in order for fascism to emerge. The first, as Gramsci points out in his 1924 article "Democracy and Fascism", is that the working class must be in a state of disorganization and passivity (Gramsci 2019 [1924]:121). The second is instability and institutional rot in the metropole (the 'homeland', specifically of a colonial empire). When the working class is passive and unorganized, reactionary movements have an open space to conduct their political schemes without challenges from communist or socialist parties, militant unions, or other leftist organizations. Fascism works to prevent the toiling masses from forming organic class-conscious organizations—workers' meetings are broken up; labor halls are smashed; organizing campaigns for class-conscious political parties are violently disrupted (Harman 2017:444–445). Fascism is characterized by an appetite for violence, rebellion against 'liberal' ideals, and above all its fanatical opposition to socialism (Bosworth 2006:152).

Socialists and communists, and the workers and peasants who organized unions connected to left-wing ideals, were viewed as the supreme enemies of the fatherland by the nationalist, anti-Marxist fascists. The savagery inflicted upon workers, working-class political parties, and class-conscious labor unions offers some insight into the reactionary bloodlust that fueled fascism's march of death in both Fascist Italy and Nazi Germany. For the Italian Fascists, particularly those who participated in the 'squadrismo' movement (*squadre d'azione*—'action squads'), violence was perceived as pleasurable and positive, a display of power and masculinity. Terror, violence, and murder were not viewed by the Fascists as unfortunate or ugly, but were encouraged by the Fascist leadership and were an integral part of the Fascist movement's war against the left and the labor movement. The 'action squads' not only broke strikes, raided and burned worker and peasant homes, and attacked leftists and labor leaders in the streets—they also took great pleasure in torturing opponents they captured, forcing them to, among other things, drink castor oil (Bosworth 2006:568–569).

In times of turmoil and crises, which in capitalism are systemic, authoritarianism and hysterical distractions from the root causes of socioeconomic instability offer the ruling class protection from working-class insurgency. This protection is what the Nazis offered the German ruling class and Mussolini's Italian Fascists offered the Italian ruling class in the period of uneasiness and uncertainty following WWI.

Germany and Italy, prior to their respective transformations into imperial fascist states, were colonial empires, and there are noticeable similarities between their colonial activities, especially in Africa, and the policies they instituted under Nazism and Italian Fascism. During the Second Reich, Germany carried out a genocide of the Herero and Nama peoples in Namibia, at the time part of German Southwest Africa, systematically murdering an estimated 80% of the Herero people and 50% of the Nama between 1904 and 1907 according to World Without Genocide (WWG 2021). The atrocities committed against the Herero and Nama included concentration camps, forced labor, forced starvation and dehydration, sexual violence, and barbaric medical experimentation. Josef Mengele, the notorious practitioner of human experiments at Auschwitz, was a protégé of Nazi geneticist Otmar Freiherr von Verschuer, who himself was a protégé of Eugen Fischer, the anthropologist and eugenicist whose field research and experiments in German Southwest Africa inspired the 'Aryan race' theory of the Third Reich (Kater 2011:515).

However, Nazi Germany's imperialist *lebensraum* ('living space') program owed much more to Fascist Italy's colonial operations than it did to the Kaiser's. SS chief Heinrich Himmler viewed the Second Reich's colonial model as outdated, and numerous Nazi officials, including Hitler, were deeply impressed by the Italian Fascists' expansionist efforts in Africa, and Libya in particular (Bernhard 2016:63). The Fascists' scheme to 'ethnically remake' Africa through the settling of millions of colonists in the territories they controlled inspired the Nazi plans for Eastern Europe.

The colonial aspirations for Nazi Germany and Fascist Italy reflected their leaders' desires to rebuild what they felt their nations had lost following WWI. Germany and Italy were both terribly embarrassed and deflated after the war, and this was crucial to the development of fascism in each country. Italy got practically nothing out of the war other than a high rate of casualties, and the Treaty of Versailles required Germany to disarm, pay reparations, and make significant territorial concessions. Germany also underwent a transformation in 1918–19, with the fall of the Second Reich and the establishment of the Weimar Republic. The instability, uncertainty, and embarrassment felt in Italy and Germany following WWI opened the door for a movement which promised to restore the fatherlands to their former greatness: fascism.

The Italian Fascists, led by Benito Mussolini, made a deal with the ruling class of Italy, which was quite nervous due to the rise of militant unions in the north and groups of radical agricultural workers in the south. In short, the deal was that, in return for political legitimacy, the Fascists would help the capitalist ruling class retain its position by crushing working-class organizations and increasing proletarian immiseration through breaking strikes, suppressing left-wing labor movements, and terrorizing communists (Tasca 2019 [1927]:313). Hitler and his Nazis made a similar appeal to the ruling class of Germany. Thus, the Italian Fascists and the Nazis gained support from their countries' ruling classes and vast segments of the petit bourgeoisie and middle classes by promising to 'restore order' through violence and authoritarianism.

Once in power, Mussolini's Fascists and Hitler's Nazis introduced programs of brutality and authoritarianism reminiscent of what Italy and the Second Reich had imposed upon their former colonial possessions. This is of the utmost importance, for if there is one brief definition of fascism, it is arguably the implementation of colonialist barbarism within the metropole. Fascism is the violent manifestations of the capitalist power structure revealing themselves.

In times of crisis, the violence which maintains the capitalist system becomes more visible and recognizable to the citizens of weary empires. One must remember, however, that this violence has long been a part of everyday life for the people living in nations exploited by the imperialist powers for cheap labor, resources, and profit. Recall, for example, the murderous right-wing dictatorships which were thrust into power with backing from the United States and other imperialist powers of the West in Latin America, Africa, and Asia, and it becomes clear that in fascism there is an element of 'chickens coming home to roost'. When it happens abroad, in a sweatshop, in a massacre carried out by a death squad, in the gang rapes of civilian women by soldiers, in mass extermination campaigns, it's business as usual for capital. When it begins to erupt in the capitalist nations themselves, it's fascism.

Authoritarianism and violence in the metropole are the refuge of the ruling class experiencing the early throes of upheaval. This explains to a large extent why the United States and other nations are witnessing a resurgence in opportunistic and fanatical reactionary movements promoting similar agendas to those of the Italian Fascists and Nazis. Neoliberal globalization has disturbed bourgeois democracy internationally, and in the midst of crises and instability, the ruling classes of nominally democratic, capitalist countries are turning toward a refurbished strain of fascism to maintain the neoliberal order (Berberoglu 2021b:277). Clearly, we are not seeing history repeating itself, but surely, it is rhyming. There may not be Blackshirts marching themselves into power, and there may not be violent Nazi putsches taking place on a global scale, but the global surge of reactionary and fascist political parties and 'strongman' leaders does at the very least indicate a concerning trend which requires immediate response from the international left.

At its core, fascism is more than a reactionary sociopolitical movement. Fascists espouse some of the same goals as mere reactionaries, this is true, but they also thirst for more than the 'turning back of the clock' that traditionalist reactionary movements desire. Fascism is a social and political ideology which places power above all else. It draws its energy from the anxious and disoriented throng by promising stability, leadership, a reactionary 'return to greatness', and restoration of order. As Wilhelm Reich notes in *The Mass Psychology of Fascism*, fascism and what Reich calls, 'führer ideology' are stimulated by the "powerlessness and helplessness of the masses of people" (Reich 1970 [1933]:234).

The fascist strongman laments the weakness of the nation and blames internal enemies for the fatherland's problems: communists, Jews, ethnic and racial minorities, shadowy cabals, and so on. So-called culture wars are waged in order to exacerbate tensions in the populace. In order to obtain and hold power, the fascists propose antidemocratic, authoritarian measures, which they claim will return order and 'greatness' to the nation. Thus, fascism is a movement which calls for the restriction of freedom for the masses but unlimited freedom (and power) for the ruling class. This point was articulated beautifully by the Duke, one of the fascist libertines in Pasolini's 1975 film *Salò, or the 120 Days of Sodom*, who says, "We Fascists are the only true anarchists, naturally, once we're masters of the state. In fact, the one true anarchy is that of power".

Today's international right-wing political movements, whether one calls them reactionary, fascist, or gives them the misnomer 'populist', are able to pursue power almost unchecked because of the glaring absence of an internationalist left, which ideally would be comprised of radical, disciplined political parties and militant labor unions/federations operating in conjunction. With no such coordinated effort in existence, the right is gaining momentum through the exploitation of pseudo-populism, the promotion of ethno-nationalism, and advocacy of authoritarianism.

The Need for a New Labor Movement

The rise of the right in its current pseudo-populist, authoritarian form is, among other things, both a flagrant consequence of the absence of a coherent, disciplined, internationalist left, and an alarm sounded for the organization of such a movement. The core of an effective left-wing response to the conspiracy-fueled, ethno-nationalist, and increasingly fascistic right must be militant, class-conscious labor unions and federations, and the reasons are clear: the opposite of pseudo-populism is *real* populism; the opposite of ethno-nationalism is internationalism; and the opposite of the right's authoritarianism can be found in the smoldering rubble of capitalist hegemony, in the seizure of power by the international working class. There is no other movement, in the United States or elsewhere, as closely connected to the masses, and no other movement with more potential to challenge the ruling class and the power structure, than the labor movement (Reed 2001:206).

There is a reason why Dulles and the other CIA operatives were so nervous about leftist labor unions in partnerships with communist parties following WWII. Labor unions are the cells of class-conscious worker organizations, and when labor adopts a sociopolitical perspective that identifies alienation, instability, and degradation as inherent to the capitalist system, unions are in a position to engage in actions which disrupt accumulation and the flow of profits to the masters of industry. Labor unions engage with the working class at the point of exploitation, in the workplace. Class consciousness is developed in conversations between workers, engaged in the same or similar daily activities, experiencing the same frustrations, uncertainties, and anxieties, and the vehicle for putting class consciousness into practice is the union.

The power of organized labor is in its ability to transcend identity barriers, bringing together workers from various backgrounds under the banner of class solidarity. To be sure, organized labor has not and does not always put this strength to use as much as it should, and one can easily recall the prejudices entrenched in the AFL, expressed in its negative attitudes regarding organizing women, racial/ethnic minorities, immigrants, and unskilled workers. However, the Industrial Workers of the World and other progressive industrial unions certainly showed labor's inclusive power in organizing the unorganized regardless of race, ethnicity, gender, skill level, or national origin. The ability of the labor movement to appeal to and unite diverse groups of people, introduce class consciousness and class solidarity, and nurture collective courage, makes it exceptionally dangerous to the right's prejudice- and fear-based agenda.

The AFL-CIO's collaboration with the CIA in toppling left-wing and center-left regimes and dismantling radical labor movements abroad might not be the sole cause of the rise of the right in its current form, but it helped the reactionary cause substantially. The labor federation, and the AFL and CIO before the merger, crushed the progressivism and revolutionary potential of organized labor by participating in purges and red-baiting as well as through deference to lopsided contracts including no-strike clauses and adherence to management prerogative. The U.S. labor movement relinquished its radicalism and its visionary potential for creating a new society in favor of the false safety of class collaborationism and a 'live-and-let-live' (or, more accurately, 'live-and-let-lose') philosophy which has plunged the labor movement into a desperate state in which unions operate like workplace arbitrators rather than class-conscious vehicles of working-class emancipation. There is now more than ever a need for a new labor movement (Geoghegan 2014:185).

Without a strong, militant, class-conscious labor movement, workers are left flounderingly grasping for explanations for the conditions which have brought alienation, instability, and insecurity to their lives. The right is readily prepared to sell the working class its pseudo-populism, conspiracy theories, chauvinism, and authoritarianism. The best way to challenge this sale is through a new, militant, internationalist labor movement capable of challenging the rise of the right with class solidarity and a program based in political activism.

Such a program might be summed up by the old labor slogan 'An Injury to One is An Injury to All'. There is no room for prejudice or petty personal squabbles when operating in the spirit of this slogan. While slogans, quips, truisms, and the like have served the working class and the left minimally, it is worth examining and appreciating this particular slogan for its strength and its brief articulation of what solidarity means. 'An Injury to One is An Injury to All' does not mean picking and choosing when to feel maligned by the mistreatment of another person; rather, it means regardless of one's personal feelings, any affront to one of us is an attack on our unity and shared objectives.

Labor solidarity is built on the shop-floor, in the warehouse or factory, on the dock, in the teachers' lounge, shared cafeteria, breakroom, or at the pub after a long day of toil. It is established by the shared experiences workers confront every day on the job, and bolstered by the recognition of common interests and antagonisms. As Marx describes in Vol. I of *Capital*, capitalist production establishes socialized labor, creates the proletariat and, as workers are "disciplined, united, organized" by their shared conditions, it begets the revolt of the working class (Marx 1992 [1887]:714–715). The fear one feels as an individual melts away with the collective courage of the union, the essence of which is solidarity—the knowledge that an injury to one is an injury to all.

The point here, despite any temptation, is not to imagine what could have been done differently by the AFL, CIO, and AFL-CIO, and how the world might have turned out another way as a result. The task of building a new labor movement, in the United States and elsewhere, means taking seriously the material conditions faced by the working class *today*, analyzing the transformations and crises within the mode of production and determining what can be done to build a movement that has the lasting power to become a central force for change.

Unions are still, despite their contradictions and limitations, and the systemic barriers to their formation and functionality, the most organic, meaningful, and capable form of working-class organization. Labor unions are the collaborative bodies which workers use to confront the daily struggles in their lives, the hardships and challenges they encounter within the material conditions surrounding them. Labor unions are also the basis for working-class participation in the political arena, as they provide the foundation for programs which promote the workers' common interests and can be articulated and fought for by a labor party. When workers have no representation in government, as is the case in the United States, the temptation to seek recognition and answers elsewhere lures them into the realm of pseudo-populism, chauvinism, and authoritarianism.

The antidote for the ugliness of the right's 'neoliberalism with a reactionary face' is a revived internationalist labor movement and the development of labor parties for pursuing the goals of the working class in political battlefields. For the working class in the United States, this means tenacious, class-conscious organizing within and beyond the AFL-CIO, an end to the unconditional labor support offered to the Democrats, and the creation of a Labor Party.

References

Beckett, Ben. 2022. Don't Trust the National Security State to Stop the next Republican Coup Attempt. *Jacobin.com*. https://jacobin.com/2022/08/gop-capitol-riot-police-trump-fbi.

Berberoglu, Berch. 2021a. Crisis of Neoliberal Globalization and the Rise of Authoritarianism in the Early 21st Century. In *The Global Rise of Authoritarianism in the 21st Century: Crisis of Neoliberal Globalization and the Nationalist Response*, ed. Berch Berberoglu. New York, NY: Routledge.

———. 2021b. Neoliberal Capitalist Authoritarianism, Resistance, and Revolution on a Global Scale. In *The Global Rise of Authoritarianism in the 21st Century: Crisis of Neoliberal Globalization and the Nationalist Response*, ed. Berch Berberoglu. New York, NY: Routledge.

Bernhard, Patrick. 2016. Hitler's Africa in the East: Italian Colonialism as a Model for German Planning in Eastern Europe. *Journal of Contemporary History* 51 (1): 61–90.

Bevins, Vincent. 2021. *The Jakarta Method: Washington's Anticommunist Crusade and the Mass Murder Program That Shaped Our World*. New York, NY: PublicAffairs.

Bonanno, Alessandro. 2021. The Crisis of Neoliberalism, Populist Reaction, and the Rise of Authoritarian Capitalism. In *The Global Rise of Authoritarianism in the 21st Century: Crisis of Neoliberal Globalization and the Nationalist Response*, ed. Berch Berberoglu. New York, NY: Routledge.

Bosworth, Richard J.B. 2006. *Mussolini's Italy: Life Under the Dictatorship, 1915-1945*. Harlow, England: Penguin Books.

Davis, Mike. 2007. *In Praise of Barbarians: Essays Against Empire*. Chicago, IL: Haymarket Books.

———. 2018. *Prisoners of the American Dream: Politics and Economy in the History of the U.S. Working Class*. London, England: Verso Books.

Dubofsky, Melvin. 1969. *We Shall Be All: A History of the IWW*. New York, NY: Quadrangle Press.

Gandesha, Samir. 2018. Understanding Right and Left Populism. In *Critical Theory and Authoritarian Populism*, 49–70. London, England: University of Westminster Press.

Geoghegan, Thomas. 2014. *Only One Thing Can Save Us: Why America Needs a New Kind of Labor Movement*. New York, NY: The New Press.

Gramsci, Antonio. 2019. Democracy and Fascism. In *Marxists in the Face of Fascism: Writings by Marxists on Fascism from the Inter-War Period*, ed. David Beetham. Chicago, IL: Haymarket Books.

Guerin, Daniel. 1973. *Fascism and Big Business*. New York, NY: Pathfinder Books.

Harman, Chris. 2017. *A People's History of the World: From the Stone Age to the New Millennium*. London, England: Verso Books.

Kater, Michael H. 2011. *The Nazi Symbiosis: Human Genetics and Politics in the Third Reich* (Review). *Bulletin of the History of Medicine* 85 (3): 515–516. https://doi.org/10.1353/bhm.2011.0067.

Kumbamu, Ashok. 2021. Saffron Fascism: The Conflux of Hindutva Ultra-Nationalism, Neoliberal Extractivism, and the Rise of Authoritarian Populism in Modi's India. In *The Global Rise of Authoritarianism in the 21st Century: Crisis of Neoliberal Globalization and the Nationalist Response*, ed. Berch Berberoglu. New York, NY: Routledge.

Marcetic, Branko. 2022. The Right Is Still the Enemy of Freedom. *Jacobin.com*. https://jacobin.com/2022/03/republican-party-right-authoritarian-freedom-censorship-protest-bds-civil-rights.

Marx, Karl. 1992. *Capital: Volume I: The Process of Capitalist Production*. New York, NY: International Publishers.

Mason, Timothy W. 1995. *Nazism, Fascism and the Working Class*. Cambridge, England: Cambridge University Press.

Montgomery, David. 1987. *The Fall of the House of Labor: The Workplace, the State, and American Labor Activism, 1865-1925*. Cambridge, England: Cambridge University Press.

Orbán, Viktor. 2018. Prime Minister Viktor Orbán's speech at the annual general meeting of the Association of Cities with County Rights – miniszterelnok.hu. *Miniszterelnok.hu.* https://www.miniszterelnok.hu/prime-minister-viktor-orbans-speech-at-the-annual-general-meeting-of-the-association-of-cities-with-county-rights/.

Partnership for Civil Justice Fund. n.d. FBI Documents Reveal Secret Nationwide Occupy Monitoring. *Partnership for Civil Justice Fund.* https://www.justiceonline.org/fbi_files_ows.

Paxton, Robert O. 2005. *The Anatomy of Fascism.* New York, NY: Random House.

Phelps, Jordyn. 2015. Donald Trump Again Says He Saw Cheering in New Jersey on 9/11. *ABC News.* https://abcnews.go.com/Politics/donald-trump-cheering-jersey-911/story?id=35355447.

Reed, Adolph, Jr. 2001. *Class Notes: Posing as Politics and Other Thoughts on the American Scene.* New York, NY: The New Press.

———. 2021. The Whole Country Is the Reichstag. *Nonsite.org.* https://nonsite.org/the-whole-country-is-the-reichstag/.

Reich, Wilhelm. 1970. *The Mass Psychology of Fascism.* 3rd ed. New York, NY: Simon & Schuster.

Róna, Dániel, Eszter Galgóczy, Judit Pétervári, Blanka Szeitl, and Márton Túry. 2020. *The Fidesz Party's Secret to Success: Investigating Economic Voting in Hungary.* Budapest, Hungary: 21 Research Center.

Smith, David. 2022. Viktor Orbán Turns Texas Conference into Transatlantic Far-Right Love-In. *The Guardian*, August 6.

Spector, Alan. 2021. Neoliberalism, Authoritarianism, and Resistance in the United States in the Age of Trump. In *The Global Rise of Authoritarianism in the 21st Century: Crisis of Neoliberal Globalization and the Nationalist Response*, ed. Berch Berberoglu. New York, NY: Routledge.

Szikra, Dorottya. 2018. Welfare for the Wealthy. *Fes.de.* https://library.fes.de/pdf-files/bueros/budapest/14209.pdf.

Tasca, Angelo. 2019. The Proletariat, Fascism and the Italian Economy. In *Marxists in the Face of Fascism: Writings by Marxists on Fascism from the Inter-War Period*, ed. David Beetham. Chicago, IL: Haymarket Books.

Togliatti, Palmiro. 1976. *Lectures on Fascism.* New York, NY: International Publishers.

U.S. Capitol Police. 2021. *January 6, 2021 Event After-Action Report.* Washington, D.C.: United States Capitol Police.

U.S. Government Accountability Office. 2022. *Capitol Attack: Additional Actions Needed to Better Prepare Capitol Police Officers for Violent Demonstrations.* Washington, D.C.: Government Accountability Office.

World Without Genocide. 2021. Genocide of The Herero and Nama, 1904-1907. *World Without Genocide.* http://worldwithoutgenocide.org/wp-content/uploads/2021/05/Namibia-One-Pager-Updated-1.pdf.

Yates, Michael. 2009. *Why Unions Matter.* New York, NY: Monthly Review Press.

CHAPTER 6

Rebuilding the Labor Movement and Prospects for the Future

In February 2020, former AFL-CIO president Richard Trumka commented on a recently released Bureau of Labor Statistics report which found that in 2019 nearly half a million workers in the U.S. had engaged in some sort of militant worker action (strikes, walkouts, work stoppages, etc.). Trumka declared, "These strike statistics represent nothing less than a sea of change in America. Working people—completely fed up with an economic and political system that does not work for us—are turning to each other and using every tool at our disposal to win a better deal" (Gruenberg 2020). There are a few points worth noting here (besides Trumka's apparent enthusiasm for worker activism that never seemed to culminate in calls for federation-wide action—let alone the use of 'every tool at our disposal') that make the reemergence of worker militancy in the U.S. of particular interest: first, that this new militancy is emerging after the Supreme Court sided with anti-union forces in the *Janus v. AFSCME* case, and second, that the workers are embracing tactics used by the industrial unions of the past—most notably the wildcat strike.

The increased militancy observed in post-*Janus* U.S. labor is worth celebrating, but the leaders of the new labor movement must find a way to maintain militancy, discipline, and a strategic program, or else they will get trapped riding 'strike waves' which inevitably crash and roll back. A strike wave is good—a sustained working-class movement is better. To be sure, the fledgling builders of the new labor movement, including the

A. Barrington, *The U.S. Labor Movement in the 20th and Early 21st Century*, Social Movements and Transformation,
https://doi.org/10.1007/978-3-031-30077-6_6

rank-and-file leaders of the Amazon Labor Union, Starbucks Workers United, the many workers and organizers involved in the Emergency Workplace Organizing Committee, and a multitude of unions, are fighting half the battle by operating (for the most part) independently of the AFL-CIO or the large unions unaffiliated with the dominant federation (e.g. Teamsters). There are exceptions, and mainstream unions are engaged in organizing activities as well, and even these campaigns are exciting in a country as anti-union and anti-worker as the United States. The fact remains that the AFL-CIO's 'play by the rules' unionism looks rusted and prehistoric to today's youthful, angry workers and organizers, who hunger for not just a better wage but a direct say in the functions of the workplace, and for more control over their lives. Involvement in organized labor is for these young workers and organizers about challenging the boss, yes, but also about challenging *all of the bosses*—that is, challenging the capitalist system.

Putting Workers Back at the Helm

For too long, the U.S. labor movement has been led by bureaucrats, political elbow-rubbers, and paid union staff. One hears labor leaders and union staff lament that workers are not involved enough in their unions, that they view the union as an external entity, among other complaints. What do they expect? The professionalization and institutionalization of the labor movement, and labor's adoption of the business model, have caused workers to view their unions as workplace arbitrators, on-the-job law firms, or even worse, as intrusive, alien entities that just want to take money out of their checks, rather than as collaborative instruments with which they can fight for their common interests and democratize their workplaces.

It would be incorrect and simplistic to suggest that all AFL-CIO unions and labor leaders in the federation are comfortable bureaucrats. After all, Sara Nelson, the International President of the Association of Flight Attendants-CWA, an AFL-CIO affiliate, declared at a 2019 AFL-CIO dinner that the government shutdown at the time could be brought to an end by a general strike (Loomis 2019). The point is that the top leadership of the federation has been unable, or more likely unwilling, to (1) articulate to workers in a meaningful way the value of unions, and (2) direct the discontent and militancy of the working class toward a program of mass organizing and struggle.

In fact, the AFL-CIO has become so institutionalized that its current president, Liz Shuler, hobnobbed with some of the most powerful union-busters in the United States at the Big Sky Labor and Employment Conference in August 2022 (Rosenblum 2022). Shuler even agreed to *open* the conference, followed by Neil Bradley, Executive Vice President, Chief Policy Officer, and Head of Strategic Advocacy for the U.S. Chamber of Commerce, a solidly right-wing lobbying institution which Shuler should know is a major enemy of organized labor (in 2021, Bradley spoke out against the Protecting the Right to Organize Act, legislation which would expand worker and union rights). Other attendees at the Big Sky conference included senior attorneys from union-busting law firm Littler Mendelson, top executives from major corporations, and right-wing Supreme Court justice Amy Coney Barrett.

There has been very little backlash after Shuler's presence at the Big Sky conference, and perhaps this is because expectations of the AFL-CIO and its top leaders are already dismal. More likely, however, is that many workers and union members are not even aware that she was present at the conference. This is largely the result of decades of timidity, class collaborationism, and worker-blaming for the state of organized labor in the United States. According to a Bureau of Labor Statistics report from January 20, 2022, only 10.3% of U.S. workers are currently represented by unions, and only 6.1% in the private sector compared to 33.9% in the public sector (Bureau of Labor Statistics 2022:1). When Shuler announced from the stage at the 2022 AFL-CIO convention in Philadelphia the formation of the Center for Transformational Organizing and the goal of organizing 1 million new workers over the next decade, she was consciously or unconsciously admitting that the AFL-CIO will oversee not the dramatic growth of organized labor but continued decline (considering Bureau of Labor Statistics estimates, 1 million new union members will account for only 8% of the workforce by 2030) (Nolan 2022). Whether Shuler meant to or not, she was admitting the federation's continued acceptance of single-digit union density.

The AFL-CIO's reluctance to use the full extent of its influence and resources to encourage and nurture bold labor activism appears counter-intuitive at a time when unions are enjoying their highest level of public support since the 1960s. An August 2022 Gallup poll showed that approval of unions among U.S. citizens is at 71%, its highest point since 1965 (McCarthy 2022). With such significant public support, why would the AFL-CIO be unwilling to throw its weight behind a more radical goal than single-digit union density? Based on the federation's history, its tendencies, and its ties with mainstream politics and industry, one can safely conclude that the AFL-CIO is more of a butterfly net for catching workers who seek to fundamentally transform their workplaces than a vehicle for class struggle and worker mobilization.

There are labor leaders and militant workers within the federation who want better things for the working class, and they are commendable for their efforts. However, the truly valuable organizing is being done by rank-and-file workers who are not willing to get stuck in the morass of the bureaucratic, safe, top-down unionism exemplified by the AFL-CIO. Militant workers and leaders who are members of AFL-CIO affiliates can assist in the construction of a new U.S. labor movement, but the heavy lifting will take place outside of the AFL-CIO. There is good reason to believe the (mostly) young workers at the helm of recent organizing efforts are aware of this fact.

In the case of the Amazon Labor Union, the organizing campaign at JFK8 was led by rank-and-file workers who meaningfully communicated with each other, maintained momentum, and when opportunities for acceleration emerged, the organizers were competent enough to take advantage of them. Starbucks Workers United, the membership of which is substantially comprised of 'millennial' and 'Gen Z' workers, has effectively organized while using social media as a type of independent labor press, posting videos of demonstrations, walk-ins on their bosses, and other union actions which have garnered tens of millions of online views (Logan 2022).

The social media component has been a significant element of the Starbucks Workers United campaign, and has been particularly useful in garnering community support and building a support system for the workers outside of the workplace. Even people who do not work at Starbucks but have watched the Starbucks workers' videos or read their online posts and sympathize with the national organizing campaign can (and do) lend their assistance to strikes, 'sip-ins', shutting down stores, and passing information along to their friends and family. The Starbucks workers conduct online trainings and communicate through a variety of mediums, keeping each other abreast of workplace conditions, plans for activities, and availability of resources. The flexibility and the aptness with which the workers and organizers in the Starbucks union drives are able to coordinate actions and sustain enthusiasm are impressive to say the least, and might show the old guard in the AFL-CIO a thing or two about what it takes to effectively organize.

There are a few other polls from Gallup worth considering. First, a November 2019 poll that showed young adults (millennials/Gen Z—ages 18–39 at the time of the poll) in the United States are split down the middle in their views regarding capitalism versus socialism (Saad 2019). Young adults (who make up a bulk of the workers and organizers leading the recent union campaigns at Amazon, Starbucks, Trader Joe's, Chipotle, REI, and other companies) have a more positive view of socialism and a more negative view of capitalism than older generations. A more recent Gallup poll from August 2022 showed that 52% of millennials and 52% of members of Gen Z identify as political independents, and another poll from August 2022 showed that a majority of U.S. citizens supports progressive taxation (higher taxes on the rich, redistribution of wealth, etc.) (Newport 2022).

Of course, one cannot assume based on a few promising polls that the U.S. working class is prepared for socialist revolution. However, that (1) the workers and organizers leading the exciting, largely independent union drives in recent times are members of generations with more positive views of socialism and negative views of capitalism than Gen X or the baby boomers, and (2) a significant majority of the U.S. public supports unions and most U.S. citizens support progressive economic policies (the redistribution of wealth) suggest that the conditions are ripe for a more ambitious left/labor political project.

UE's work with DSA (EWOC) shows a promising path forward for collaborative efforts between independent, progressive labor unions and left-wing political organizations. There is no reason why such efforts cannot bloom into something more permanent, and more active in the political arena. UE's political independence makes such a collaboration possible. While most unions in the United States are sutured to the Democratic Party, UE does not offer its support to the Democrats, Republicans, or any other political party, but rather endorses individual candidates who champion the working class (for example, UE has long supported Bernie Sanders), and unlike most unions, UE does not have a political action fund. UE offers its political support through rank-and-file participation in get-out-the-vote efforts and actions that apply pressure to legislators (Schuhrke 2020). By remaining politically independent, UE continues to be untethered and unbeholden to the interests of the ruling class, which are expressed through the mainstream capitalist parties.

In August 2022, young workers in Lansing, Michigan, led a successful campaign which for the first time brought a union to a Chipotle store. Though the workers voted to join the Teamsters rather than build an independent union, the heavy lifting was largely done by the workers themselves. The workers at Chipotle used the classic, reliable organizing tactics—one-on-one conversations with coworkers, mapping their workplace, inoculation, and so on—but also maintained momentum through consistent communication via social media (Blanc 2022). By the time the rank-and-file organizers got in touch with the Teamsters, most of the organizing work had already been done.

The decision to go with the Teamsters rather than form an independent union was based on the resources and legal support that could be offered to the Chipotle workers which might not have been available if they had decided to go the route of the ALU. The workers explained in a recent interview in *Jacobin* that they had reached out to other unions and were either ignored or told their campaign was not worth the time or resources for union involvement (Blanc 2022). The Chipotle workers are not alone in this regard. Although there is no database kept for tracking how many workers seeking union representation reach out to union representatives only to be let down or told they are not worth the union's energy, one can safely assume there are more workers who want union representation than obtain it. Because many (if not most) mainstream unions operate according to the business model, the cost-benefit analysis conducted when deciding whether to support an organizing campaign often results in the union opting to reject workers in need of assistance. This reluctance to fund organizing and bring new workers into the labor movement comes at a terrible cost to unions, and the working class as a whole (Moody 2007:101).

The business model and the calculating timidity it has instilled in the mainstream U.S. labor movement have made worker-led organizing drives and independent unions inevitable. Just as the CIO broke from the AFL when the dominant federation was unwilling to do the necessary work of organizing the unorganized, independent unions and the more progressive unions within the AFL-CIO will need to chart their own paths. Workers who want to organize on the job and form unions will need to take up the burden themselves, as they cannot rely on docile, institutionalized unions or the AFL-CIO to effectively fight for their interests. Even in the case of the Chipotle workers who joined the Teamsters, had the workers not done the organizing work themselves, there may have been only a slim chance the Teamsters would have agreed to get involved.

Another recent organizing campaign illustrates the growing appeal of independent unionism in the United States. In July 2022, workers at a Trader Joe's store in Hadley, Massachusetts, formed the first union representing U.S. Trader Joe's employees, and another store in Minneapolis, Minnesota, followed suit in August. Rather than affiliate with an existing union, the workers formed an independent union, Trader Joe's United. Following the uncertain course of independent unionism is not a decision easily made by workers at Trader Joe's or elsewhere, and not every shop will go the same way. Workers at a Trader Joe's in Boulder, Colorado, for example, opted to affiliate with United Food and Commercial Workers (UFCW). However, the workers withdrew their union petition after filing charges against the company for coercion and intimidation (Furman 2022). A Trader Joe's wine shop in New York City abruptly closed on August 11, 2022 after workers there began an organizing campaign with UFCW.

So far, the two successful organizing drives at Trader Joe's stores have been those led by rank-and-file workers who took the path of independent unionism. This is not to say that independent unions will not face challenges and defeats, but the organic, close-knit nature of independent unions make them a lot harder to intimidate and break apart. The workers involved in organizing independent unions feel the union as a natural outgrowth of their inherent interests as individuals and as members of a class, and there is no chance for the boss to 'third-party' the union when the union was built by the workers themselves. Independent unions will be the lifeblood of the new labor movement, and this is because independent unionism puts workers in control of their unions and their destinies.

What Will a New Labor Movement Look Like?

In looking to the past for inspiration, there are at least two models which, while not without shortcomings, offer meaningful insight into what kind of labor movement workers and organizers can build today. In addition to the UE's democratic, rank-and-file-led unionism, still alive and ahead of its time, today's militant workers and organizers might look to the radical, egalitarian unionism of the Industrial Workers of the World and the politically engaged, community-minded Trade Union Unity League.

The Wobblies: Radical Solidarity

The IWW, like UE, is still around today despite the Red Scares, and has done some commendable organizing work in recent years. According to data from the Department of Labor, the IWW's membership experienced significant growth between 2016 and 2021, rising to nearly 9000 members in 2021 from a little over 3000 in 2016 (DOL Annual Reports 2016, 2021). The Wobblies, while relatively small in number and certainly less powerful than they were in the past, continue to organize and fight for the One Big Union, and their efforts have led to union contracts in a variety of workplaces including restaurants, movie theaters, charter schools, coffee shops, warehouses, and grocery stores, among others. In 2011, when reactionary Wisconsin Governor Scott Walker proposed a bill that would eliminate automatic dues-checkoff, cut pay for public sector workers, and implement an austerity budget for social services, the IWW introduced proposals to the South-Central Federation of Labor (SCFL) calling for preparation for a general strike and staunch opposition to Walker's bill (Conatz and Sawyers 2011). The IWW's proposals passed unanimously.

Though the general strike never happened and Walker's bill was signed into law, the IWW's presence during the battle in Wisconsin showed if nothing else that the Wobblies have not disappeared, and remain an active, committed force in the labor movement. In the IWW, the young workers leading the campaigns that will build the new labor movement can find inspiration in Wobbly tenacity and the One Big Union's long history of egalitarianism and opposition to racism, sexism, homophobia, and all other forms of chauvinism and prejudice. While other unions were quick to dismiss women, immigrants, non-whites, and 'unskilled' workers, the IWW, since its inception in 1905, distinguished only two kinds of people: workers and bosses. Divisions in the working class are still more strident than one may like to think, but the Wobblies showed how such divisions can be overcome and how suspicion and enmity can be turned into solidarity.

There were times when the Wobblies had to take up arms and physically confront racists and right-wing militia organizations, including the Ku Klux Klan. An old Wobbly poster depicting an armed Klansman proclaimed "Protect yourself from this menace – the Ku Klux Klan is anti-Jew, anti-Negro, anti-Catholic, anti-Foreigner, and anti-Labor. Organize industrially; Line up! Join the I.W.W.". In February 1924, nearly 200 armed Wobblies patrolled Greenville, Maine, anticipating violent conflict with the KKK. The IWW workers had already clashed with the Klan in Maine, the members of which were used as hired guns by the lumber bosses to chase the Wobblies out of Greenville, but the militant workers stayed put. IWW delegate Bob Pease of Bangor, Maine, told the *Portland Press Herald* "We are going to stick, and if the Klan starts anything, the IWW will finish it" (Portland Press Herald February 5, 1924).

The IWW's willingness to risk harm and even death in battles with reactionaries and bigots can inspire beyond the labor movement, but the point is that the Wobblies showed that workers and their unions must be at the forefront of egalitarian and civil rights efforts. When other unions would not look twice at an immigrant or black worker, the IWW was there with open arms to defend and fight for any worker regardless of race, sex, ethnicity, national origin, religious beliefs, or skill level. This was not some kind of cheap, faux progressive attempt to appear 'diverse' and welcoming, which is all too common in numerous left-liberal organizations today. The class-conscious Wobbly philosophy simply does not have room for prejudice. When a worker joins the IWW, they do not join as a 'woman worker', 'black worker', 'immigrant worker', and so on—they join as a *worker*. When the IWW declared at its founding convention that the working class and the employing class have nothing in common, they meant the entire working class. The Wobbly spirit of inclusivity and solidarity, and the willingness to defend the dignity of all workers by any means necessary, must guide the embryonic new labor movement.

TUUL: Organizing the Unorganized and Unemployed

In late August through early September 1929, the Trade Union Educational League (TUEL) held its fourth national conference in Cleveland, Ohio. At the conference, TUEL was reorganized and rebranded as the Trade Union Unity League (TUUL). The convention also saw a change in the labor organization's program, which had been mainly focused on organizing workers in existing unions ('boring from within') in order to push the AFL to the left (Cochran 1977:44–45). It was decided that, in addition to working in already existing unions, workers had to be organized into new, independent industrial unions.

This decision came about largely out of necessity. The AFL's conservative leadership had little patience for the TUEL and the political left in general, and thus progressive voices in the labor movement found that they had to develop their projects independently of the dominant federation (Stepan-Norris and Zeitlin 2002:33–34). The TUEL had a policy opposing 'dual-unionism', when workers paid dues in an AFL affiliate but organized independent unions as well. With the TUUL, this attitude changed. Workers and organizers were encouraged to push existing unions to the left while also building independent unions to challenge AFL hegemony.

There was much discussion at the Cleveland convention regarding what would be included in the Constitution and Program of the TUUL. The leaders of the TUEL, including William Z. Foster, who would continue his role as general secretary in the new organization, emphasized the importance of organizing black workers, and combating racism was an integral part of the TUUL's vision for the labor movement (Foner 2022:2). The League also made organizing women, youths, 'unskilled' laborers, and foreign-born workers priorities in its program. The TUUL's Constitution distinguished three types of national organization which would provide the foundation for the TUUL platform: (1) industrial unions, (2) industrial leagues, and (3) trade union minority groups.

The AFL's response to the League and its platform was predictably hostile, and the threat to the dominant federation posed by the left-wing labor organization caused the AFL to reconsider its longstanding opposition to admitting 'unskilled' workers into its ranks. The League's efforts in the U.S. south were particularly concerning to the AFL's leadership. Having been customarily neglected by the AFL, it was feared that the 'Communist destructionists' (as AFL president William Green called them) would gain a foothold in the south, and so it was determined that each affiliate of the AFL would send down an organizer to prevent the TUUL from achieving any kind of organizational advantage.

Green and the other conservative leaders of the AFL found a sympathetic friend in capital. In October 1929, the president of the National Association of Manufacturers, John Edgerton, said at a conference of the National Industrial Council that while the workers in the south were ignorant, they were also patriotic, and so there was little need to fear that they would adopt communism or the radical principles of the TUUL. In addition, Edgerton suggested that if the workers were to unionize, they would "'accept the sedative of the American Federation of Labor as a cure for radicalism'" (Foner 2022:8).

Edgerton's words at the National Industrial Council conference summed up how capitalists generally perceived organized labor at the time, and it is more or less how capitalists view unions today. If there are going to be unions, they should be moderate, timid, and willing to adhere to management prerogatives. Having no union in the workplace at all is the best-case scenario for the boss, but the next best thing to no union is a conservative union. The obvious worst-case scenario for employers was and is a workforce organized in a militant, class-conscious union that is prepared to go to war with capital.

The TUUL also differed from the AFL in its approach to unemployment and the unemployed. Under the presidency of Samuel Gompers, the AFL openly opposed any assistance for the unemployed. William Green followed in his predecessor's footsteps, opposing unemployment insurance legislation until the Great Depression had made it impossible for the federation to retain such a position. In the months leading up to the beginning of the Great Depression, the AFL simply parroted President Hoover's inattentive optimism regarding the economy. The AFL's approach to unemployment and economic crises was predominantly just echoing the sentiments of the government and corporations.

In contrast to the AFL's attitude, the TUUL prioritized the organization of unemployed workers. As the growing number of victims of the Depression inundated soup kitchens and charities, the TUUL and the Communist Party launched a campaign to organize councils of the unemployed. The councils, discriminating against no unemployed worker regardless of race, sex, or nationality, fought against evictions and led 'hunger marches' to pressure the government to provide unemployment insurance and other forms of much needed relief. The League's organizing efforts and demonstrations were met with violence. For example, in March 1932, the Detroit unemployed council joined TUUL autoworkers in a demonstration in front of the Ford factory in Dearborn. The three thousand demonstrators at the factory demanded that Ford rehire laid-off workers and slow down assembly lines. The police and company guards responded by firing into the crowd, killing 5 workers and injuring 60 others (Murolo and Chitty 2018:157).

The Communist Party, while still in its 'underground stage', attempted to organize unemployed workers prior to the Depression-era, but internal struggles prevented the Party from making significant gains. The primary factional dispute in the Communist Party was between William Z. Foster and Jay Lovestone, who would go on to lead a breakaway opposition group and later collaborate with the CIA to crush leftists and radical unionism.

The Communist Party was still healing from the Foster-Lovestone schism when it began developing its program for organizing the unemployed, a program which would take center stage in the TUUL's operations before and during the Great Depression. 'Red-baiting' may have been a method of disparaging unions and union leaders by associating them with the communists or the left more broadly, but for the TUUL, having ties to the Communist Party was a point of strength.

The TUUL, unlike the AFL, had a vision of a future in which the working class did not need to sell its labor to employers to survive, and did not depend on the charity of churches or a sympathetic capitalist government in times of crisis. The AFL had criticized unemployment insurance in terms familiar to right-wing hardliners and reactionaries: it would make one dependent on the government, and so on (Yates 2009:116). The TUUL, on the other hand, sought to confront the very system which produces unemployment, lack of shelter, and other forms of humiliation and desperation.

The Communist Party ran into trouble after adopting the Popular Front strategy. The TUUL was dissolved, and the CIO emerged as the dominant force in industrial unionism. Rather than organizing independent, left-wing unions while developing progressivism in mainstream unions, the Popular Front strategy encouraged radical workers and organizers to drop all talk of revolution, join the ranks of CIO unions, and nudge workers to the left without breaking with liberal, Democratic Party politics. The Popular Front strategy did lead to some significant victories for CIO unions, but once the communists and other leftists in the labor movement urged workers to abandon Roosevelt liberalism in favor of something more, many workers were not up to the task.

Much of the gains won by the Communist Party happened prior to the adoption of the Popular Front strategy, and those that followed were largely to the benefit not of the political left but of centrists and the labor bureaucrats who ran the CIO (Davis 2018:93). By partnering with liberals and conservative unionists and concealing their radicalism, the left-wingers in the labor movement undermined their own efforts, crushing any hope of a labor party and making the ensuing purges a simpler undertaking for the class-collaborationist labor aristocracy.

The Communist Party's political contortionism and self-contradiction did considerable damage to its influence and revolutionary project within the U.S. labor movement. The Communist Party went from calling FDR a fascist to declaring him a friend of the working class after the adoption of the Popular Front strategy (Post 2017). When labor forged its alliance with the Roosevelt administration, the Communist Party was emphatically opposed to the formation of alternative political parties, a position which the CP unsuccessfully tried to reverse when the party urged labor to support Wallace and the Progressives against the Democrats in 1948 (Moody 1993:37). The absence of independent, left-labor political institutions has been disastrous for labor and the left, but greatly beneficial for employers, labor bureaucrats, and capitalist political hegemony.

Today's young, politically independent workers and union organizers face a different situation. The dominance of a bureaucratic, defanged labor federation is still here, but it does not have the 'backroom deal' rapport with employers enjoyed by the AFL. The young workers are also organizing their independent unions in a political environment in which the working class has little reason to trust the Democratic Party, and the enthusiasm that workers felt for the FDR administration has no resemblance to the frustration and hostility many workers feel towards Democratic Party politicians today.

The builders of the new labor movement must take note of these differences and take steps untaken by militant unionists and political radicals in the past. While continuing the TUUL/Communist Party project(s) of organizing the unemployed alongside employed workers, today's organizers have the ability to implement political strategies that were unconsidered or unimaginable during the years of the Popular Front. The new labor movement must represent the working class beyond the limitations of this or that workplace, and boldly enter the political arena, when the time is right, with a genuine, revolutionary labor party.

Councils of the unemployed are arguably more of a relevant project today than at any point since the Great Depression, as the COVID-19 pandemic made the insecurity of unemployment a more frightening reality for the working class in the United States and elsewhere. The young workers organizing independent unions should, as the TUUL did, prioritize organizing the unemployed and building class-conscious partnerships between militant, independent unions and representative councils of unemployed and unsheltered workers.

U.S. labor's attachment to the Democratic Party has been a dead end for workers and unions, so much so that even former AFL-CIO political director Steve Rosenthal had to admit that unions '"basically have become an ATM for the Democrats. There is a sense of taking unions for granted, no place else to go, don't need to do much for them"' (Jacoby 2021:20).

However, because the U.S. working class today, and especially its youth, has no devotion to the Democratic Party (or at least a diminished sense of devotion compared to the past), there is no need for the workers and organizers building the new labor movement to fall into the trap of a 'Popular Front'. They can, and should, courageously distance themselves from the Democratic Party while laying the groundwork for what could become an independent political party of the working class in the United States. The establishment of a labor party is not a new goal, but it has been unrealized due to violence against the political left in the United States, mishaps and mistakes committed by the leaders of labor party movements themselves, and the absorption of the labor movement into the Democratic Party. The builders of the new labor movement have an opportunity to accomplish this task which has been put off or rejected for far too long.

New Labor, New Politics

The absence of a labor party in the United States is largely the consequence of the labor movement being co-opted by the Democratic Party during the FDR years. To be sure, there have been numerous attempts at establishing left/labor political parties in the United States, including multiple socialist parties, the Communist Party of the United States of America (CPUSA, which used to be called the Workers' Party), the Socialist Labor Party, a few Trotskyist parties, and others that never gained support beyond the political fringe. The most recent attempt at forming a party of the working class was in 1996, when progressive members of various unions, including ILWU, UE, United Mine Workers (UMW), the American Federation of Government Employees (AFGE), the Oil, Chemical and Atomic Workers International Union (OCAW), among others, gathered with independent activists at a convention in Cleveland, Ohio, to form the Labor Party (Reed 2001:208–209).

At that time, U.S. labor was rightfully feeling sold-out by President Clinton's embrace of neoliberalism, and thus it appeared that the conditions were ripe for an exodus of labor support from the Democratic Party and for unions and workers to finally build a political party of their own. The Labor Party had considerable potential, and much of its strength was rooted in its base of union workers and organizers—people who had experience leading campaigns and organizing drives in addition to the discipline and foresight that are necessary in the development of a lasting, competent working-class movement. However, several factors contributed to the decline and eventual suspension of Labor Party activities, including the deterioration of labor power in the United States (a result of neoliberal globalization) and the perceived riskiness in the complete abandonment of the Democratic Party (Dudzic and Isaac 2012).

Convincing workers to leave the Democrats behind without a coherent, competent alternative is a terribly difficult task, as it amounts to suggesting workers risk their material interests and needs in the hopes that an unprepared left will triumph in the electoral political arena. In the case of the Labor Party, even the most militant unionists were understandably reluctant to take such a plunge, and with the arrival of 'Obamamania' leading up to the 2008 presidential election, the inability of the Labor Party to produce the alternative political force so badly needed in the United States became undeniable.

The conditions confronted by today's progressive unionists are quite different, and while the U.S. labor movement (at least its mainstream current) remains meek, the political independence of the young organizers and workers leading the charge toward a labor renaissance offers more assurance to the prospect of building a party of the working class. The young workers organizing and joining fresh independent unions do not feel the same sense of devotion to the Democratic Party that characterized previous generations of workers, nor do they feel that the Democrats are their best bet for meaningful representation in the political arena. In other words, the architects of the new labor movement must embrace an attitude toward the Democratic Party that is similar to the logical position toward the AFL-CIO: if the Democratic Party and AFL-CIO are unprepared, unwilling, or unable to lead the working class to victory, then they had better get out of the way.

Labor Organizing Is Political Organizing

Class consciousness is the engine that drives the formation of the union, the labor federation, the party, the international—workers recognizing their common interests, common struggles, and common enemies serves as the basis upon which they build the movement toward the resolution of systemic contradictions and the attainment of social, political, and economic power. That the U.S. labor movement's dominant federations, from the AFL to the CIO to the AFL-CIO, have been unable or unwilling to take the necessary next step forward in establishing a party of labor speaks to the larger problem of the untenable barrier between labor and *labor politics.*

In a way this problem is a consequence of the general confusion regarding the purpose of politics that plagues U.S. society, confusion rooted in the decline of politics as an arena for debate between coherent parties with concrete programs (Mills 1956:274). In U.S. electoral politics, to be 'partisan' carries a negative connotation, while being 'bipartisan', willing to compromise with one's adversaries, is viewed as admirable. Rather than using the party as a body with which to fight opponents in the political battling pit, is it not the case that each of the dominant parties has historically attempted to appear not as representative of a particular class or group but rather 'the American people' as a whole? Admittedly, the Republican Party has, in its conspicuous lurch to the extreme right, abandoned much of the 'bipartisan' ideal which characterizes U.S. politics, but the Democratic Party has to its detriment continued to practice an asinine, almost religious, deference to the principle of nonpolitical politics.

The purpose of a political party is to be *partisan*—that is, to take sides, to represent the interests of a class, and to fight political opposition in a competition for power. The working class in the United States has no such political party. The Democratic Party has shown since its adoption of neoliberalism in the Clinton-era (although it had already started its rightward turn much earlier, and even before then it rested mostly in the center) that it is unwilling to exercise the partisanship necessary to combat the increasingly extreme Republican Party, with which it shares more politically than one may want to admit. After all, how many times has a Democratic candidate campaigned on their ability to work 'on both sides of the aisle'? The working class can only suffer under the leadership of a political party which finds virtue in friendliness with the right.

Despite the labor bureaucracy's undying fondness for the Democrats, the failure of labor's alliance with the Democratic Party to promote the interests of the working class and build worker power means the discussion regarding alternative forms of political engagement is far from over (Yates 2009:49). This is not to say that workers should prematurely throw their weight behind an underdeveloped labor party that is unprepared, strategically and in terms of resources, for the political/electoral arena. However, the young, politically independent workers who are organizing today's independent unions must consider their struggle as one with political connotations, and ramifications beyond the confines of the workplace. The battle between workers, organized into unions, and their employers is class struggle, and class struggle is political struggle. The workers may at first organize in order to fight for shared on-the-job interests against the boss, but the union is an organism which must evolve into a more vigorous and dynamic political unit, the party of the working class, which the workers will use to engage in the struggle for power against capital and the capitalist state.

Marx made similar observations regarding labor unions in his writings to delegates of the International Workingmen's Association. In examining the 'past, present, and future' of the 'trades' unions', Marx found that unions emerged at first as a means to reject or at least control the competition between workers forced upon them by the capitalist mode of production (Marx 1866). The focus of the trades' unions, as Marx called them, was restricted to the everyday problems and necessities facing the workers—wages and labor, confronting capitalist intrusion in their lives, and so on. However, Marx suggested that, without being aware of it, the workers establishing trades' unions were building the centers of working-class organization, bodies which would eventually become the agencies with which the working class would do away with wage slavery and capitalism entirely (Marx 1866).

The workers organizing the new labor movement must have this historical mission in mind as they engage in their imperative struggle to resurrect militant unionism. The AFL-CIO, and the AFL and CIO before their combination, long ago rejected the notion that labor unions could ever be more than associations of workers for bargaining for a better wage or shorter hours on the job. Refusing the real task of the labor movement, that of challenging the whole capitalist mode of production, means admitting that the working class will forever be confined to exploitation, alienation, and degradation. Today's workers and organizers, particularly the young, politically independent leaders of the embryonic new labor movement, must refuse such an admission of defeat, and organize with the full knowledge that so long as there is capitalism, workers will not have control over their lives—they will be at the mercy of a ruling class which cares little, in fact, whether they live or die.

Building a Labor Party

Developing a political party that represents the interests of the working class is going to take more than enthusiasm and will. The capitalist parties' financial resources alone make the task daunting, and there is little use in founding a labor party that is incapable of challenging the Democratic-Republican hold on U.S. politics on an electoral level. Workers may have the ruling class outnumbered, but if the working class cannot eliminate competition between workers and build strong bonds of solidarity (including solidarity with the international working class), its numbers will amount to nothing.

There is no getting around the grueling work that must be done to organize a base of support sturdy enough to withstand the pressures and challenges of the political arena. Organizing through sustained, disciplined workplace- and community-based campaigns involving consistent self-critique and flexible, strategic planning is how the foundation for a labor party will be established. Workers and organizers who understand the necessity of a working-class political party may feel out of a legitimate sense of urgency that there is no time to engage in the careful, tiresome, and oftentimes disappointing slog of building a base of popular support, but there is no other way. The working class has been either encouraged to stay out of political affairs or corralled into the capitalist parties (historically the Democratic Party, but over the past few decades into the GOP as well). Nurturing class consciousness and solidarity in the working class through union organizing is not only a fine place to start; there is little reason to believe there is any other starting point for this massive undertaking (Reed 2001:206).

Insofar as there is a 'left' in U.S. politics, it has, for the most part, been restricted to running and/or endorsing progressive candidates against centrists in Democratic Party primary elections. This task has largely been taken up by the DSA, which, to its credit, has assisted in important (and occasionally unexpected) electoral victories of progressives. At best this program has advanced the left-leaning wing of the Democratic Party in opposition to the party's dominant neoliberal ideology, but at worst it has kept the left trapped and impotent inside the Democratic Party (Davis 2018:269–270). The project of building enough of an internal progressive presence to push the Democratic Party to the left is, I argue, a project destined for failure.

The progressive representatives in the Democratic Party have been unable to achieve practically all of their goals—no national healthcare system, no 'Green New Deal', no elimination of 'right-to-work' laws, no cutting of the military budget, no expansion of public housing, no federal employment program, and so on. Certainly, having progressives in office, even if they are Democrats, is better than the alternative, but if they are not able to effectively change the fundamental structure of the Democratic Party, how much use are they to the working class?

Still, the Democratic Party finds its appeal primarily in two areas. First, the increasingly extremist and unhinged policies of the Republican Party make the Democrats at least appear as a sane alternative. Second, the Democratic Party has efficaciously latched itself onto social movements and used popular momentum to its advantage. The cynicism and half-heartedness of the Democratic Party's proclaimed commitment to the interests of workers, minorities, women, and LGBTQIA+ citizens matter little when there is no other legitimate political option for people to turn to. Even more alarming than the Democrats' moderation on the social movement front is the party's unwillingness to seriously address and combat the accelerated threat posed by fascism in the United States and around the world.

The Republican Party has mastered its obstructionist technique, and appears to be developing a political framework which will allow it to maintain its power and influence regardless of elections or other democratic processes (Reed 2021). By failing to effectively realize and confront the approaching dangerous political situation, the Democratic Party is complicit in the capitalist state's disturbing lurch to the far-right. The only answer is a new, unabashedly left-wing party with mass popular support and a commitment to internationalism—in a word, a labor party.

Again, the real need for a labor party is not a reason for working-class organizers to prematurely found a political party that declares itself the representative of the toiling masses. The tough but necessary work that must be done in building a base of mass support cannot be avoided. However, there is hope in the new labor movement, in the politically independent, class-conscious young organizers and workers who are engaged currently in struggles for union recognition in workplaces that were neglected by the AFL-CIO and most mainstream labor unions. The hard work is already underway, but maintaining momentum, coordinating organizing campaigns on a national scale, and building strong relationships with militant, working-class organizations abroad will make all the difference, and indeed will determine what comes next.

References

Blanc, Eric. 2022. Chipotle Workers on How They Won the First Chipotle Union in the United States. *Jacobin.com*. https://jacobin.com/2022/09/chipotle-workers-lansing-michigan-union-teamsters.

Bureau of Labor Statistics. 2022. *Union Members - 2021*. https://www.bls.gov/news.release/pdf/union2.pdf. Washington, D.C.: U.S. Department of Labor.

Cochran, Bert. 1977. *Labor and Communism: The Conflict that Shaped Labor Unions*. Princeton, NJ: Princeton University Press.

Conatz, Juan, and Brendan Sawyers. 2011. The General Strike That Didn't Happen: A Report on the Activity of the IWW in Wisconsin. *IWW Historical Archives*. https://archive.iww.org/history/library/iww/general-strike-didnt-happen-report-activity-iww-wisconsin/.

Davis, Mike. 2018. *Prisoners of the American Dream: Politics and Economy in the History of the U.S. Working Class*. London, England: Verso Books.

Dudzic, Mark, and Katherine Isaac. 2012. Labor Party Time? Not Yet. *The Labor Party*. http://www.thelaborparty.org/d_lp_time.htm.

Foner, Philip. 2022. *The History of the Labor Movement in the United States, Vol. 11: The Depression*. New York, NY: International.

Furman, Jonah. 2022. Trader Joe's Workers Are Unionizing — and the Company Is Union Busting. *Jacobin.com*. https://jacobin.com/2022/09/trader-joes-united-union-busting-ufcw.

Gruenberg, Mark. 2020. Trumka: 19-Year High in Strikes Shows 'Sea Change in America.' *People's World*. Retrieved December 16, 2022 https://www.peoplesworld.org/article/trumka-19-year-high-in-strikes-shows-sea-change-in-america/.

Jacoby, Sanford M. 2021. *Labor in the Age of Finance: Pensions, Politics, and Corporations from Deindustrialization to Dodd-Frank*. Princeton, NJ: Princeton University Press.

Logan, John. 2022. Why Starbucks Workers United May Offer a Key to Labor's Revitalization. *Jacobin.com*. https://jacobin.com/2022/09/starbucks-workers-united-labor-union-organizing-model.

Loomis, Erik. 2019. Sara Nelson Calls for a General Strike to End Shutdown. *Atlantic Monthly (*Boston, Mass.*)*, January 25.

Marx, Karl. 1866. The International Workingmen's Association, Instructions for the Delegates of the Provisional General Council. *Marxists.org*. https://www.marxists.org/history/international/iwma/documents/1866/instructions.htm.

McCarthy, Justin. 2022. U.S. Approval of Labor Unions at Highest Point since 1965. *Gallup*. https://news.gallup.com/poll/398303/approval-labor-unions-highest-point-1965.aspx.

Mills, C. Wright. 1956. *The Power Elite*. New York, NY: Oxford University Press.

Moody, Kim. 1993. *An Injury to All: The Decline of American Unions*. New York, NY: Verso Press.

———. 2007. *U.S. Labor in Trouble and Transition: The Failure of Reform from Above, the Promise of Revival from Below*. London, England: Verso Books.

Murolo, Priscilla, and A.B. Chitty. 2018. *From the Folks Who Brought You the Weekend: A Short, Illustrated History of Labor in the United States*. New York, NY: New Press.

Newport, Frank. 2022. Average American Remains OK with Higher Taxes on Rich. *Gallup.com*. https://news.gallup.com/opinion/polling-matters/396737/average-american-remains-higher-taxes-rich.aspx.

Nolan, Hamilton. 2022. The AFL-CIO's Official New Goal: Continued Decline. *In These Times*. https://inthesetimes.com/article/afl-cio-union-federation-organizing-goal-workers.

Portland Press Herald. 1924. KKK and IWW Wage Drawn Battle in Greenville, 1924. *Libcom.org*. https://libcom.org/article/kkk-and-iww-wage-drawn-battle-greenville-1924.

Post, Charlie. 2017. The Popular Front Didn't Work. *Jacobin.com*. https://jacobin.com/2017/10/popular-front-communist-party-democrats.

Reed, Adolph, Jr. 2001. *Class Notes: Posing as Politics and Other Thoughts on the American Scene*. New York, NY: The New Press.

———. 2021. The Whole Country Is the Reichstag. *Nonsite.org*. https://nonsite.org/the-whole-country-is-the-reichstag/.

Rosenblum, Jonathan. 2022. Why Is This Union Leader Schmoozing with the Enemy? *Nation*, July 20.

Saad, Lydia. 2019. Socialism as Popular as Capitalism among Young Adults in U.S. *Gallup*. https://news.gallup.com/poll/268766/socialism-popular-capitalism-among-young-adults.aspx.

Schuhrke, Jeff. 2020. The US Labor Movement Needs More of the UE's 'Them and Us' Unionism. *Jacobin.com*. https://jacobin.com/2020/08/united-workers-labor-unions.

Stepan-Norris, Judith, and Maurice Zeitlin. 2002. *Left out: Reds and America's Industrial Unions*. Cambridge, England: Cambridge University Press.

U.S. Department of Labor. 2016. 070-232 (LM2) 06/30/2016. *Dol.gov*. https://olmsapps.dol.gov/query/orgReport.do?rptId=627901&rptForm=LM2Form. Washington, D.C.: U.S. Department of Labor.

———. 2021. 070-232 (LM2) 06/30/2021. *Dol.gov*. https://olmsapps.dol.gov/query/orgReport.do?rptId=783018&rptForm=LM2Form. Washington, D.C.: U.S. Department of Labor.

Yates, Michael. 2009. *Why Unions Matter*. New York, NY: Monthly Review Press.

CHAPTER 7

Conclusion: A World to Win

The U.S. labor movement from its earliest days has been a force with the revolutionary potential to dismantle oppressive socioeconomic structures and reshape society. To the detriment of the working class in the United States, as well as in nations which have been targeted by transnational corporations for capitalist expansion through the global neoliberal project, the dominant trends in U.S. labor (the AFL, CIO, and AFL-CIO) have opted to ignore the revolutionary historical mission of the working class in favor of forging, on unequal terms, non-combative relationships with the ruling class and the state. The labor movement's conservative leaders, from Gompers to Schuler, have chosen backroom deals with employers, management prerogative, professionalization and institutionalization, and even conspiring with agents of the state's intelligence apparatus—in a word, class collaborationism—instead of nurturing the militancy and class consciousness from which the labor movement obtains its strength and revolutionary potential.

Throughout U.S. labor's history, there has been an internal struggle between the class conscious and class-collaborationist factions, between those who view unions as vehicles for radical change and those who view them merely as mediators in the workplace. The conditions have fluctuated with time, but the struggle remains largely the same. Rank-and-file militants in the labor movement today face many of the same challenges that union militants confronted in the past—namely, the struggle of

A. Barrington, *The U.S. Labor Movement in the 20th and Early 21st Century*, Social Movements and Transformation,
https://doi.org/10.1007/978-3-031-30077-6_7

developing and maintaining class consciousness and worker solidarity while avoiding the 'trap' of co-optation. Just as the labor bureaucrats in the CIO harnessed the energy that erupted with the rank-and-file organizing drives of the 1930s only to stifle it later with boss-friendly contracts and anticommunist purges, there is a great risk of today's young, aggressive organizers and their campaigns being muzzled by the AFL-CIO and/or class collaborationist labor leaders. That is not to say that the bureaucrats running the AFL-CIO are knowingly pernicious. There is no evidence that Shuler or anyone else at the top of the AFL-CIO pyramid is patiently waiting for the day the dominant federation can step in to discipline the young organizers and force them to accept U.S. labor's status quo. Some existing unions are even assisting the young organizers (e.g., Workers United, an affiliate of SEIU, is helping the workers behind the Starbucks campaigns), and there is no reason that this assistance cannot be appreciated and used to the advantage of workers. However, the plain truth is that if U.S. labor is going to flourish, not just survive, new methods for organizing workers, building solidarity, and invigorating worker power, must be developed.

On the labor front, the architects of a new labor movement must completely reject old labor's relationship with the Democratic Party. A new labor movement should use resources, financial and otherwise, for building worker power, organizing new unions, establishing centers for worker education, providing assistance for the unemployed, and forming collaborative relationships with international working-class organizations (militant unions, revolutionary political parties, etc.), among various other worthy projects that do not involve donating money to or knocking doors for capitalist politicians. Rather than donating millions of dollars to the campaigns of political candidates, the AFL-CIO could be spending money on projects like those listed above. That the dominant federation has not undertaken such an ambitious program speaks to why U.S. labor is in the trouble it is in today. Thus, it is up to a new generation of labor organizers, rank-and-file workers, and their activist allies to take up this monumental task.

In terms of dealing with employers, a new labor movement could find inspiration in past examples of working-class militancy while developing fresh strategies for implementing and maintaining union actions. Direct action, as it has been said time and again, gets the goods—but only sustained, worker-led programs that challenge the power of the capitalist class and its guardian, the state, have the potential to fundamentally change the workplace, relations of production, and the socioeconomic skeleton which preserves the power structure.

During organizing drives and other labor campaigns, it is certain that employers (often with the help of the state via police, repressive labor laws, etc.) will retaliate. Using employer retaliation as an opportunity for maintaining an organizing drive, which the organizers behind the ALU campaign did masterfully, is one example of a successful tactic to counter the boss. Another is building strong enough relationships with workers in one's community to debilitate the power of the employer, as seen in the case of the West Virginia wildcat teacher strikes. Forging collaborative alliances with other unions and working-class organizations in one's city, town, neighborhood, and so on can similarly bring a struggle in a given workplace out into the streets, making the conflict between the workers and the employer one of significance even to those who do not work there. The point is that a new labor movement will have to nurture solidarity and build coalitions beyond the workplace, although the workplace is of course the starting point.

These coalitions will necessarily be internationalist in character. With neoliberal globalization, the entirety of the international working class faces instability and turmoil which have produced on the one hand widespread poverty, illness, and death, and on the other, an accelerated threat of labor repression under reimagined fascism. The task of the U.S. labor movement today is one it shares with labor federations, unions, and working-class organizations around the world: establishing a radical, internationalist response to neoliberal global capitalism and (re)building a coherent, disciplined global left that is capable of disrupting the rise of the right on a world scale.

For the young workers and organizers building new independent unions in the United States, there is still much work to be done at home. However, the new labor movement must have a global perspective, as the spread of capitalism across the face of the earth has already determined that the confrontation between the working class and ruling class will be international in scale. The only way to combat the interests of capital is to organize workers globally, and this requires the new labor movement to take the daunting step toward a labor party that is capable of articulating the interests of the working class in the United States and connecting these interests to those of the working classes of other nations around the world. The embryonic new labor movement is admittedly far from being able to accomplish this task, but it remains necessary all the same.

Capital does not limit itself to one nation, for it is impossible for it to do so. Likewise, today it is impossible for a labor movement to limit itself to its home country and expect the needed results. One can organize a strong union in a factory in Ohio, or Pennsylvania, or any other U.S. state, but when the employer is able to move the factory out of the country, of what good is a domestic union without comrades abroad to apply the same pressure on the boss? If the AFL-CIO's work with the CIA helped make the world safe for capitalism, the responsibility of the new labor movement is to make the world dangerous for capitalism. This is easier said than done, but it must be done. It is no exaggeration to say that capitalism will drive humanity to oblivion, as one can see from the increasingly alarming effects of climate change. Thus, in the fight between labor and capital, the world is at stake.

There are multiple promising trends in the United States and abroad that can and should provide energy to the project of rebuilding the U.S. labor movement as part of a larger effort to revitalize the international left. As mentioned earlier, the popularity of unions and socialism, particularly among young U.S. citizens, gives cause for optimism. In Chile, the nation which served as the womb in which neoliberalism formed, a new left-wing government has taken power with popular support. While the new progressive government in Chile is struggling to throw out all of the debris left over by the fascist Pinochet dictatorship, unionists and activists around the world should pay close attention to the militant labor movement and activist organizations in Chile that helped bring the new left-wing government to power. Latin America has experienced exciting political shifts to the left elsewhere, including in Colombia, where the election of progressive economist Gustavo Petro as president has brought confidence to a country with a long history of right-wing governments, violent paramilitary organizations, and collaboration with U.S. imperialism. In Mexico, President Andrés Manuel López Obrador (AMLO) has called for Latin American unity against U.S. domination, and recently refused to attend U.S. President Biden's June 2022 Summit of the Americas in Los Angeles in protest of the exclusion of Cuba, Venezuela, and Nicaragua. On the labor front, Mexican workers have started organizing their own independent unions in opposition to the boss-friendly Confederación de Trabajadores de México (CTM). On September 1, 2022, it was announced that 350 auto workers voted to join the Mexican Workers' League (la Liga Sindical Obrera Mexicana) at the VU Manufacturing plant in Piedras Negras, Coahuila.

The architects of the new labor movement in the United States must view the struggles of workers around the world as extensions of their own struggles, and likewise their own struggles as extensions of the struggles of workers around the world. Building relationships with unions, labor federations, and radical working-class organizations in Latin America, where the AFL-CIO's collaborations with the CIA inflicted significant damage, is a natural place to begin establishing the groundwork for a militant, internationalist labor movement.

One of the imperative components of this program will be rectifying a catastrophic and derogatory blunder committed by yesterday's labor movement: the debasing, insulting, and/or ignoring of non-white, rural, and immigrant workers. The new labor movement must be on the frontline of civil rights struggles. New labor must offer tangible opportunities and support for combating racism and chauvinism, disrupting the landlord/developer-driven deterioration of inner-city working-class enclaves, and providing real assistance to economically ravaged communities, among other projects, while building solidarity between workers of all backgrounds.

When the CIO's Operation Dixie flopped, it all but destroyed the potential for meaningful organizing in the rural south, at the time home predominantly to black workers. The result was that the labor movement (or at least its dominant trend) remained disconnected, for the most part, from the Black liberation struggle. The new labor movement must become organically (as opposed to *opportunistically*) connected to the Civil Rights movement, an unfinished revolution in the United States, and work side by side with left-wing Black liberation activists and organizations in combating the capitalist power structure.

Similarly, the new labor movement must build meaningful, organic coalitions with radical Latino/a activists and organizations, particularly in the Southwest, where Latino/a communities are antagonized and abused by a racist immigration law enforcement system and socioeconomic marginalization. The new labor movement must also show solidarity with Indigenous communities, and establish alliances with militant Native American/First Nation activists and organizations. Indigenous communities fighting against U.S./Canadian government and corporate encroachment and the poverty and decay inflicted upon their communities by the capitalist class and state(s) deserve a devoted friend and collaborator in the labor movement. Labor should earn the respect and collaboration of Native American/First Nation communities, activists, and organizations to sustain such alliance.

This is an area where labor can also join forces with the environmentalist movement, with which labor must also develop close ties. As Indigenous communities struggle against pipelines, for example, environmentalist organizations join Native American/First Nation activists on the frontline. The labor movement has a particularly influential place in this struggle, and has the moral responsibility to become part of it. Union workers should refuse to participate in work that jeopardizes the environment, or (further) invades Indigenous lands.

The new labor movement must make the protection of the environment and combating climate change its priorities, and is in a unique position to have a tremendous impact. Railroad workers, especially those involved in the progressive labor organization Railroad Workers United (RWU), have already shown a clear path toward forging an alliance with environmentalist causes. On October 5, 2022, the RWU steering committee adopted a resolution supporting the public ownership of North American railroads, and urged labor unions, environmentalist organizations, community groups, and social justice activists to push for public ownership and control of the rail system.

The new labor movement must also forge coalitions with progressive LGBTQIA+ and Asian American advocacy organizations. LGBTQIA+ and Asian American citizens have been increasingly victimized in recent times by the right. Racist attacks on Asian Americans since the start of the COVID-19 pandemic demand a militant, coordinated response from the left, and labor should be at the forefront of advocating for Asian Americans and offering resources and protection against violence from right-wing bigots. LGBTQIA+ citizens have experienced similar violent attacks from the right. Although violence against minority groups is nothing new, the labor movement has not committed itself to the level of coalition-building and fostering of organic solidarities with such groups and the progressive activist organizations representing their interests that are necessary for developing a mass movement capable of challenging the power structure. The new labor movement must recognize the importance of developing such a mass movement and act as the bridge which connects progressive activist organizations directly to the struggle against capitalism.

The mission of the new U.S. labor movement starts essentially with turning old labor's anticommunist program on its head. Where old labor purged left-wing workers and organizers from unions, the new labor movement must bring such militants into its ranks, and develop class consciousness and radical solidarity in the rank and file. Where old labor conspired with the U.S. government and the capitalist class to crush militant labor and progressive political movements abroad, new labor must join forces with the international left and revolutionary labor movements around the world to combat neoliberalism and right-wing authoritarianism. Old labor's class collaborationism must be replaced with class consciousness and a commitment to class struggle in the new labor movement. Finally, old labor's allegiance to the capitalist political structure, a major point of weakness in U.S. labor, must be abandoned by the new labor movement in favor of building a working-class party with mass popular support.

A tall order, to be sure. There is, however, little hope for labor in the United States and elsewhere if workers cannot effectively organize to confront the disastrous political, social, and economic currents which grow more monstrous each day. The catastrophic effects of neoliberal globalization—namely, the accelerated destruction of the environment and the rise of the authoritarian right—give urgency to the project described above, and there is no comfort to be found in any deterministic notion of the inevitable victory of the working class. Everything is uncertain, nothing is predetermined, and power waits patiently for those who dare to seize it. In these times of uncertainty and turbulence, the working class must tenaciously exclaim, as Eugene V. Debs did before the court prior to his imprisonment, "the midnight is passing, and joy cometh with the morning".

Bibliography

Agee, Philip. 1975. *Inside the Company: CIA Diary*. American ed. New York, NY: Stonehill.

Alvarado, Siboney. 2022. Define VU Manufacturas titularidad de contrato. *Periódico Zócalo | Noticias de Saltillo, Torreón, Piedras Negras, Monclova, Acuña*. https://www.zocalo.com.mx/define-vu-manufacturas-titularidad-de-contrato/.

AP-NORC. 2018. American Attitudes toward Teacher Pay and Protests. *AP-NORC*. https://apnorc.org/projects/american-attitudes-toward-teacher-pay-and-protests/.

———. 2022. Immigration Attitudes and Conspiratorial Thinkers: A Study Issued on the 10th Anniversary of The Associated Press-NORC Center for Public Affairs Research. *AP-NORC*. https://apnorc.org/projects/immigration-attitudes-and-conspiratorial-thinkers/.

Aronowitz, Stanley. 1973. *False Promises: The Shaping of American Working-Class Consciousness*. New York: McGraw-Hill Co.

———. 1983. *Working Class Hero: A New Strategy for Labor*. New York, NY: Adama Books

Avrich, Paul. 1984. *The Haymarket Tragedy*. Princeton, NJ: Princeton University Press.

Beckett, Ben. 2022a. After Buffalo, Great Replacement Theory Isn't Going Anywhere. *Jacobin.com*. https://jacobin.com/2022/05/buffalo-shooter-great-replacement-theory-carlson-gop.

A. Barrington, *The U.S. Labor Movement in the 20th and Early 21st Century*, Social Movements and Transformation, https://doi.org/10.1007/978-3-031-30077-6

———. 2022b. Don't Trust the National Security State to Stop the next Republican Coup Attempt. *Jacobin.com.* https://jacobin.com/2022/08/gop-capitol-riot-police-trump-fbi.

Beetham, David, ed. 2019. *Marxists in the Face of Fascism: Writings by Marxists on Fascism from the Inter-War Period.* Chicago, IL: Haymarket Books.

Berberoglu, Berch. 2021a. Crisis of Neoliberal Globalization and the Rise of Authoritarianism in the Early 21st Century. In *The Global Rise of Authoritarianism in the 21st Century: Crisis of Neoliberal Globalization and the Nationalist Response*, ed. Berch Berberoglu. New York, NY: Routledge.

———. 2021b. Neoliberal Capitalist Authoritarianism, Resistance, and Revolution on a Global Scale. In *The Global Rise of Authoritarianism in the 21st Century: Crisis of Neoliberal Globalization and the Nationalist Response*, ed. Berch Berberoglu. New York, NY: Routledge.

Bernhard, Patrick. 2016. Hitler's Africa in the East: Italian Colonialism as a Model for German Planning in Eastern Europe. *Journal of Contemporary History* 51 (1): 61–90.

Bevins, Vincent. 2021. *The Jakarta Method: Washington's Anticommunist Crusade and the Mass Murder Program That Shaped Our World.* New York, NY: PublicAffairs.

Blackstock, Nelson. 2000. *Cointelpro: The FBI's War on Political Freedom.* 3rd ed. New York, NY: Pathfinder Books.

Blanc, Eric. 2022. Chipotle Workers on How They Won the First Chipotle Union in the United States. *Jacobin.com.* https://jacobin.com/2022/09/chipotle-workers-lansing-michigan-union-teamsters.

Blum, William. 2003. *Killing Hope: US Military and CIA Interventions since World War II.* London, England: Zed Books.

Bonanno, Alessandro. 2021. The Crisis of Neoliberalism, Populist Reaction, and the Rise of Authoritarian Capitalism. In *The Global Rise of Authoritarianism in the 21st Century: Crisis of Neoliberal Globalization and the Nationalist Response*, ed. Berch Berberoglu. New York, NY: Routledge.

Bosworth, Richard J.B. 2006. *Mussolini's Italy: Life Under the Dictatorship, 1915-1945.* Harlow, England: Penguin Books.

Boyer, Richard O. and Herbert M. Morais. 1984. *Labor's Untold Story*, 3rd edition. New York: United Electrical, Radio, and Machine Workers of America.

Broder, David. 2022. Italy's Centrists Are Failing to Take the Fight to the Far Right. *Jacobin.com.* https://jacobin.com/2022/08/italy-fratelli-ditalia-giorgia-meloni-fascism.

Brooks, Chris. 2022. How Amazon and Starbucks Workers Are Upending the Organizing Rules. *In These Times.* https://inthesetimes.com/article/amazon-starbucks-workers-organizing-unions-momentum-movement-moment.

Calamur, Harini. 2021. 'Hindu Khatre Mein Hai' Is Analogous to the Narrative That Fostered Partition, Writes Harini Calamur. *Free Press Journal.* https://www.freepressjournal.in/analysis/hindu-khatre-mein-hai-is-analogous-to-the-narrative-that-fostered-partition-writes-harini-calamur.

Cantú, Francisco. 2019. The Fingerprints of Fraud: Evidence from Mexico's 1988 Presidential Election. *The American Political Science Review* 113 (3): 710–726. https://doi.org/10.1017/s0003055419000285.

Cochran, Bert. 1977. *Labor and Communism: The Conflict that Shaped Labor Unions.* Princeton, NJ: Princeton University Press.

Conatz, Juan, and Brendan Sawyers. 2011. The General Strike That Didn't Happen: A Report on the Activity of the IWW in Wisconsin. *IWW Historical Archives.* https://archive.iww.org/history/library/iww/general-strike-didnt-happen-report-activity-iww-wisconsin/.

Davis, Mike. 2007. *In Praise of Barbarians: Essays Against Empire.* Chicago, IL: Haymarket Books.

———. 2018. *Prisoners of the American Dream: Politics and Economy in the History of the U.S. Working Class.* London, England: Verso Books.

De Caux, Len. 1978. *The Living Spirit of the Wobblies.* International.

De Leon, Daniel. 1913. 1913: Industrial Unionism. *Marxists.org.* https://www.marxists.org/archive/deleon/works/1913/130120.htm.

Directorate of Intelligence. 1983. Mexico: Labor-Government Relations. *Freedom of Information Act Electronic Reading Room.* https://www.cia.gov/reading-room/docs/CIA-RDP84S00897R000100040007-7.pdf.

Dixon, M., V.J. Roscigno, and R. Hodson. 2004. Unions, Solidarity, and Striking. *Social Forces; a Scientific Medium of Social Study and Interpretation* 83 (1): 3–33. https://doi.org/10.1353/sof.2004.0107.

Domingos, Charles Sidarta, and Machado. 2018. Ligações Perigosas: A Deterioração Das Relações Entre Os Governos de João Goulart e John Kennedy No Ano de 1962. *Tempo (Rio de Janeiro, Brazil)* 24 (3): 525–545. https://doi.org/10.1590/tem-1980-542x2018v240306.

Dubofsky, Melvyn. 1969. *We Shall Be All: A History of the Industrial Workers of the World.* Chicago, IL: Quadrangle Books.

Dudzic, Mark, and Katherine Isaac. 2012. Labor Party Time? Not Yet. *The Labor Party.* http://www.thelaborparty.org/d_lp_time.htm.

Dulles, Allen W. 1951. Analysis of the Power of the Communist Parties of France and Italy and of Measures to Counter Them. *Freedom of Information Act Electronic Reading Room.* https://www.cia.gov/readingroom/docs/CIA-RDP80R01731R003200020013-5.pdf.

Eagleburger, Hart, and Jack Rusk. 2017. Deliver Us to the Lesser Evil: How Social Movements Bury Themselves in the Democratic Party. *Left Voice.* http://www.leftvoice.org/deliver-us-to-the-lesser-evil-how-social-movements-bury-themselves-in-the-democratic-party.

Engels, Friedrich. 1887. *The Condition of the Working Class in England*. New York, NY: Stanford University Press.

Faux, Jeff. 2013. NAFTA's Impact on U.S. Workers. *Economic Policy Institute*. https://www.epi.org/blog/naftas-impact-workers/.

Federal Reserve Bank of Atlanta. 2022. Wage Growth Tracker. *Federal Reserve Bank of Atlanta*. https://www.atlantafed.org/chcs/wage-growth-tracker.

Fletcher, Ben. 2021. The Negro and Organized Labor. In *Ben Fletcher: The Life and Times of a Black Wobbly*, ed. Peter Cole. Oakland, CA: PM Press.

Foner, Philip. 1965a. *History of the Labor Movement in the United States: V. IV: The Industrial Workers of the World, 1905-1917*. International.

———. 1965b. *The Case of Joe Hill*. International.

———. 1983. *Mother Jones Speaks: Collected Writings and Speeches*. Monad Press.

———. 2022. *The History of the Labor Movement in the United States, Vol. 11: The Depression*. New York, NY: International Publishers.

Foreign Broadcast Information Service. 1962. Espionage Record of U.S. Agent Exposed. *Freedom of Information Act Electronic Reading Room*. https://www.cia.gov/readingroom/docs/CIA-RDP75-00149R000100500026-1.pdf.

Francia, Peter L. 2010. Assessing the Labor-Democratic Party Alliance: A One-Sided Relationship? *Polity* 42 (3): 293–303. https://doi.org/10.1057/pol.2010.7.

French, Nick. 2019. A Different Kind of Teachers' Strike Wave. *Jacobinmag.com*. http://jacobinmag.com/2019/03/a-different-kind-of-teachers-strike-wave.

Furman, Jonah. 2022. Trader Joe's Workers Are Unionizing — and the Company Is Union Busting. *Jacobin.com*. https://jacobin.com/2022/09/trader-joes-united-union-busting-ufcw.

Gandesha, Samir. 2018. Understanding Right and Left Populism. In *Critical Theory and Authoritarian Populism*, 49–70. London, England: University of Westminster Press.

Geoghegan, Thomas. 2014. *Only One Thing Can Save Us: Why America Needs a New Kind of Labor Movement*. New York, NY: The New Press.

Glaberman, Martin. 1952. *Punching Out*. Edmonton, Alberta: Thought Crime.

Godard, John. 2009. The Exceptional Decline of the American Labor Movement. *Industrial & Labor Relations Review* 63 (1): 82–108. https://doi.org/10.1177/001979390906300105.

Gramsci, Antonio. 1971. *Selections from the Prison Notebooks of Antonio Gramsci*. New York, NY: International.

———. 2019. Democracy and Fascism. In *Marxists in the Face of Fascism: Writings by Marxists on Fascism from the Inter-War Period*, ed. David Beetham. Chicago, IL: Haymarket Books.

Green, James. 2007. *Death in the Haymarket*. New York, NY: Anchor Books.

Gruenberg, Mark. 2020. Trumka: 19-Year High in Strikes Shows 'Sea Change in America.' *People's World*. Retrieved December 16, 2022 https://www.peoplesworld.org/article/trumka-19-year-high-in-strikes-shows-sea-change-in-america/.

Guerin, Daniel. 1973. *Fascism and Big Business.* New York, NY: Pathfinder Books.

Harman, Chris. 2017. *A People's History of the World: From the Stone Age to the New Millennium.* London, England: Verso Books.

Haskins, James. 1976. *The Long Struggle: The Story of American Labor.* Louisville, KY: Westminster John Knox Press.

Henwood, Doug. 2022. No Strike Wave in 2021. *LBO News from Doug Henwood.* https://lbo-news.com/2022/01/17/no-strike-wave-in-2021/.

Hirsch, Fred. 1977. In *The CIA and the Labour Movement*, ed. R. Fletcher. Nottingham, England: Spokesman Books.

Immerman, Richard H. 1982. *The CIA in Guatemala: The Foreign Policy of Intervention.* 1st ed. Austin, TX: University of Texas Press.

Industrial Workers of the World. 1905. Preamble, Constitution, & General Bylaws of the Industrial Workers of the World. *Iww.org.* https://www.iww.org/resources/iww-constitution-en.pdf.

Jacoby, Sanford M. 2021. *Labor in the Age of Finance: Pensions, Politics, and Corporations from Deindustrialization to Dodd-Frank.* Princeton, NJ: Princeton University Press.

Jenkins, Philip. 1998. *Moral Panic: Changing Concepts of the Child Molester in Modern America.* New Haven, CT: Yale University Press.

Kallas, Johnnie, Leonardo Grageda, and Eli Friedman. 2022. Labor Action Tracker. *The ILR School.* https://www.ilr.cornell.edu/worker-institute/blog/reports-and-publications/labor-action-tracker-annual-report-2021.

Karp, Stan, and Adam Sanchez. 2018. The 2018 Wave of Teacher Strikes. *Rethinking Schools.* http://www.rethinkingschools.org/articles/the-2018-wave-of-teacher-strikes.

Kater, Michael H. 2011. *The Nazi Symbiosis: Human Genetics and Politics in the Third Reich* (Review). *Bulletin of the History of Medicine* 85 (3): 515–516. https://doi.org/10.1353/bhm.2011.0067.

Kimeldorf, Howard. 1999. *Battling for American Labor: Wobblies, Craft Workers, and the Making of the Union Movement.* Berkeley, CA: University of California Press.

Kirkwood, Burton. 2000. *The History of Mexico.* Westport, CT: Greenwood Press.

Kolin, Andrew. 2019. Repression, Resistance, and Development of the Labor Movement in the United States. In *The Palgrave Handbook of Social Movements, Revolution, and Social Transformation*, ed. Berch Berberoglu. New York, NY: Palgrave Macmillan.

Kumbamu, Ashok. 2021. Saffron Fascism: The Conflux of Hindutva Ultra-Nationalism, Neoliberal Extractivism, and the Rise of Authoritarian Populism in Modi's India. In *The Global Rise of Authoritarianism in the 21st Century:*

Crisis of Neoliberal Globalization and the Nationalist Response, ed. Berch Berberoglu. New York, NY: Routledge.

Kurlander, Eric. 2018. *Hitler's Monsters: A Supernatural History of the Third Reich*. New Haven, CT: Yale University Press.

Lembcke, Jerry. 1998. *The Spitting Image: Myth, Memory and the Legacy of Vietnam*. New York, NY: New York University Press.

Lenin, Vladimir. 1920. 'Left-Wing' Communism: An Infantile Disorder. *Marxists.org*. https://www.marxists.org/archive/lenin/works/1920/lwc/ch06.htm.

Lens, Sidney. 1961. *The Crisis of American Labor*. Beaminster, England: Barnes.

Lichtenstein, Nelson. 2021. Are We Witnessing a 'General Strike' in Our Own Time? *Washington Post*. https://www.washingtonpost.com/outlook/2021/11/18/are-we-witnessing-general-strike-our-own-time/.

Lipset, Seymour Martin. 1998. American Union Density in Comparative Perspective. *Contemporary Sociology* 27 (2): 123. https://doi.org/10.2307/2654769.

Logan, John. 2022. Why Starbucks Workers United May Offer a Key to Labor's Revitalization. *Jacobin.com*. https://jacobin.com/2022/09/starbucks-workers-united-labor-union-organizing-model.

Loomis, Erik. 2019. Sara Nelson Calls for a General Strike to End Shutdown. *Atlantic Monthly*. January 25.

Lynd, Staughton. 2015. *Solidarity Unionism: Rebuilding the Labor Movement from Below*. 2nd ed. Oakland, CA: PM Press.

Marcetic, Branko. 2020. Stories for the End of the World. *Jacobin.com*. https://jacobin.com/2020/11/stories-for-the-end-of-the-world.

———. 2022. The Right Is Still the Enemy of Freedom. *Jacobin.com*. https://jacobin.com/2022/03/republican-party-right-authoritarian-freedom-censorship-protest-bds-civil-rights.

Marx, Karl. 1866. The International Workingmen's Association, Instructions for the Delegates of the Provisional General Council. *Marxists.org*. https://www.marxists.org/history/international/iwma/documents/1866/instructions.htm.

———. 1877. Letters: Marx-Engels Correspondence 1877. https://www.marxists.org/archive/marx/works/1877/letters/77_07_25.htm.

———. 1992. *Capital: Volume I: The Process of Capitalist Production*. New York, NY: International Publishers.

Marx, Karl, and Friedrich Engels. 2005. *The Communist Manifesto and Other Writings (Barnes & Noble Classics Series)*. New York, NY: Fine Communications.

Mason, Timothy W. 1995. *Nazism, Fascism and the Working Class*. Cambridge, England: Cambridge University Press.

McCarthy, Justin. 2022. U.S. Approval of Labor Unions at Highest Point since 1965. *Gallup*. https://news.gallup.com/poll/398303/approval-labor-unions-highest-point-1965.aspx.

McKenzie, Rob. 2022. *El Golpe: US Labor, the CIA, and the Coup at Ford in Mexico*. London, England: Pluto Press.

Mills, C. Wright. 1948. *The New Men of Power: America's Labor Leaders*. London, England: Harcourt, Brace & Co.

———. 1956. *The Power Elite*. New York, NY: Oxford University Press.

Montgomery, David. 1987. *The Fall of the House of Labor: The Workplace, the State, and American Labor Activism, 1865-1925*. Cambridge, England: Cambridge University Press.

Moody, Kim. 1993. *An Injury to All: The Decline of American Unions*. New York, NY: Verso Press.

———. 1995. NAFTA and the Corporate Redesign of North America. *Latin American Perspectives* 22 (1): 95–116. https://doi.org/10.1177/0094582x9502200107.

———. 2007. *U.S. Labor in Trouble and Transition: The Failure of Reform from Above, the Promise of Revival from Below*. London, England: Verso Books.

Morris, George. 1967. *CIA and American Labor: The Subversion of the AFL-CIO's Foreign Policy*. New York, NY: International Publishers.

Murolo, Priscilla, and A.B. Chitty. 2018. *From the Folks Who Brought You the Weekend: A Short, Illustrated History of Labor in the United States*. New York, NY: New Press.

National Security Archive. 2004. Chile 1964: CIA Covert Support in Frei Election Detailed. *Gwu.edu*. https://nsarchive2.gwu.edu/news/20040925/index.htm.

Newport, Frank. 2022. Average American Remains OK with Higher Taxes on Rich. *Gallup.com*. https://news.gallup.com/opinion/polling-matters/396737/average-american-remains-higher-taxes-rich.aspx.

NLRB. 2022. Union Election Petitions Increase 57% in First Half of Fiscal Year 2022. *National Labor Relations Board*. https://www.nlrb.gov/news-outreach/news-story/union-election-petitions-increase-57-in-first-half-of-fiscal-year-2022.

Nolan, Hamilton. 2022. The AFL-CIO's Official New Goal: Continued Decline. *In These Times*. https://inthesetimes.com/article/afl-cio-union-federation-organizing-goal-workers.

Office of Current Intelligence, CIA. 1952. Current Intelligence Bulletin. *Freedom of Information Act Electronic Reading Room*. https://www.cia.gov/reading-room/docs/CIA-RDP79T00975A000900240001-5.pdf.

Orbán, Viktor. 2018. Prime Minister Viktor Orbán's speech at the annual general meeting of the Association of Cities with County Rights – miniszterelnok.hu. *Miniszterelnok.hu*. https://www.miniszterelnok.hu/prime-minister-viktor-orbans-speech-at-the-annual-general-meeting-of-the-association-of-cities-with-county-rights/.

Parenti, Michael. 2001. *Blackshirts and Reds: Rational Fascism and the Overthrow of Communism*. San Francisco, CA: City Lights Books.

Partnership for Civil Justice Fund. n.d. FBI Documents Reveal Secret Nationwide Occupy Monitoring. *Partnership for Civil Justice Fund*. https://www.justiceonline.org/fbi_files_ows.

Paxton, Robert O. 2005. *The Anatomy of Fascism*. New York, NY: Random House.

Phelps, Jordyn. 2015. Donald Trump Again Says He Saw Cheering in New Jersey on 9/11. *ABC News*. https://abcnews.go.com/Politics/donald-trump-cheering-jersey-911/story?id=35355447.

Pitkin, Daisy. 2022. Interview: Starbucks Workers Are in the Fight of Their Lives for a Contract. *Labor Notes*. https://labornotes.org/blogs/2022/08/interview-starbucks-workers-are-fight-their-lives-contract.

Portland Press Herald. 1924. KKK and IWW Wage Drawn Battle in Greenville, 1924. *Libcom.org*. https://libcom.org/article/kkk-and-iww-wage-drawn-battle-greenville-1924.

Post, Charlie. 2017. The Popular Front Didn't Work. *Jacobin.com*. https://jacobin.com/2017/10/popular-front-communist-party-democrats.

Reed, Adolph, Jr. 2001. *Class Notes: Posing as Politics and Other Thoughts on the American Scene*. New York, NY: The New Press.

———. 2021. The Whole Country Is the Reichstag. *Nonsite.org*. https://nonsite.org/the-whole-country-is-the-reichstag/.

Reich, Wilhelm. 1970. *The Mass Psychology of Fascism*. 3rd ed. New York, NY: Simon & Schuster.

Richman, Shaun. 2018. The West Virginia Teachers' Strike Has Activists Asking: Should We Revive the Wildcat? *In These Times*. http://inthesetimes.com/working/entry/20987/west_virginia_teachers_strike_wildcat_janus.

Roman, Richard, and Edur Velasco Arregui. 2017. The NAFTA Consensus. *Jacobin.com*. https://jacobin.com/2017/08/nafta-trans-pacific-partnership-trump-free-trade.

Róna, Dániel, Eszter Galgóczy, Judit Pétervári, Blanka Szeitl, and Márton Túry. 2020. *The Fidesz Party's Secret to Success: Investigating Economic Voting in Hungary*. Budapest, Hungary: 21 Research Center.

Rosenblum, Jonathan. 2022. Why Is This Union Leader Schmoozing with the Enemy? *Nation*, July 20.

Ryan, Paul William. 1979. *The Big Strike*. New York, NY: International.

Saad, Lydia. 2019. Socialism as Popular as Capitalism among Young Adults in U.S. *Gallup*. https://news.gallup.com/poll/268766/socialism-popular-capitalism-among-young-adults.aspx.

Savage, Marion Dutton. 1922. *Industrial Unionism in America*. New York, NY: The Roland Press Company.

Schaal, Dennis. 1981. Unions Blunt U.S. Salvador Policy. *Freedom of Information Act Electronic Reading Room.* https://www.cia.gov/readingroom/docs/CIA-RDP90-00806R000100070005-8.pdf.

Schuhrke, Jeff. 2020. The US Labor Movement Needs More of the UE's 'Them and Us' Unionism. *Jacobin.com.* https://jacobin.com/2020/08/united-workers-labor-unions.

———. 2022. Trader Joe's Workers Have Won Their First Unions in America. *Jacobin.com.* https://jacobin.com/2022/08/trader-joes-union-minneapolis-ma-interview.

Segraves, Mark. 2019. Suspect in Arson at 'Pizzagate' Restaurant Arrested during Caught-on-Camera Brawl with Officers at Monument. *NBC4 Washington.* https://www.nbcwashington.com/news/local/arson-at-comet-ping-pong-arrested-fight-with-police-washington-monument/4717/.

Selcer, Richard F. 2006. *Civil War America, 1850 to 1875.* New York, NY: Facts On File.

Servicio Sismológico Nacional. n.d. El Sismo de 1985: En Cifras. *Internet Archive.* https://web.archive.org/web/20080610175800/http://www.ssn.unam.mx/website/jsp/Carteles/sismo85.jsp.

Smith, David. 2022. Viktor Orbán Turns Texas Conference into Transatlantic Far-Right Love-In. *The Guardian*, August 6.

Somayajula, Pranay. 2022. From Buffalo to India, the Right's Demographic Paranoia Fuels Deadly Violence. *Jacobin.com.* https://jacobin.com/2022/06/far-right-modi-india-us-great-replacement.

Spector, Alan. 2021. Neoliberalism, Authoritarianism, and Resistance in the United States in the Age of Trump. In *The Global Rise of Authoritarianism in the 21st Century: Crisis of Neoliberal Globalization and the Nationalist Response*, ed. Berch Berberoglu. New York, NY: Routledge.

Stark, Louis. 1935. Fist Fight puts A.F. of L. in Uproar; Lewis and Hutcheson, Labor Leaders, Trade Punches on Convention Floor. Climax to Bitter Row, Constitution Amended to Bar Reds from State and Central Labor Groups. *The New York Times*, October 1935. P. 22

Stepan-Norris, Judith, and Caleb Southworth. 2010. Rival Unionism and Membership Growth in the United States, 1900 to 2005: A Special Case of Inter-Organizational Competition. *American Sociological Review* 75 (2): 227–251. https://doi.org/10.1177/0003122410365308.

Stepan-Norris, Judith, and Maurice Zeitlin. 2002. *Left out: Reds and America's Industrial Unions.* Cambridge, England: Cambridge University Press.

Szikra, Dorottya. 2018. Welfare for the Wealthy. *Fes.de.* https://library.fes.de/pdf-files/bueros/budapest/14209.pdf.

Szymanski, Albert. 1978. *The Capitalist State and the Politics of Class.* Cambridge, MA: Winthrop.

Tasca, Angelo. 2019. The Proletariat, Fascism and the Italian Economy. In *Marxists in the Face of Fascism: Writings by Marxists on Fascism from the Inter-War Period*, ed. David Beetham. Chicago, IL: Haymarket Books.

Theweleit, Klaus. 1987. *Male Fantasies: Volume 1: Women Floods Bodies History.* Minneapolis, MN: University of Minnesota Press.

Tigar, Michael E. 2016. Job Loss, the Clintons, NAFTA, and a New Progressive Labor Rights Agenda. *MR Online.* https://mronline.org/2016/11/17/tigar171116-html/.

Torlina, Jeff. 2011. *Working Class: Challenging Myths about Blue-Collar Labor.* Boulder, CO: Lynne Rienner Publishers.

U.S. Capitol Police. 2021. *January 6, 2021 Event After-Action Report.* Washington, D.C.: United States Capitol Police.

U.S. Department of Labor. 2016. 070-232 (LM2) 06/30/2016. *Dol.gov.* https://olmsapps.dol.gov/query/orgReport.do?rptId=627901&rptForm=LM2Form. Washington, D.C.: United States Department of Labor

———. 2021. 070-232 (LM2) 06/30/2021. *Dol.gov.* https://olmsapps.dol.gov/query/orgReport.do?rptId=783018&rptForm=LM2Form. Washington, D.C.: United States Department of Labor

U.S. Senate Select Committee to Study Governmental Operations with Respect to Intelligence Activities (Church Committee). 1975. *Covert Action in Chile 1963-73.* Washington, D.C.: U.S. Government Printing Office.

United Electrical, Radio and Machine Workers of America (UE). n.d. *Member-Run Unionism: The Democratic Alternative That Works.* Pittsburgh, PA.

United States Government Accountability Office. 2022. *Capitol Attack: Additional Actions Needed to Better Prepare Capitol Police Officers for Violent Demonstrations.* Washington, D.C.: Government Accountability Office.

Weber, Brandon. 2018a. When Workers Say 'No!': A Whirlwind Tour of Wildcat Strikes. *Progressive.org.* http://progressive.org/dispatches/when-workers-say-no180831/.

———. 2018b. *Class War, USA: Dispatches from Workers' Struggles in American History.* Chicago, IL: Haymarket Books.

Werstein, Irving. 1969. *Pie in the Sky: An American Struggle: The Wobblies and Their Times.* New York, NY: Dell Publishing.

World Without Genocide. 2021. Genocide of The Herero and Nama, 1904-1907. *World Without Genocide.* http://worldwithoutgenocide.org/wp-content/uploads/2021/05/Namibia-One-Pager-Updated-1.pdf.

Yates, Michael. 2009. *Why Unions Matter.* New York, NY: Monthly Review Press.

Index

A. Barrington, *The U.S. Labor Movement in the 20th and Early 21st Century*, Social Movements and Transformation,
https://doi.org/10.1007/978-3-031-30077-6

L

M

N

O

FSC
www.fsc.org
MIX
Papier | Fördert
gute Waldnutzung
FSC® C083411

Kolibri 360 GmbH
Ferdinand-Jühlke-Straße 7
99095 Erfurt, Deutschland
produktsicherheit@kolibri360.de